M. & J. Walzer
Princeton
1986

Human
Conditions

Human Conditions

The Cultural Basis of Educational Development

Robert A. LeVine and Merry I. White

ROUTLEDGE & KEGAN PAUL

New York and London

First published in 1986
by Routledge & Kegan Paul Inc
in association with Methuen Inc
29 West 35th Street, New York NY 10001

and in the UK by
Routledge & Kegan Paul plc
11 New Fetter Lane, London EC4P 4EE

Set in Linotron 202 Times, 10 on 12pt
by Inforum Ltd, Portsmouth
and printed in Great Britain
by Billing & Sons Ltd, Worcester

Library of Congress Cataloging in Publication Data

LeVine, Robert Alan. 1932–

Human conditions.
Bibliography: p.
Includes index.
1. Education—Social aspects. 2. Social change.
3. Educational anthropology. I. White, Merry I.,
1941– . II. Title.
LC192.L48 1986 370.19 85–19340

ISBN 0-7102-0568-6

CONTENTS

NOTE ON THE PROJECT ON HUMAN POTENTIAL

The Bernard van Leer Foundation of The Hague, Netherlands is an international non profit-making institution dedicated to the cause of disadvantaged children and youth. It supports innovative projects that develop community approaches to early childhood education and child care, in order to help disadvantaged children to realize their potential.

In 1979, the Foundation asked the Harvard Graduate School of Education to assess the state of scientific knowledge concerning human potential and its realization. Proceeding from this general directive, a group of scholars at Harvard has over the past several years been engaged in research exploring the nature and realization of human potential. Activities sponsored by the Project on Human Potential have included reviews of relevant literature in history, philosophy, and the natural and social sciences, a series of international workshops on conceptions of human development in diverse cultural traditions, and the commissioning of papers and books.

The principal investigators of the Project represent a variety of fields and interests. Gerald S. Lesser, who chaired the Project's steering committee, is an educator and developmental psychologist, a principal architect in the creation of educational television programs for children. Howard Gardner is a psychologist who has studied the development of symbolic skills in normal and gifted children, and the impairment of such skills in brain-damaged adults. Israel Scheffler is a philosopher who has worked in the areas of philosophy of education, philosophy of science, and philosophy of language. Robert LeVine, a social anthropologist, has worked in

vii

sub-saharan Africa and Mexico, studying family life, child care and psychological development. Merry White is a sociologist and Japan specialist who has studied education, formal organizations and the roles of women in the Third World and Japan. This wide range of interests and disciplines enabled the Project to take a multi-faceted approach to issues of human potential.

The first volume published under the aegis of the Project was Howard Gardner's *Frames of Mind* (Basic Books, 1983), a study of human intellectual potentials which drew not only on psychological research but also on the biological sciences and on findings about the development and use of knowledge in different cultures.

Israel Scheffler's *Of Human Potential* (RKP, 1985) was the second book of the Project to appear, and it offers a treatment of philosophical aspects of the concept of potential. Sketching the background of the concept and placing it in the context of a general theory of human nature, this treatment then proposes three analytical reconstructions of the concept and offers systematic reflections on policy and the education of policy-makers.

To provide background for the study of diversity in development, the Project established teams of consultants in Egypt, India, Japan, Mexico, the People's Republic of China, and West Africa. Selected papers presented by these consultants in Project workshops will appear in a third volume, *The Cultural Transition*, to be published in November, 1985, under the editorship of Merry I. White and Susan Pollak. Representatives of international development agencies were also engaged as consultants and correspondents over the five-year period of the Project. Through such international dialogue and research, the Project has sought to create a new multidisciplinary environment for understanding human potential.

The present (and fourth) volume is *Human Conditions: The Cultural Basis of Educational Development*, by Robert A. LeVine and Merry I. White. Emphasizing the crucial role of cultural factors in the progress of human development, the book offers new models for development based on the social anthropology of the life span and the social history of family and school.

The Hague
Netherlands
September, 1984

PREFACE

How shall we think about education, in a world that bases so many hopes on it, yet is often dissatisfied with its outcome? Much contemporary thinking views education as an investment to be evaluated by its economic returns. Alternative perspectives are given little attention in the most influential policy forums. This book presents the case for including a cultural perspective – encompassing historical, anthropological, and psycho-social information – in the analysis of educational policies and their effects throughout the world.

Our perspective is frankly relativistic in insisting that culture-specific traditions of thought and indigenous models of the life span are more important for understanding what education means in a particular country than 'universal' models of rational choice or social progress. Thus the 'human conditions' of our title is offered not only as a corrective to the idea of a single human condition but also as a reference to the role of culturally organized ideas in mediating the influence of economic, demographic and political conditions. The 'hard facts' of quantitative social science are heavily conditioned in their most significant impacts by the subjective realities described in ethnography and history.

The analysis of education and human development as global phenomena requires specific information on the cultural contexts in which lives are led, but it must be based on a conceptual framework for approaching cultural diversity. In this book, we present such a framework, grounded in the particulars of anthropological and

1

historical data but venturing beyond them to generalize about trends and processes. In developing and illustrating this framework, we deliberately alternate between theory-building and an empirical critique of generalizations.

We need both culture-specific knowledge and a comparative perspective to inform policy. This middle ground between the formal abstractions of theoretical social science and the descriptive richness of area studies is relatively unexplored and provides a perilous but exciting new focus for discourse among social scientists and policy-makers.

Policy statements on international development since 1960 have recognized that the economic goals of growth and distribution are not ends in themselves but means to other goals – variously called satisfaction, fulfillment, self-realization, quality of life and the realization of potential – which cannot be understood through economic analysis alone. It has often been assumed that formal education provides the institutional means through which each individual can define and attain these desired ends in personal terms, leaving their description and analysis outside the bounds of social policy. As the value of schooling to the individual and society is increasingly and fundamentally questioned, however, this dubious assumption becomes less tenable. Explicit and systematic attention to the meanings of life as experienced by the world's peoples has become a necessity in the international development field; concepts and data from all of the relevant social sciences must be brought to bear on the possible and actual effects of policy on the individual. The task of assembling our knowledge to analyze global problems of human development represents a major challenge to the social sciences today.

The challenge is taken up in this book, which shows cultural factors to be crucial in the implementation of policies and programs intended to promote individual development. This book uses case material from specific cultural settings – Japan, Third World countries and the historical West – to generate theory and guidelines for practice. Abstract models of educational success and failure represented by statistical indicators are revealed as less valuable for theory and practice than examination of educational patterns seen at different times and places.

Part I examines agrarian cultures, past and present, as our most important source of alternative conceptions of education and human development, conceptions which underwent radical change in the West during the nineteenth century and which continue to change throughout the world today. Chapter 2 presents the findings of recent social anthropology concerning models of the human life span in agrarian societies. Despite their diversity in other respects, these societies have in common moral codes favoring filial piety and intergenerational reciprocity, gender-specific ideals of social and spiritual virtues rather than specialized intellectual ones, concepts of childhood learning that emphasize the acquisition of manners and work skills without competitive evaluation, and concepts of the adult years as the prime period for significant cognitive development. Cultural variations on these themes are reviewed and their persistence as traditional sources of contemporary variation, even among industrial countries, is demonstrated.

Chapter 3, viewing the demographic and social history of the West, tells the story of how models of parent-child relations have changed since 1800, in terms of the material and ideological conditions that underlie agrarian assumptions, thus ushering in new concepts of child development, new strategies of parental investment conducive to educational mobilization, and a new sense of political community transcending sectional and class interests in its concern with the nation's children.

Chapter 4 describes schooling as an institutional form related to craft apprenticeship in the urban sectors of literate pre-industrial societies of the Old World, which was transformed from a model of education and individual development based on agrarian premises to one predicated on a competitive labor market, social mobility and mass participation in national government. The rise of the occupational career as an organizer of the identities of individuals and of career development as the primary responsibilities of parents and teachers under the conditions of mass competitive schooling are seen as major outcomes of this transformation. While contemporary school systems and occupational structures impose a certain uniformity on the world, there are enough variations among countries, stemming in part from their differing agrarian traditions, to consider what alternative pathways for human development exist at the present time and what their costs and benefits are.

In Part II, a general model of educational mobilization is proposed, in which differences in academic achievement between countries, social classes and ethnic groups are attributed not to intellectual potential but to processes that motivate an investment (of time, space, attention, money) in teaching and learning at both microsocial and macrosocial levels and especially to ideological commitments that help coordinate activities at the two levels. At the microsocial level, parent involvement is crucial in providing a long-term commitment to the career development of the child; at the macrosocial level, it is the sense of a community of interest in the welfare of children outside one's primary group that broadens the base for educational mobilization. But the personal costs of successful mobilization are exposed, leading to a consideration of the alternative goals for education found in societies that have not been mobilized for learning and performance.

Japan is offered, in Chapter 5, as a recognized case of educational development, where indigenous concepts of learning and performance were harnessed to Western goals in mobilizing the nation for education. The social and historical preconditions and consequences of this mobilization are reviewed, with particular attention to collaboration between the microsocial (parent-child and teacher-pupil) and macrosocial (political and bureaucratic) components of the educational system and the cultural context in which collaboration occurred. The cognitive achievements of Japanese children are shown to be wrongly construed as the product of a top-down national program stressing acquisition of large amounts of knowledge through rote memorization and drill. Motivation, initiative and goals are generated in the parent-child relationship, and the content and process of primary schooling are focused on the engagement of the child's interest and excitement rather than on an accumulation of facts. Japanese educational planners were and are sensitive to local individual contexts and goals; there is a congruence between the interests of policy-makers and the motivation of families to participate in long-term commitment to children's development. Political goals inform education in China (Chapter 6) which represents alternative models for educational mobilization based on the idea of virtue. Chapter 7 discusses life chances in Third World countries in terms of the unevenness of development. This development cannot build on Western pre-conditions, nor does it promise to re-create in the future Western patterns and correlations of industrialization, educational development, and changes in fertility and mortality.

Part III is concerned with questions of life chances and costs in

Preface

present and future educational development. Chapter 8 treats the problems incurred when policies based on Western assumptions concerning human betterment are adopted in non-Western environments. The introduction of mass schooling arouses hopes that cannot be fulfilled. The reduction in mortality creates massive population growth that threatens a country's resource base. The cases of child labor and women's rights are particularly examined in terms of policies predicated on the universal applicability of human rights.

The final chapter considers, in the light of the evidence analyzed in the volume, how and toward what ends policy-makers might act to improve human development and what place education should have in their efforts. Universal solutions are rejected in favor of a framework attuned to specific settings and historical conditions. Educational interventions advanced without regard to the socio-economic and cultural contexts in which they are being introduced are shown to be doomed to failure in their local and long-range implementation. The roles of motivation and mobilization are emphasized. Policy planners need to analyze their particular social systems with particular attention to the cultural factor, if their innovations are to succeed.

In such a statement as this book makes there is ample room for argument, and in its genesis in the Bernard van Leer Foundation's Project on Human Potential, there have been many viewpoints reflected. The perspective this book presents is the product of reading and discussion across a wide swath of literature and specialists. We have had to ignore a wealth of scholarship, nonetheless, and have not done justice to that from which we have learned. To review all the relevant literatures, would, we feel, have been diversionary from the themes and messages we have developed here, but we hope that in constructing a new model for considering the context of human development we have added more to the field than we distorted or ignored.

This book was generated in discussions at the Project on Human Potential, where, as described in the Note on page vii, a five year study of the conditions of human development was undertaken at the Harvard Graduate School of Education from September 1979 to September 1984, sponsored by the Bernard van Leer Foundation of The Hague. Our greatest debts are to the Executive Director of the Foundation, Dr. Willem Welling, and to the Chairman of the

Board of Directors, Mr. Oscar van Leer, for having conceived this challenging study and for supporting us as we attempted to meet the challenge.

The substance and import of this book was conceived in our relationships with our colleagues in many countries. A mere 'acknowledgment' is insufficient here since without the stimulus and perspectives drawn from our several international workshops the book would not exist. These workshops in Japan, Egypt, the Gambia, India, Mexico and the People's Republic of China, engaged us in the issues of culture and development with people whose perspectives and experiences enriched us greatly. Our relationship with the Social Science Research Council's Group for the Study of Alternative Psychologies of South Asia, organized by McKim Marriott of the University of Chicago provided us with the impetus to work with other such groups of social and behavioral scientists and practitioners in other societies, and we established similar groups in the above countries. Papers by several participants are included in the volume, *The Cultural Transition: Human Experience and Social Transformation in the Third World and Japan*, edited by Merry White and Susan Pollak. It is appropriate here to list some of our colleagues to whom we are so grateful for sharing with us their expertise and thoughtfulness. In the India group, besides McKim Marriott, we would like to thank Sudhir Kakar, B.K. Ramanujam, A.K. Ramanujan, Alan Roland, and Prakash Desai. In Japan, Akira Hoshino, Sumiko Iwao, Shigefumi Nagano and Michiko Fukazawa were generous and hard working. In Egypt, we would especially like to thank Nawal and Asaad Nadim, Salah Kotb, Kadry Hefny, Farag A. Farag and Roshdy Fam. In West Africa, Lamin Sanneh of the Harvard Divinity School assembled an exciting group of people for our workshop in the Gambia: Cheikh Ba, Boubacar Barry, Amechi Anumonye, Felicia Ekejiuba, Christopher Bakare, and Kadja Mianno.

In the People's Republic of China, we are especially grateful to Fei Xiaotong, Xia Shuzhang, Zeng Xingchu, Zhang Suwo, He Bingzi, and Zhang Tian-an. Our Latin American study was especially benefited by the work of Carlos Eduardo Vasco, Carlos Corona, Marta Arango, Glen Nimnicht, Juan Lafarga, Carlos Garcia, Josefina Quintanilla, Ezequiel Nieto-Cardozo and Raul Magana.

Besides these workshops, our consideration of the work of international development was enlightened by discussions with people associated with the United Nations and other agencies in New York, Washington and Geneva. Our several meetings at the World Bank were implemented by D. Davies and Stephen Heyneman. In New York, David Burleson of UNESCO arranged sessions with UNICEF officers and researchers such as Mansour Ahmed, Nico van Oudenhoven, Dorothea Banks and Mary Hollensteiner. We also met with Orlando Olcese and Abebe Ambatchew at the UNDP. At the Ford Foundation, Robert Myers offered advice and critical reading of our work. David Szanton, Sophie Sa, Kenneth Prewitt and others at the Social Science Research Council offered their expertise and thoughtfulness to the pursuit. Kenneth King of IDRC was also helpful. In Geneva, many helped: at UNRISD Solon Barraclough; at UNICEF Regional Headquarters, Yves Pelle and Thierry Lemaresquier were among those who engaged in very fruitful discussions with us.

Our colleagues at the Project, especially the principal investigators, Howard Gardner, Gerald Lesser, Israel Scheffler, and Harry Lasker engaged us actively over the years in provocative cross-disciplinary debate. Our research colleagues, Susan Pollak, Lois Taniuchi, Liz Fine, Sara Taber, Suzanne Kirschner, Paul Fulton, Bill Skryziniarz, Claudia Strauss, Linda Levine, and Julia Shiang ensured that we were exposed to a broad array of data and perspectives. We are also grateful for the help of Deborah Davis-Friedmann and Daniel Wagner. Dolly Appel, Laura Stephens-Swannie and Damaris Chapin have cheerfully worked on many drafts of our work and have offered creative suggestions as well. Margaret Herzig brought a questing philosophic context to the editing of our manuscript, as well as providing a stable administrative environment against all odds. Leonie Gordon gave us enthusiastic and critical support while managing the complexities of our workshops in China, Japan and West Africa. Her scholarly treatment of traditional and modern Chinese education provided an important contribution to Chapter VI of this volume. Susan Pollak's encyclopedic studies of traditional education were particularly important as background to Chapter IV.

Two of our most valued supporters and friends over the years were Dr. William Wall, whose energy and nurturance helped us at the earliest, most chaotic stages of our thinking, and Dr. Leo Fernig, whose friendship we count as one of the most cherished outcomes of the Project, and whose probing clarity of thought has helped us in the final stages of writing.

Our editor at Routledge & Kegan Paul, Stratford Caldecott, has offered calm and confident indulgence, as well as perceptive advice, that we have sorely needed in preparing the final manuscript.

The community of people who worked with us to write this book is the best evidence of the power of relationships which we claim has always given meaning to people's lives and potentials: this volume is the product of the balance between the motivating support of ligatures and the creative tension of options.

I: Cultural and Human Development in World History

Theories which, because of their high level of abstraction, look perfectly neutral as between one kind of economic system and another, often are primarily relevant to the conditions under which they were conceived. They usually originate in attempts to illuminate possible solutions to specific problems encountered at a given time, and are sometimes directly designed to do so. If they are useful theories, they will have focused on variables that in a particular setting are both strategic and subject to change by policy-makers. Therefore, the more useful they are in one setting, the less they are likely to be so in a completely different one.

Albert O. Hirschman,
The Strategy of Economic Development, 1959, p.29.

1

HUMAN DEVELOPMENT AS A GLOBAL PROBLEM

Europeans have been spreading their own models of personal and societal development in other parts of the world since the sixteenth century, usually on the assumption that they were introducing better conditions for the far-flung peoples involved. Christian missionaries, colonial administrators and development planners alike have sought to re-educate the inhabitants of Asia, Africa, the Americas and the Pacific, to re-form their aspirations as well as their institutions in accordance with the latest advances in Western thought. As long ago as 1531, the Spanish official and Franciscan missionary Vasco de Quiroga borrowed the model of Christian community described in Thomas More's *Utopia* to re-organize Mexican Indians whose indigenous social life had been shattered by the Conquest. The French Enlightenment gave such intercultural reform efforts their modern rationale, that of civilizing those peoples left behind in man's progress toward civilization. In the immediate aftermath of the French Revolution, the Société des Observateurs de l'Homme sent an expedition to Australia to study the customs of the aborigines and share the blessings of European cultural superiority, 'to show them the route which will conduct them to our state', not only in matters of science and technology but even in style of dress (Degerando, quoted in Stocking, 1968). Mounted in 1800, the ill-fated expedition never reached Australia, but the idea of a civilizing mission gained momentum in the nineteenth and twentieth centuries, inspiring a myriad of movements for reform and revolution and policies aimed at national and international development.

11

Education was central to the civilizing mission from the beginning and has remained so, with a variety of philosophical and scientific rationales. 'Backward' peoples have been seen as lacking knowledge and motivation along with technology, wealth, organization and power. Their personal, as well as societal, potentials have been regarded as unrealized. Such deficit models permit an easy transfer of educational ideas and methods from one place to another, regardless of their different social and cultural settings. But growing evidence of human diversity in the ends of life, and the place of education in achieving them, challenges the assumption that any given model will be universally applicable and suggests the need for a pluralistic social science of human development to guide policy formation. In this book we make the case for such a pluralistic social science, review the evidence for cultural diversity in human development and indicate the directions a new analysis should take.

In the past, social scientists and policy analysts have sought to define the Human Condition as a basis for informed action. Simple dichotomies – e.g. developed/less developed, modern/pre-modern, capitalist/pre-capitalist – served to conceptualize global variations and historical tendencies in terms that were at once comprehensible and comprehensive. It was natural to extend these categories to the person at the center of the educational process and view those who lived in less developed countries as lacking in development themselves until exposed to formal schooling. They were, implicitly or explicitly, educational 'have-nots' in contrast with the 'haves' of the developed world. Their children in particular represented the life-long potentials that might be realized with greater access to education. The aim of a rational and just policy was to supply what they lacked, to remedy their deficiencies, to provide access to advantages they had not experienced.

This view left out the multitude of advantages and benefits that do not fit into the categories of desired outcomes in Western educational thought but which anthropological research has shown are experienced by non-Western peoples in the course of their lives. Literate or illiterate, their traditions provide alternative utopias – or at least distinctive and coherent images of well-being, public virtue and personal maturity that guide the education of children and motivate the activities of adults. These diverse models of the good life, which can be thought of as 'life plans,' 'blueprints for living' or 'cognitive maps of the life course,' are embedded in vernacular codes of conduct and local survival strategies that endow the life span with culture-specific potentials for personal development. Grounded in economic, moral and spiritual considerations, cultural conceptions of potential set goals for men and women and organize pathways for their realization. Parents experience their lives and those of their children in terms of these indigenous conceptions, which constitute frameworks for the re-interpretation of imported models.

Thus non-Western peoples, largely agrarian in their current adaptations or recent background, are not waiting for Western models of personal development to fill a void in their lives. On the contrary, *there is no void*; they are busily pursuing potentials richly symbolized in their traditional models. Furthermore, evidence reviewed in this book shows that they do not give up traditional aspirations upon borrowing Western institutions but infuse the latter with new combinations of indigenous and imported meanings. There is no other way of understanding educational development in Japan, China and the Third World as described in Chapters 5, 6 and 7. The particular agrarian culture indigenous to each country or province sets the stage for an interaction with foreign ideas that continues for centuries, creating distinctive contexts for life span development. To ignore these contexts, their historical roots and their influence on personal experience, when designing policy is to court failure in its implementation. Cultural, historical and psychosocial understanding is a practical necessity for the policy-maker, but it has not yet found a secure place in the analysis of educational policy and practice.

THE LADDER AND THE AUCTION: THEORETICAL MODELS OF DEVELOPMENT

Policy analysis related to education and other aspects of human development has been based largely on economic models of the Human Condition, each offering a unitary and elegantly simple explanation for the most evident divisions among the world's peoples. Universality is a largely unproven premise of these models, and its validity has as often been tested retrospectively (and expensively) by the success or failure of policies inspired by the models as by prior empirical research. Policy failures have led some economic development specialists like Albert O. Hirschman (1959) to skeptical opinions such as that quoted at the beginning of this chapter, and to consider paradigms, i.e., general theoretical frameworks as a 'hindrance to understanding' in this field (Hirschman, 1971). Yet economic paradigms have continued to be as influential in our time as theological paradigms were at the time of Thomas More and Vasco de Quiroga.

Most economic models of personal and societal development can be classified as based on one of two metaphors: the ladder and the auction. The ladder metaphor represents all societies as ranked by their positions in a historical progression, with some temporarily more advanced than others, though moving in the same ameliorating direction. Contemporary variations are attributed to differing (earlier and lower, later and higher) stages in an invariant sequence. While the nineteenth-century forms of such societal evolutionism, as formulated by Spencer, Morgan, Marx and Engels, were definitively refuted in anthropology (Boas, 1911; Steward, 1953), more sophisticated forms emerged in mid-twentieth century economics (Rostow, 1952), demography (Notestein, 1945; Caldwell, 1982) and sociology (Inkeles, 1974; Levy, 1966; Parsons, 1977), as the theories of economic development, demographic transition and modernization, respectively. The newer theories characterize backward societies in terms of what is absent in them but present in the more advanced societies, i.e., self-sustaining economic growth, control over fertility and mortality and the structural and psychological features of a complex social order. This perspective conceptually homogenizes all societies lacking the characteristics of advancement (though they actually differ widely on other dimensions) and emphasizes what they need to acquire as prerequisites for progress.

Steven Jay Gould (1977) has pointed out that the ladder metaphor, and the concept of unilinear evolution that lies behind it, misrepresents Darwin's theory and is not supported by modern biological research. He recommends the bush as a more appropriate metaphor for the divergent tendencies in the evolution of species: upward, to be sure, but also outward in adaptive response to diverse environments. The same is true of human societies, i.e., empirical research has not confirmed a ladder-like progression toward socio-economic modernity but has uncovered a wide array of divergent tendencies at all levels, advanced as well as backward, and documented the existence of multiple routes to varied destinations. The idea that Third World societies, for example, are or should be replicating the history of the West or more recent advances in East Asia is no longer tenable in the light of the evidence now available, as we shall show in succeeding chapters. In social research as in evolutionary biology, the bush is better than the ladder in representing what we know.

Disillusionment with models of economic and societal development based on the ladder metaphor has helped revive the influence of classical economics on policy analyses concerned with education and international development. Neoclassical economics, as Lester Thurow (1983) has pointed out, assumes the universality of a 'price-auction model' for economic behavior, and the auction metaphor has infiltrated recent theory and research concerning education, the family and human development. The world as a whole can be seen as an auction, with the nations as bidders for a common but expanding pool of resources and consumer goods. Those nations that are wealthier outbid the others and acquire more of the resources and goods for themselves. Thus the most significant division of the world is into rich and poor nations. Since they are all bidding for the same kinds of things, the problem is how to strengthen the bidding position of the poor nations so they can do better at the auction and acquire more of what they want but do not, at present, have. The solution is investment that builds their productive capacity and gives them more wealth to bargain with. According to the human capital school of Becker (1962, 1976) and Schultz (1981), the best investment is in the education and health of the population, which increases both national productivity and the lifetime earnings of the individual. Gaining in wealth and life expectancy, the individual in a poor country benefits by approximating the life of someone in a rich country. Economics provides the mathematical guidance for national and even family investment strategies designed to enhance life through wealth.

The world-as-an-auction metaphor assumes not only that everyone wants the same things from life, all measurable in monetary terms, but that all humans make important life decisions on a 'rational' basis, i.e., with the purpose of maximizing economic returns. Unlike some of the unilinear evolutionists, neoclassical economists (particularly of the human capital school) do not believe that some peoples are more rational than others, but that all are

15

equally so within the constraints that keep the poorer bidders in less advantageous situations. This can be treated as a technical economic problem, in which the unlocking of human potential through investment in education (human capital formation) is seen as strictly parallel to the exploitation of minerals and other natural resources. Research in this paradigm is consequently focused on topics such as the efficiency of school systems in meeting labor market needs (Psacharopoulos, 1983).

Inequalities among the bidders can, alternatively, be treated as a political problem (as Marxist analysts tend to treat it), in which the rich nations, and richer groups within all countries, try to protect their privileged positions against efforts of the poor to liberate themselves from oppressive exploitation. In either case – technical or political – the auction metaphor guarantees that theorists will not confront the possibility of diversity in what is desired or considered beneficial. No people is thought to reject the auction as an arbiter of value. Peoples may manifest varying 'tastes' that are either beyond scientific analysis or symptomatic of a 'false consciousness' in which they do not recognize where their real economic interests lie. Education as cognitive training or indoctrination can help agrarian peoples update their economic rationality in terms of understanding the options and constraints of new markets for their goods and labor and how they might take advantage of them – or in terms of understanding how they are exploited and what political steps they must take to do something about it. The purpose of education is either skill development for human capital formation or consciousness–raising for economic liberation, or both. Human purposes are defined simply as the adaptive pursuit of material interests.

Economic analysis frequently operates with assumptions adopted mainly for the ease with which they permit model-building, measurement and comparisons; their empirical validity may be assessed later, often indirectly. Thus economists using the auction metaphor do not know as empirical fact that benefits are experienced similarly in diverse cultures or that the maximization of economic utility is accorded the same weight among non-Western peoples as it is in the West, but they find those assumptions convenient to make. In recent years, some economists (e.g., Thurow, 1983, p. 216) have questioned the value of abstract models based on unverified assumptions in the formation of domestic economic policy. As Hirschman (1959) foresaw, the attempt to generalize them to other countries is even more questionable. We contend that the problem of realizing individual potential cannot even be confronted, let alone resolved, by assumptions – however compelling their metaphorical appeal – made in advance of inquiry into the variety of conditions in which humans live.

EDUCATION FOR WHAT?

In a narrowly economic framework, the objectives of educational policy are not at issue and the problem for research is how to attain them. The productive employee earning an income, setting his own goals, and spending or investing rationally to achieve them – this is the ideal held out for developing societies from the experience of Europe and North America. Schooling must be organized to develop the skills needed for economic production and rational household management, while relations between the school system and the labor market should be organized toward creating jobs and hence earnings for the largest number of people and toward high productivity for national economic growth. To hold a job and earn an income is the major improvement conceivable in the life of a person from the Third World, who is imagined as otherwise 'unemployed,' unhealthy, poor, ignorant and disadvantaged – a prime case of unrealized potential.

Debates among educational development specialists who share these objectives center on how to create the largest reservoir of skills, the greatest number of jobs to utilize them and the most equitable distribution of earnings. Since development policies have failed to create enough jobs or equality of income to satisfy anyone, there is much scope for research on these topics without investigating what happens after a person gets a job, or whether his life and that of his family are genuinely improved by earnings and employment. It is assumed that earnings will expand his options and therefore constitute a benefit. Expansion of options is conceptualized either as increased choice in a free market situation or as welfare entitlements that reduce material deprivation, prolong life expectancy and provide the literate skills needed to live a meaningful life as a civilized person. Non-Western peoples have their own traditions, to be sure, but these can be classified as either compatible with educational development – and therefore unnecessary to understand in detail – or as incompatible with it – and therefore obstacles to be eliminated. Educational development thus conceived is a universal form of progress consistent with all human aspirations regardless of ideology or culture.

A more complex and realistic alternative to this conception of educational policy goals development can be based on Ralf Dahrendorf's concept of life chances (1979). Dahrendorf is less sanguine in his view of the 'modernization process' in general, which he sees as involving losses as well as gains for humanity. In attempting to conceptualize the potentials of societies for providing their members with meaningful and satisfying lives, Dahrendorf proposes life chances as the joint product of the options (choices) and ligatures (social attachments) made available by the social structure. At any given historical moment it is (theoretically) possible to identify an optimal balance between these two structural factors, and that balance defines the maximum of life chances attainable for members of that society at that time. Unlike income or even happiness, life chances are not easily measured or clearly defined in the abstract; to say that they are 'possibilities to realize needs, wants and interests in, or at times against, a given social context,' (p. 53), is rather vague and general. In specific cases, however, the balance or imbalance is often clear. Where options have been expanded at the expense of ligatures, the likelihood is increased that individuals will face lives of isolation and loneliness; where ligatures have been developed at the expense of options, it is more likely that individuals will suffer restriction and coercion. Liberal political theory has favored extending options and demolishing ligatures, and the processes of modernization have brought this about in the West, but Dahrendorf suggests that it has gone too far.

Dahrendorf distinguishes three historical processes – the emergence, enhancement and extension of life chances – and illustrates them (briefly) with the educational history of the West (pp. 78–9).

1 The emergence of a new life chance is a genuine innovation, like a technological invention. For education, Dahrendorf identifies the founding of Plato's Academy with the emergence of education as a new life chance. Although this idea is offered briefly and cautiously, we believe what he means is that the

Academy created a new prototype for educational activity as a self-conscious means of integrating individual learning with social goals. This prototype permanently altered the course of European educational history.

2 The enhancement or development of an existing life chance is incremental progress, refinement and re-structuring of the prototype, as in the development of schools and curricula in Europe between the classical period and the nineteenth century.

3 Extension 'consists in making life chances which have been invented and developed available to more people.' The expansion of schooling since the early nineteenth century to cover the entire population of a country and eventually the world is an example from educational history.

Dahrendorf implies that the emergence, development and extension of education resulted not merely in an expansion of options for the individual but in a strengthening of ligatures: it offered the possibility of new linkages as well as new choices. His critique of Western thought and policy, however, is that – at least since the Enlightenment – the expansion of options has been paramount and ligatures have not been sufficiently valued in theory or practice, with the result (particularly in the contemporary period) that the net improvement in life chances from 'modernization' (including educational development) has been less than could have been expected. Furthermore, the drive to extend education at all levels to more and more people has begun to result in a diminution rather than improvement in life chances even for the highly educated. Thus Dahrendorf views educational development as a potential for increasing life chances which can be fully realized only if its effect on ligatures is not entirely destructive and if its extension does not vitiate its central purposes.

This view is applicable to world educational development and is consistent with the major critiques of educational expansion programs. Extending education in the Third World has had negative social and psychological consequences (Dore, 1976; Simmons, 1980) that are due in part to over-extension and the destruction of linkages in the social surround of the individual. Dahrendorf's concepts supply a critical framework for evaluating educational development comparatively and – more importantly in the context of this book – for incorporating an understanding of social, cultural and historical contexts into such an evaluation.

Dahrendorf's framework, in contrast with much of development economics, suggests the need for comparative and historical evidence concerning the optimization of life chances. In development theory, the practical objective is to extend to the rest of the world life chances that emerged and have been developed in the West. This is conceptualized as a technical and organizational problem, like the transfer of technology, requiring no alteration in the original prototypes. We now know, however – and this book will show – that alternative prototypes for education and other life chances have emerged in non-Western societies (Chapters 2 and 4) and also that prototypes borrowed from the West have undergone radical change in those societies (Chapters 5, 6 and 7). These alternative cultural inventions and differing directions of historical change constitute the great neglected resource for evaluating educational policy, because they raise fundamental questions about the *status quo* and provide empirical contact with possible futures. Most importantly, they challenge the dominance of prototypes derived from the West as the only possibilities for life chances in human societies.

The nature of this challenge is clarified by Dahrendorf's concepts, for life chances in non-Western societies differ from those of the West primarily in the ways they balance options with ligatures. Through cultural models of personal development in which individual choice and social attachment are united rather than opposed and through social processes that resolve conflicts between these two potentials for action, non-Western cultures represent possible solutions to problems and dilemmas of educational development long recognized by Western scholars.

In Dahrendorf's view, it is the ligatures – the social linkages and attachments of the individual – that make choices meaningful. The freedom to choose a career, a spouse, a place to live and consumer goods, may be considered inherently desirable as a matter of principle, but it is only experienced as satisfying or beneficial in a social context established by a reference group with shared values. In so far as modernization diminishes the permanence, stability and normative authority of reference groups and the support networks that are typically embedded in them, it may provide the individual with more freedom of choice than can be enjoyed or even tolerated. The responsibility of autonomous decision-making, self-evaluation and constructing a personal identity to replace conventional orthodoxy – however cherished in Western thought – leaves many (including those who have successfully pursued available options) feeling more isolated and lonely than satisfied or contented. This is the Western experience – an improvement in life chances, but at a cost in the linkages and attachments that endow choice and success with their most deeply satisfying meanings. It is not so common an experience among non-Western peoples, and their means of striking a different, perhaps better, balance between options and ligatures commands our attention in this book.

Many Western thinkers have deplored the loss of community and the isolation and loneliness of the individual in European and North American societies; it is a major theme in literature and experience over the last hundred years. Dahrendorf's framework requires that we conceptualize the ways in which ligatures contribute to life chances, without romanticizing that contribution or its loss. Their contribution can be thought of in terms of the benefits persons can receive from the social linkages made available to them in their societies, benefits classifiable as support, structure and motivation.

1 *Support* The social interdependencies organized by kinship, neighborhood and other forms of affiliation provide ties on which individuals count for goods, services and emotionally significant symbols of permanence, particularly at times of crisis and deprivation. This kind of support provides a minimal sense of long-term security which most individuals need, particularly where their needs are not anticipated by government programs.

2 *Structure* A normative order publicly defines virtue and vice, establishes a predictable moral environment and provides unambiguous conditions for interpersonal trust and positive self-regard. This kind of order can give the individual both the satisfaction of living a good life according to community standards and the comfort of being able to trust others in the community.

3 *Motivation* Relationships define the purposes of adult activities, motivating individuals to direct their efforts toward

the benefit of others (e.g., their families), toward the approval of those whom they respect (e.g., their sponsors) and toward recognition within groups they value (e.g., their communities). Such motivation can benefit society (e.g., in improved production and political leadership). It benefits the individual by setting personal achievement in a collective context that gives it additional meanings (e.g., pride, morale).

Thus personal security, community trust, positive self-regard and group morale are all benefits possible from social linkages, through the support, structure and motivation they provide for individuals of a given society. These benefits are conditions of the good life by anyone's definition – their importance can be assessed by imagining life without them – and their increase must be counted as improvement in life chances as much as an increase in the options made accessible by income, education and a longer life expectancy. Social linkages, however, are not so easily controlled by policy-makers as income, education and health; hence they have not received the attention they deserve.

By explicating the benefits possible from social linkages, we seek a better balance in the comparative assessment of life chances, which has been heavily weighted in favor of the options cherished in Western thought. That many in the West, ourselves included, have benefited from the blessings of freedom of choice in an affluent society with a complex culture, is acknowledged. That the same experience is possible or desirable in societies with differing cultural traditions is questionable, and is the question that provoked this book. The information to answer it is at hand in the studies of anthropologists, comparative sociologists and historians, which we synthesize in the following chapters.

We begin with an overview of what life means in agrarian societies past and present (Chapter 2); how agrarian family life was transformed in the West by socio-economic, demographic and cultural change (Chapter 3); and how schooling has changed from its agrarian forms and functions over the centuries (Chapter 4). Then we present profiles of historical change and continuity in educational purposes and patterns in Japan (Chapter 5) and the People's Republic of China (Chapter 6), involving alternative models of educational mobilization based on differing cultural traditions and social conditions. Chapter 7 considers the diverse ways in which Third World countries currently combine models of human development from their agrarian traditions and their borrowed educational-occupational structures. In Chapter 8, we consider the dilemmas of formulating policies related to human development in diverse cultures. Chapter 9 explores what conclusions concerning life chances and the realization of potential are justified by the comparative and historical evidence reviewed in the book.

2

VIRTUES AND VICES: AGRARIAN MODELS OF THE LIFE SPAN[1]

For at least 3,000 years, a majority of the world's families have lived by their own agriculture or animal husbandry, embedded in local associations of kin and neighbors, conducting their lives according to local standards of maturity, morality and personal well-being. Rural population growth in the Third World during this century has so outpaced the spread of urban-industrial patterns that agrarian life – with domestically organized food production as its basis – remains the majority condition of humanity. The agrarian cultural traditions of Asia, Africa, Oceania and Latin America are still the most widely used guides to the purpose of life, the nature of human development and the relations between individual and society. In descriptions of particular agrarian societies and cultures, anthropologists have documented diversity in beliefs, values and forms of adaptation. Here we take a broader comparative perspective, an overview of agrarian models of the life span as they differ from those of the urban-industrial West and as they constitute an alternative framework for defining benefits, life chances and human potentials. From the large body of ethnographic and historical evidence available, we present the common elements of agrarian life that shape individual experience.

A PREVIEW OF THE ARGUMENT

An 'agrarian society' in our definition refers to a population the majority of which lives in small communities and engages in domes-

24

tically organized food production, regardless of what other institutions exist there. An 'agrarian culture' is a collective organization of ideas shared by an agrarian population, in which some of the basic premises are derived from the routines of their productive and reproductive lives. An agrarian culture, like all cultures, supplies a vocabulary, a logic, a moral symbolism and a plan of action for a community and its members. Every culture includes ideal models of the good life, maturity and other goals for the life span that motivate adult activities. We have chosen to call these personified images of valued and disvalued characteristics 'virtues' and 'vices.' Individuals seek to be identified as virtuous and to avoid identification as vicious in evaluation by self and community. In other words, they seek to optimize their own social identities in terms of community standards. Agrarian cultures, though varying widely in many respects, recognize virtues and vices differing from those of the urban-industrial West and inspire a distinctive range of social identities.

The social identities of agrarian adults are organized by a local age-sex hierarchy that offers support, structure and motivation: support from the reciprocal obligations of kin and neighbor relationships; structure from the conventions of interpersonal morality that unambiguously define virtue and vice and underlie trust and positive self-regard; and motivation from the possibility of advancement in the hierarchy, with corresponding increments of wealth, security, prestige or power. Advancement in the local hierarchy defines optimization of life chances in the agrarian cultural context. Agrarian societies are, in Dahrendorf's terms, rich in social linkages. They do not, for the most part, offer social identities that transcend or reject existing linkages in the pursuit of individual fulfillment as do contemporary Western societies, or they at most reserve such identities for a few exceptions at the top of the age-sex hierarchy.

The potentials of the individual that agrarian peoples select for optimal development are accordingly different from those of the urban-industrial West. They include, as we shall show in this chapter, child-bearing, a variety of social skills (e.g. obedience, cooperation), and religious piety. All of these are framed in terms of social ties of kinship and neighborhood and are designed to maximize the connectedness of the individual to a community that can confer the benefits of security, trust and continuity – benefits that cannot be purchased in the economic marketplace.

Concepts such as optimal development and maximization are of course alien in an agrarian context, where the Enlightenment conceptions of human perfectibility and progress, with their implications of hope for the fulfillment of individual aspirations, do not form part of the basic assumptions about life. Agrarian discourse tends to presume as known the benefits of social and moral order and to foster realistic expectations of reciprocity within a predictable pattern of life span experience. If its norms sound oppressive to the ears of contemporary Western intellectuals, they must nevertheless be recognized as having provided material as well as moral benefits to agrarian peoples over the centuries and as having generated the codes of the world's great religions. While they recognize a place for individual ambition, agrarian cultures limit its horizons to a point within reach of the average person, while at the same time imagining higher ideals that may not be realized by anyone in the community. This is a different way of structuring human aspirations than one centered on an occupational hierarchy for which all are prepared to compete through years of formal schooling. Given a view of life chances in which ligatures weigh as much as options, however, it is not clear that the agrarian way is less beneficial to the individual than that of urban-industrial societies.

What *is* clear from the anthropological evidence is that agrarian models of the life span are not consistent with Western assumptions concerning the autonomous decision-maker and freedom of choice, assumptions embedded in the abstract models on which so much educational policy is based. The evidence reviewed in this chapter suggests that the peoples affected by policy interventions hold a different set of assumptions.

AGRARIAN SOCIETIES AND CULTURES

Though hardly uniform in their institutions, agrarian societies resemble each other in the economic and demographic conditions of family life, which are accompanied by broadly similar moral codes for parent-child relations and similar cultural models of the life span in which parenthood symbolically occupies the central place. This view of parenthood, more than anything else, distinguishes agrarian peoples as a whole from the urban-industrial world in thinking about human potential.

Agrarian populations raise their own food through the cultivation of crops, the rearing of domesticated animals, or a combination of the two, while residing in small rural communities. Each family or domestic group produces food for its own consumption without recourse to the market, although it may also sell or barter some of the produce to others. This relative autonomy of the family in producing the food it consumes is a defining feature of agrarian societies. (Thus we regard the contemporary People's Republic of China as a heavily *rural* society because the majority live in small communities devoted to food production, but one that is no longer agrarian because agriculture is collectivized and for the most part subject to direct bureaucratic control.) Until recently, agrarian communities were largely without schools, which meant the autonomy of the family extended to full control over the activities of children.

The common economic and demographic conditions of agrarian families can be considered under the headings of *child labor* and *natural fertility*, both of which reflect widespread adaptive solutions in agrarian settings that affect concepts of parenthood and parent-child relationships.

Child labor

In contrast with advanced industrial societies, agrarian societies not only use the labor of children aged six to fourteen in essential productive activities but are dependent on the economic contributions of child labor. The agrarian family operates as a team in which each individual is responsible for task performance in one or more phases of the productive process. The bonds of primary kinship – i.e., the parent-child, husband-wife and sibling bonds – serve as hierarchical work relationships according to customary norms, giving agrarian family life a somewhat formal character by modern Western standards.

Child labor is a necessity in the economic adaptation of agrarian peoples. Their techniques of agriculture and animal husbandry are labor-intensive and relatively inefficient, i.e. they require large inputs of human labor for the number of calories of food produced. In particular phases, e.g. the harvest, everyone capable of helping

27

must be mobilized to get the job done. Many other tasks (herding and feeding animals, carrying seeds and implements, certain kinds of planting and weeding) are particularly suitable for children, as they involve little skill or strength and can be carried out at or near home. Furthermore, children can perform necessary household tasks (fetching water, grinding, cooking, caring for infants) that free adults for directly productive work. Given the low-technology system of agrarian food production, the child contribution is both essential and readily available. Second, children form a very large proportion of agrarian populations because of a high death rate and low life expectancy for adults. If they were freed from work, children's food consumption would not be offset by a contribution to production, thus straining the limited adult work force to feed entirely dependent children. In the labor-intensive economy of the agrarian family, there is pressure to achieve a favorable cost-contribution ratio for each family member, who becomes engaged in the domestic work force at the earliest feasible age.

Agrarian societies are not all dependent on child labor to the same degree. Some experience less subsistence pressure than others, for reasons of climate, geography and technology. In some parts of Oceania, for example, food from the sea and a relatively undemanding agriculture combine to make it less imperative than elsewhere in the agrarian world that children contribute at early ages. In sub-saharan Africa, on the other hand, poor soil, unreliable rainfall and shifting cultivation with the hand-held hoe create an intense demand for routine labor including that of young children. The use of draft animals in plowing and other agrarian activities, as in rural areas of South Asia and Latin America, eases the demand and permits postponement of labor contributions to a later age. Certain specified crafts such as the weaving of Persian carpets depended on children to make knots too small for adult hands. Thus there is no given level of child involvement in domestic production that is common to all agrarian societies. It would be rare, however, to find an agrarian society in which the majority of children aged ten to fourteen were not making a significant contribution to the family economy. This means that agrarian parents in general expect from children obedience to their commands, respect for their status and responsibility for delegated tasks. These expectations are central to the status of children and to definitions of the parent-child relationship.

Natural fertility

In agrarian populations women and their mates do not deliberately curtail their period of child-bearing. While the women of contemporary industrial societies typically cease bearing children well before the age of thirty, agrarian women continue giving birth until menopause. Births are spaced, with an interval of two or three years and prolonged breast-feeding, in the interests of child health. Extended reproduction with a lengthy birth interval maximizes the number of surviving children possible among peoples with high infant and child mortality rates.

Children are wanted in part because of their labor contribution. Given high adult mortality, distributing births over twenty to thirty years has the added advantage of providing the younger children with adult siblings who can act in *loco parentis* after the real parents die. Thus 'natural' fertility, as demographers call child-bearing continued until menopause, is adaptive in terms of the family economy and the care of children. It is the reproductive arm of the agrarian system of domestic production, raising a work force as the family workers raise crops.

One typical consequence of natural fertility in the agrarian context is that every woman is expected to bear children, and those who do not are exceptional and are likely to be pitied and feared. Another consequence is that reproduction and child care are expected to involve much of a woman's adult life span, with relatively few women living many years beyond the last child's infancy. In general, reproduction is not seen as optional for individuals or the family but as a need of the highest priority and a lifelong process of family growth.

The phenomena of child labor and natural fertility show that agrarian families operate under economic and demographic conditions that give them a common interest in prolonged child-bearing and the raising of obedient children, leading to some common assumptions about parenthood and parent-child relations. These basic patterns of domestic production and reproduction, however, can be embedded in a wide variety of institutional forms.

Agrarian societies vary widely in their organization, both at the local level and in the wider structures of socio-economic and political integration. At the local level, there is variation in kinship –

i.e. in the reckoning of descent, the classification of kin, patterns of marriage and residence, rules of inheritance and the structure of authority and responsibility; there is also variation in the composition and governance of face-to-face communities. At levels beyond the locality, there is variation in the size, scale and complexity of political units, in the presence and penetration of market trade and economic specialization, and in the presence or absence of urban centers in which populations are concentrated and from which economic transactions and administrative decisions are coordinated.

The larger, more centralized and internally specialized organizations depend on an agricultural surplus which frees some people from the demands of food production to devote themselves to crafts, trade, administration and religious activities. The surplus is sometimes due to a bountiful environment, but more often to advances in extractive technology that make food production more efficient, or to military-political expansion that extracts surplus from one group to support another. Thus greater organizational complexity and coordination at translocal levels among agrarian societies is almost invariably associated with technological progress in cultivation (e.g., the plow, manuring), transportation (e.g., wheeled vehicles), food processing (e.g., the water mill), military weaponry and building construction; and with large-scale empires based on conquest and the collection of tribute.

Agrarian societies can be broadly classified by complexity into two categories: those with large-scale political integration, urban centers, networks of market trade, occupational specialties and advanced (but pre-industrial) technologies – and those without. Before AD 1500, the more complex agrarian societies were concentrated on the Eurasian land mass (stretching from Ireland and Portugal to Japan and Thailand), in North and West Africa, Malaya and Indonesia, Mesoamerica and Peru. The agrarian societies which were simpler in terms of their translocal organization were concentrated in sub-saharan Africa, the Pacific Islands and the Americas (except for Mesoamerica and Peru). The distance between these two broad classes in terms of social differentiation was considerable. For example, in the simpler societies, the life span was differentiated largely by sex and age, with certain specially marked exceptions for chiefs and ritual practitioners. The more complex societies, however, recognized occupational (largely craft and governmental) specialization and socio-political stratification – differences in skills and power – as the basis for distinct social identities with divergent patterns of life span experience.

On the other hand, it is easy to exaggerate the direct impact of societal complexity on the lives of the majority in agrarian societies. Even in the more complex societies, the majority were peasants or yeoman farmers, living in small rural villages, reproducing on a natural fertility schedule and depending on child labor. Urban centers, occupational specialization and political centralization unquestionably affected them but did not alter their basic adaptation to life. Towns were small, transportation was poor, and even many craftsmen grew their own food at home. The government neither provided welfare services nor tried to limit parental control of children, so it was possible to maintain a model of the parent-child relationship not very different from that of the simpler societies. Craft organization involved apprenticeship (usually in early adolescence) and the development of social mechanisms for children to be trained and make labor contributions outside the domestic group into which they were born or adopted at an early age. But the extent of apprenticeship or the sending of children to other homes varied widely among the complex agrarian societies and was nowhere as common as in pre-industrial Britain.

Along with the differences in organization between simple and complex agrarian societies there were corresponding differences in culture, based on literacy. The simpler societies lacked writing, while the more complex societies not only had writing as a means of notation and communication but a distinctly different development of culture associated with it. There were written texts, considered not only sacred in religious terms but also as embodying and defining cultural traditions – the codes of belief and conduct according to which life was to be lived. Literate specialists who could read these texts applied them to current situations. Each text-based religion spread far beyond the locality in which it had originated, through military conquest or peaceful proselytization, creating a distinction between prototypes embodied in sacred texts and their local variants adjusted to the unwritten folk cultures of the converts. Thus each of the great world religions of Eurasia – Hinduism, Buddhism, Confucianism, Islam and Judaeo-Christianity – provided a common set of ideals for agrarian peoples of previously diverse cultural backgrounds.

31

What is most striking about the great world religions from the perspective of parenthood and parent-child relationships is how compatible they were with what we have proposed as the common agrarian view: fertility and respect for parents are central values, now codified and elaborated in myth and a variety of other symbolic forms. However diverse these religious doctrines in their cultural origins and in their cosmological and theological assumptions, their family moralities have much in common. These were, and are, the religions of agrarian peoples, attuned to the pragmatic needs of domestic relationships in small food-producing communities while providing a universal symbolic code for their interpretation. In the scriptures of the world religions, the local conventions of non-literate agrarian societies were dramatized as virtues and vices of transcendent significance, principles of an order not merely social and moral but divine or cosmic. The forms of communication vary among agrarian societies – complex and simple, past and present – but the message is the same: multiply, and honor thy father and thy mother. This support from the most advanced and widespread religious doctrines for ancient norms and assumptions helped to perpetuate agrarian concepts of virtue and models of the life span for much of the past two thousand years.

AGRARIAN CONCEPTS OF VIRTUE

In an agrarian village, both organizational and cultural factors support fertility and filial loyalty as central to the group's evaluation of a person and the person's evaluation of self. The social ties of kinship and locality are defined by concepts of reciprocal obliga-tion, i.e. rules prescribing reciprocation between persons and fami-lies in providing needed resources to each other. Neighbors and brothers may recognize reciprocity in house-building, harvesting, defense against attack, and funerary rituals. These activities can be organized by village, kinship or a combination of both. Kin contri-bute to the bridewealth or dowry of a sibling's child, knowing the others will contribute to their children's marriages. Families in specified kin relationships, or who reside in the same village, can call upon each other's food stocks when one or the other is running low. In the more complex societies, reciprocal obligations also involve transfers between persons of unequal status, often using the idiom of kinship – e.g. caste and *jati* relationships in India, *compadrazgo* (godparenthood) in Mexico, and feudal ties between landlords and peasants in much of the pre-industrial Old World. Almost everywhere in the agrarian world, significant local relationships outside the domestic family are defined by mutual obligation, and a person's position in the community depends in part on meeting local standards of reciprocity.

The same principle applies within the domestic family, particularly in the parent-child relationship, although the time period for expectable reciprocation is often longer. Parents are seen as the nurturers and sponsors of their children, giving unilateral support and care for their young offspring for which they deserve a subsequent return. Child labor in this context, far from being exploitation, is the first installment of a child's reciprocation for what the parents have already given, namely, the gift of life and survival through infancy and early childhood. (If the child moves away, dies or becomes disaffected from the parents, child labor may also be the last installment; in many cases it is the only one of which a parent can be certain.) When the child marries, which usually involves feasts, gifts and ceremonies, the parents again provide crucial material and social support, for which later reciprocation may be expected. Where land is passed on from father to sons, the inheritance is considered (in advance) a major parental contribution for which a return from the child is expected. The most frequently expected return is material and social support from children in the parent's old age, though a proper burial (performed by the children themselves) is another often mentioned in African societies. Whatever the specifics, children are seen as owing their parents old-age support within the terms of a long-term relationship that follows the general rules of social reciprocity.

The parent-child relationship, however, is not simply a matter of obligation. Adult children support their parents for a variety of reasons that make sense in an agrarian context. Working with and under their parents during childhood and adolescence gives many children a lifelong sense of loyalty to their elders. If they live in the same village as their parents, the children will continue to share a familial identity and a sense of common fate with their family of origin. If they are waiting to inherit, they may try to please the parents in order to get more. Even if they move away at marriage, as women do in India, traditional China and much of Africa, children may cherish one or both of their parents above the relationships established by marriage and continue to visit and help as long as the older people are alive. The affection in such a relationship is accompanied by respect, for agrarian children have learned to respect their parents as well as obey them. In other words, the pattern of socialization that gives children the obedience and compliance to function effectively as child laborers frequently imbues them with lifelong positive feelings, varying in conceptual and emotional quality from one culture to another, but amounting to a filial loyalty that maintains reciprocity between child and parent.

Agrarian filial loyalty is thus voluntary as well as obligatory, representing individual self-interest as well as altruism, involving rational calculation as well as emotional attachment. It is a mark of public virtue and may also be a sign of religious piety. Confucian doctrine links filiality with the basic principles of order in society and the universe. While other agrarian ideologies may not give it such a central place or connect it so explicitly with social and cosmic order, they consider filial loyalty a moral value of the highest priority, often surrounded by sacred symbolism.

This analysis of filial relationships in agrarian societies clarifies the meaning and function of child labor and natural fertility in several ways. First, child labor is not simply a compulsory economic contribution but part of a lifelong relationship between child and parent that is conceptualized as consistent with the reciprocal moral order of the community. This order entails filial loyalty to parents as they grow older, an obligation particularly emphasized in the great world religions and implemented on a voluntary basis throughout the agrarian world. Parents are normally limited in exploiting their immature children by the desire to maintain a long-term relationship in which old-age support can be reasonably expected from them as adults. The normative order of agrarian society creates a setting in which moral duty and economic self-interest can be congruent.

Second, reciprocity is not necessarily achieved within a generation. It may well be that agrarian children give more to their parents than they receive in terms of the hypothetical market value of goods and services. It is assumed, however, that every child will become a parent, thus correcting the imbalance in exchange with his own parents.

Third, it is in the interests of each parent to bear as many children as possible, since children acquire a lifelong loyalty benefiting parents: more children mean more security. Yet this is not naked self-interest, for the proliferation of progeny multiplies relationships, each of which widens the circle of reciprocation and expands the moral community of kinship. In agrarian settings particularly afflicted by intergroup violence and instability, reproduction may be the only reliable way of expanding the circle of people one can trust.

All of this means that parents in agrarian villages pursue the goals of bearing many children and securing their compliance and loyalty – which benefit parents economically – with the sense that they are not only morally virtuous by community standards but are realizing the highest and most sacred potential of human life as conceptualized in religious doctrine and celebrated in ritual. The religiously validated moral ideals and economically based practical requirements of family life find common ground in the social conventions of a small community, through which public images of vice and virtue are propagated. Gossip stigmatizes those who are infertile, speculating on the immorality that might have led to their affliction and the witchcraft (based on envy) that might follow from it. Sons who oppose their fathers are subjected to more formal sanctions, and even if applied in private they are soon known throughout the village, adding to the stock of horror stories about deviants from filial piety.

What is most important about agrarian concepts of virtue, however, is not that they are used to punish deviants and reward conformists to community standards in the manner of a legal code that is being enforced, but that they offer rich models of the good life and the good person that inspire identification in boys and girls and motivate adults to realize the cultural ideals in their own lives. These cultural influences are effective because: 1) the models are so deeply grounded in the pragmatics of the agrarian family situation that they are consistent with common-sense conclusions an intelligent villager could reach in an independent appraisal – i.e., they are reinforced by experience; 2) the symbols in traditional models are more elaborated conceptually and more appealing emotionally than those of any other available ideology (if indeed any other is available); 3) through the conventions of the small community, the cultural models, even if originating in distant religious doctrines, have become accommodated to the contingencies of village life, so that the ideals they embody are viewed as locally realizable.

Thus rejection of fertility and filial loyalty as personal goals is not regarded as a possibility for a normal person; it would be considered symptomatic of madness (acting against one's obvious self interest) as well as immorality. Agrarian men and women construct their social identities from the cultural models available to them, with fertility and filial loyalty as salient themes in their images of personal advancement, moral virtue and sacred duty. The means by which agrarian social identities are constructed, however, can only be understood by examining, in overview, the representations of self and the organization of the life course in the cultures of agrarian peoples.

THE SELF AND THE LIFE COURSE IN AGRARIAN CULTURES: BEYOND WESTERN ASSUMPTIONS

In this section we explore at a deeper level the assumptions agrarian peoples bring to the construction of social identities in which fertility and filial loyalty are so salient. We have until now used terms such as 'reciprocity' and 'identity' as if they had the same meanings in agrarian contexts as they do in our own culture. This may have been misleading, however, because Westerners often assume the prior existence of a separate self that enters into reciprocal relationships like a sovereign state committing itself to an international treaty, and agrarian peoples do not think about their reciprocal obligations that way. Similarly, Westerners often view the construction of an identity as a matter of individual choice, and this, too, is not the way agrarian villagers see the development of their identities. It is difficult to find a terminology free of culture-specific assumptions, but unless we try to do so we may mistakenly attribute our own beliefs to others simply because we cannot conceptualize alternatives.

This has been a common mistake in psychology, as indeed in all disciplines that have sought to generalize about the thought, feelings and behavior of humanity on the basis of evidence drawn exclusively from Western populations and settings. We are now fortunate, however, in that some anthropologists have inquired into the ethnopsychologies (i.e., the indigenous psychological concepts) of diverse peoples, many of them agrarian, in order to describe in painstaking detail the different cultural perspectives that exist about human behavior and development.

Fundamental questions have been raised about the universal applicability of Western psychological concepts. Hsu (1971) has argued that the concept of personality represents Western in-dividualism in its assumption of a strongly bounded person with a sharp distinction between what is inside and outside. He states that 'personality' is a manifestly inadequate term in a Chinese context, where the Western assumption does not hold, and he suggests the Chinese concept of *jen*, referring to the person and his proximate environment, as a more appropriate term for capturing (in all cultures) the psycho-social homeostasis that includes significant others in the conditions of emotional sta-bility. Marriott and Inden (1977) have objected to the term 'individual' as carrying the Western assumption of a person's indivisibility; this assumption is not applicable in Hindu India, where a more fluid concept of the person – which they refer to as 'dividual' – is dominant.

These challenges to psychological terminology of the most basic sort represent the general position that Western psychology does not operate from a privileged location independent of culture but shares many of its assumptions with the Western folk and philo-sophical traditions of thought from which it grew. It is charged, in effect, with being one of many ethnopsychologies rather than the universal science it has claimed to be.

We are not ready to reject all of the claims of Western psycholo-gy, but we do believe 1) that non-Western peoples operate with premises about human behavior radically different from those of the West, 2) that these premises and their consequences have not been anticipated in Western psychological theory or research, and 3) that understanding these premises is essential to understanding how non-Western peoples experience their lives and what consti-tutes improvement or fulfillment in those lives.

At the most general level it can be said that Western thought is dualistic – it posits dichotomies regarding psychological phenomena (mind *v.* body, thought *v.* feeling, person *v.* situation) – that are not recognized in non-Western cultures, that this difference is symp-tomatic of divergent assumptions about the person and interperson-

37

al relations, and that the divergence is greatest between Western thought and all other cultures studied to date. In other words, most non-Western cultures resemble each other more than any of them resembles the West – or so it seems so far. This suggests that skepticism of Western psychology as a guide to human experience as a whole may well be justified.

The conclusions we draw from anthropological research on concepts of the personal and interpersonal relations in diverse (largely agrarian) societies are summarized below:

    1   There are concepts of the person and the self in all cultures. Self-awareness and a sense of one's continuity over time are universal in human experience, and all human adults distinguish between actions of the self as opposed to those of another.

    2   Thoughts, feelings and behaviors described in psychological terms in the West are located by some cultures either in bodily organs or social situations. They are accounted for in what we would call biological or sociological terms, and set in a broader framework that we would call religious. The distinctions between medicine, biology, psychology, sociology and religion current in the West are not replicated throughout the world; the phenomena involved are most frequently referred to in agrarian cultures through what might be called moral-medical discourse, i.e. in terms of social norms that involve bodily processes which can require the attention of healers.

    3   Every culture has a lexicon of character traits, but there is wide variation in their elaboration, purpose and frequency of use, and in their implications of stability, personal distinctiveness and personal responsibility. Agrarian cultures have lexicons of life stages, social roles and local relationships that are often given precedence over idiosyncratic traits in describing a person. In agrarian societies the most frequent purposes for describing a person are to locate his or her position in relation to others in the community, for which a history of family exchanges may be considered the most relevant context, or to evaluate his or her moral conduct, for which the conventions of social interaction provide the terms of reference. Apparent exceptions are found where socially organized competition – e.g., the struggle for leadership in some Oceanic

societies – has made invidious distinctions salient in social comparison; there an elaborate vocabulary of individual traits comparable to that of Western societies (also notable for their socially organized competition and the salience of invidious distinctions in their social comparisons) seems to be more frequently used.

4   Anthropological field workers have long reported that diverse non-Western peoples, ranging from Eskimos, Hopi and Tahitians to Hindu Indians and Japanese, do not make so sharp a distinction between the person and the group as is made in the West. In the cultures of small communities, hunting and gathering as well as agrarian, the social sharing of responsibility is so fundamental in normal thought, behavior and discourse that Western field workers are frequently confronted by instances of it that contrast with Western norms: A person is punished, along with others, for a crime committed by another member of his or her kin group. People entertain kinsmen who arrive without prior notice, although it interrupts their ongoing activities for days at a time and involves considerable expense. A young woman who is asked for her opinion on an issue refers the investigator to her father-in-law, the head of the family, rather than answering herself. A child falls ill or an adult becomes psychotic, and the affliction is attributed to spiritual neglect by the head of the domestic group or his deceased grandfather. In these instances, the autonomy of the individual as conceived in Western thought seems to be denied at a very basic level.

5   In agrarian contexts, morality and intelligence are conceptually fused rather than distinguished in the evaluation of social performance (Lutz and LeVine, 1983). The idea of intelligent behavior that is contrary to or independent of moral norms is treated as novel and even a contradiction in terms: If you are intelligent, you behave according to the moral norms of the community because to do otherwise would antagonize those with whom you are permanently connected – which no intelligent adult would want to do (unless driven mad by external influence). Those who behave in accordance with social convention are assumed to be intelligent in the way that counts the most, i.e., in their maintenance of the social linkages that mean long-term security, though this implies normal rather than

exceptional intelligence. Those in the community who are most respected for their moral virtue are credited with being wisest and most intelligent when the question is asked by an outside observer, though the separation between moral and cognitive qualities would not be made spontaneously in discourse among community members.

6   The skills involved in productive work and in arts and crafts among agrarian peoples are not normally the focus of global evaluation of the person by self or others. Skilled performance is required in adult sex roles and is taken for granted as characteristic of the normal man or woman. Those with exceptional skills are admired for them but gain no increment in social rank unless the skills contribute directly to success in a socially organized competition. In many agrarian societies, however, overt competition of all kinds is avoided. Prestige is more likely to be based on success in both managing relationships and acquiring wealth or power rather than on demonstrated competence in a specialized skill.

The social identities of agrarian peoples are thus constructed in ways not encompassed by Western psychological concepts. They are based on one's location in a network of social linkages rather than on personal qualities defined independently of linkages. This often involves assuming as part of one's identity characteristics of one's family with whom one is linked in the eyes of the community. Although this locational identity is not lost, it changes as one grows older, forges new links and acquires more status. Conformity to the social conventions of village life, rather than performance in a role requiring specialized skill, is central to the acquisition of higher status in adulthood. Such conformity is interpreted as moral virtue, reflecting not the sacrifice of self but the good sense to see that one's personal interests are best advanced through the maintenance and cultivation of reciprocal relationships. This entails avoiding interpersonal antagonism and even overt competition in many settings, but agrarian adults who have been raised as compliant children to identify and cooperate with others are not only accustomed to avoiding conflict; they have come to feel more secure in doing so than they would in jeopardizing linkages through public self-assertion. The avoidance of interpersonal conflict is experienced not as damaging to one's evaluation of self (as many Americans would experience it) but as an automatic act of adaptation that is consistent with both the pursuit of virtue and improvement of one's position in life.

What constitutes improvement in the agrarian setting? In every agrarian community there is a local age-sex hierarchy, i.e. a ranked social order in which positions are determined by age and sex, though other criteria are also involved. The adult men and adult women form separate reference groups within which seniority in age means higher status. The men as a whole are ranked higher than the females and usually comprise the more socially visible grouping, though the women as a group and in individual cases may have more social power than their public positions convey. This hierarchy may include a formal decision-making group, settling disputes and allocating resources. It may involve patron-client and caste relationships in addition to the ties of kinship and neighborhood. Whatever its specific organization, however, the local age-sex hierarchy is the stage on which the agrarian drama of life is played, with the players moving through age-graded roles in search of fulfilment.

Advancement in the local age-sex hierarchy of an agrarian community is quite predictable, since one's sex is fixed at birth and the stages of life are culturally established before one reaches them. In the life plan for men there is a pre-adult, usually premarital, stage, sometimes involving warrior status; a young adult, usually married stage, that involves hard work and provision for young children; and an elder stage, that involves the highest respect, leisure and often a major role in the governing of the community. The plan as a whole offers hope to each boy of increasing honor as he grows older; it provides a cognitive map for future aspirations. The greatest uncertainty concerns survival, for in a population with a high death rate, many men do not live to enjoy the last and best stage, and this is something outside of their control.

Aging by itself does not guarantee a man the best rewards possible in each of these stages, for he must acquire the respect of his seniors and peers in the hierarchy by demonstrating his maturity according to local standards: 1) reproductive maturity, i.e. begetting the expected number of children and grandchildren of the valued age and sex by the time his cohort reaches a given stage; 2) moral maturity, i.e. visible adherence to the normative conventions relevant to his age and stage; and 3) economic maturity, some

41

minimum level of affluence expectable at a given age. (A man does not ordinarily gain more respect if his wealth is due to his own efforts rather than to his inheritance; in the agrarian context, the inheritance belongs to him as much as his 'earnings' would in a Western society.)

There is a similar life plan for women but its status gradient with age has an even steeper upward slope, as young married women frequently begin at the bottom of the adult hierarchy and undergo a sharp improvement after menopause as they are freed from earlier constraints and gain the honor of grandparenthood – which, it must be remembered, is a recognized contribution to production and family security in an agrarian community.

For agrarian men and women, the life plan offers rewards that are highly significant. Having acquired their earliest identities in a local context established by the age-sex hierarchy, they experience the chance to ascend that hierarchy and enjoy the privileges of its higher positions as a singularly meaningful benefit, realizing potentials they learned to cherish long ago. They have a good chance to reach the top providing they survive – an important qualification where mortality is high, but one that at least does not expand the numbers of those with frustrated ambitions. Furthermore, if they do live long enough, agrarian men and women enjoy public honor in their later years rather than (as in industrial societies) at an intermediate point with a substantial decline to follow.

There is a religious component in the agrarian villagers' experience of the local hierarchy. Fertility and filial loyalty are celebrated in their myths and ceremonies, giving larger meanings to their reproductive lives and interpersonal relationships. Furthermore, their life plan moves the person not simply toward death but toward an immortality in which they remain permanently connected with their descendants and ancestors. Thus growing old and moving up in the local hierarchy mean not only gaining social respect but improving one's place in a larger order symbolized in terms of divinity or cosmology.

The great world religions provided, for the more complex agrarian societies, theologically-derived life plans which involved a sequence of stages that gave structure to the expectations of men and women. Although their models of the life course vary among themselves and are not merely replicas of the folk models found in the simpler agrarian societies, there is significant concordance, particularly in the emphasis on honoring elders, thus giving an upward sweep to the life span in terms of anticipated rewards.

AGRARIAN EXPERIENCE: PRELIMINARY CONCLUSIONS

This overview suggests in broad strokes the differences between agrarian and Western urban-industrial peoples that help account for the divergent goals they pursue in life, the differing benefits they obtain, and their differing constructions of the life span. Our basic argument has been that the social identities of agrarian peoples are founded on permanent social relationships they seek to expand and enhance through a lifetime of child-bearing, domestic food and craft production and increasingly mature reciprocity in the setting of a small community. This agrarian pattern has its origins in the ecology of labor-intensive family food production, which favors high fertility and the use of child labor, giving rise to cultural values supporting filial loyalty and extended child-bearing. These values, built into the moral and religious fabric of agrarian cultural traditions, including the doctrines of the great world religions, create a different sense of what is worth pursuing in life than is current in the West. For agrarian peoples, reciprocity occurs in a context established by the assumption of prior interdependency rather than prior separateness, and identity is less a matter of personal choice than one of progression along a predictable pathway. By the same token, the improvements in life that are sought and the realization that is imagined are conceptualized in terms of the quality of relationships with the living, the dead and the divine.

This agrarian pattern has often been classified by sociologists as 'particularism' and contrasted with the 'universalism' that makes Western bureaucracies work and allegedly represents the next stage in the global evolution of society. What has been overlooked is that agrarian particularism provided rural inhabitants with a level of social security – including goods and services, emotional confidence and a sense of worth – that may never be replaced for most of the world's peoples by the bureaucratic governments and economic markets to which they have access.

43

LIFE CHANCES IN AGRARIAN SOCIETIES

What benefits could individuals expect from agrarian societies as they existed in the past – before 1500 for the world as a whole, but also as recently as 1900 for much of Africa, mainland Asia and the Pacific – and what costs did they experience in their social lives? It is not impossible to attempt this assessment in economic terms, but this would cover only a small part of what agrarian peoples found rewarding in their lives and what they expended or contributed to others. This is not only because they exchanged so many goods and services through the reciprocal relationships of kinship, neighborhood and clientage rather than through market transactions, or because so many material resources crucial to survival were often available without payment to all members of an agrarian community – though these conditions often prevailed. Rather it is because, for agrarian peoples as for the rest of us, economic goods and services were only meaningful as means towards other ends – and it is agrarian conceptions and experience of these ends that we seek to understand.

The productive and medical technologies of agrarian societies were clearly inefficient by modern standards. This meant agrarian peoples faced subsistence hazards, work demands and health conditions that were severe compared with contemporary urban-industrial peoples. On the other hand, in many cases relatively low food production *per capita* was balanced by high mortality rates, i.e., the economy was limited but so was the population, so that subsistence was not threatened by reproduction. Agrarian populations that outgrew their resource base, however, turned to warfare for plunder and tribute, establishing conquest states and empires (Fried, 1967). But the question remains how the capacities and limitations of agrarian societies were translated into subjective benefits and costs for their members.

Our answer to this question, which cannot be complete on the basis of available evidence, is that agrarian societies provided their members with the benefits of security, respect and continuity – through means that entailed substantial costs.

44

Security

Agrarian social structures provided means of keeping predictable risks, hazards and uncertainties within bounds, and agrarian cultures provided symbolic representations of ideal states of security which even if not attainable were pleasurable to imagine or experience vicariously. The reciprocities of kin and neighborhood networks, and patron-client relations, could be called upon to share responsibility at times of need and crisis, e.g., when famine, attack from enemies, or interpersonal conflict threatened family survival or unity. In the absence of the state or under it, those structures of mutual responsibility gave emergency help in terms of food and labor, acted as a military defense force and gathered to settle disputes. They were activated frequently enough so that each individual knew from experience that their responsible action was not merely hypothetical but a predictable part of reality itself. Furthermore, parents could look to their children for support in old age, based on filial loyalty as obligation and voluntary commitment.

Thus local relationships operated as systems of social and military security, affording (at their best) material support and protection in time of need as well as an expandable moral community within which responsibility was shared. Dramatized in religion and local belief, this moral system of filiality and mutual responsibility was the dominant ideology of the community, encouraging individuals to feel secure in the interdependencies and reciprocities of local ties. This feeling of security must be classified as a personal benefit of great value to any adult in an agrarian society.

Respect

As we have suggested earlier in this chapter, agrarian models of the life span included a hierarchy of age-graded roles in which those of highest status could be occupied only by elder men and women. While many did not live to an age in which they could occupy such respected roles and not all who survived that long were entitled to do so, statuses commanding a good deal of community respect were frequently available to the majority. Even those who did not qualify as notables of the village commanded the respect of their adult children as their parents, of their kin as senior members of a descent group, and of their peers as bearers of children and respectable participants in the community. There is every indication that agrarian men and women experienced this respect as a benefit worth having, seeking, and holding onto, whether or not it afforded actual power.

Continuity

Agrarian cultures offered powerful social identities grounded in the same permanent reference groups that provided security and respect in one's own adult years, and a sense of continuity over the generations. Lineages, for example – in Africa as well as China – encompassed dead ancestors and future descendants in a conception of intergenerational permanence and renewal that placed each male in a genealogical succession of which he could be proud. Where social organization was non-lineal, it gave women as well as men a sense of permanent membership in an entity larger than themselves, even when they travelled, and a sense of participation in a group, a history or a cosmos that transcended the human life span.

Social identities such as these are deeply satisfying for reasons that are not obscure but have not been investigated in sufficient detail: they enhance one's sense of self-worth through identification with public figures and divinities; they deny the finality of death and enable each person to imagine himself immortal; they therefore enable one to believe that wishes unfulfilled in this life have another chance, through future generations, an afterlife or reincarnation. The resultant sense of continuity is experienced as uniquely beneficial. Perhaps this is why cost-conscious Europeans and Americans go on bearing children, however low their fertility, when it is not economically rational to do so: children provide the sense of continuity for secular Westerners. This may also be why modern urban Japanese often maintain a small altar in their homes at which they communicate with deceased parents and spouses: relationships, even after death, can be continued and even improved, whatever Western scientific education might propound. In agrarian settings, however, the desire for progeny and contact with departed forebears were given a level of public support and symbolic elaboration that is missing in urban-industrial societies. In other words, agrarian societies satisified what appears to be a general human need more fully and wholeheartedly than the rich nations of the contemporary world.

Thus agrarian peoples, despite their short life expectancies and poverty of material goods, enjoyed the benefits of security, respect and continuity as provided by their social structures and represented in the symbols of their cultural traditions. They cannot be validly portrayed as disadvantaged and deprived simply because their technology and economy were inefficient relative to ours. The wealth of urban-industrial peoples is meaningless if not translated into security, respect and continuity for individuals and families. This argument, however, raises many questions for future research, questions concerning the specific ways in which social structures past and present have provided benefits that cannot be measured through conventional economic indicators.

What about the costs exacted by agrarian societies, their inadequacies in terms of subjective well-being and suffering? Rather than focus on the obvious deficiencies in technology, economy, health and literacy, it is instructive to examine the categories of benefit just reviewed – security, respect and continuity – to assess their limitations and the requirements they imposed. In regard to security, for example, there are the severe limits of agrarian societies in providing physical safety. Many agrarian societies were afflicted by internal feuding, warfare and banditry which created chronic fear of being killed, robbed or abducted if one ventured outside the community. Social anthropologists have identified and emphasized the social connections through which agrarian peoples maintained and mobilized defensive alliances that afforded protection under the circumstances. In many cases, however, the imposition of colonial rule and emergence of national states – whatever their disadvantages in other respects – brought an unprecedented peace of mind to ordinary people: relief at last from the insecurity of violent conflict between local groups. Despite the struggles of pastoralists and foragers to remain independent of national governments, the sedentary majority of agrarian societies across the world welcomed the protection they gained only when violence was centrally controlled by an effective government. This had happened under secure agrarian-based empires for varying periods of time, but agrarian societies, generally speaking, could not safeguard their local communities from the risk of group violence.

Thus the security found in local ties was severely limited by the fragility of interlocal government. This could be said of economic security too, in that the local interdependence and reciprocities of agrarian communities were limited in their response to famines and other failures of food production once they became widespread. Furthermore, it could be argued that the security for an old person possible in dependence on adult offspring could not match that provided by the predictability of bureaucratically administered old-age assistance in contemporary industrial societies. That does not settle the issue, however, for security is ultimately a function of subjective experience rather than economic transfers, and its beneficial aspects may derive as much from the interpersonal and ideational context as from the stability and magnitude of resources involved. Is a check in the mail necessarily preferable to a continuing relationship with one's children? The economic security of agrarian societies was more limited and fragile than bureaucratic assistance provides, but the radical differences in context keep the question of benefit and cost open to future investigations.

Respect raises similar issues. In many agrarian societies a large number of people were able to experience being a 'big frog in a little pond,' due to the small size of the community and its local age-sex hierarchy. (In the case of slaves, serfs, untouchables and other pariahs, this benefit is of course not available.) Generally speaking, agrarian ambitions were kept within the bounds of possible realization. This counts as a benefit in subjective terms, for it permitted men and women to treasure the respect available to them and experience fulfillment within their reference groups. Once agrarian peoples came to believe that alternative – and higher – forms of respect were available to them in the world outside their local reference groups, their aspirations expanded and they sought to improve the status of their children – largely through formal education, as subsequent chapters show.

Did the lower aspirations of the agrarian condition induce agrarian peoples to settle for less respect than would have benefited them? To answer in the affirmative is to argue that living with virtuous but unrealizable aspirations is more beneficial than aspiring only to those within reach – an answer supported by Western mythology from Icarus to John F. Kennedy but alien to the reflective social thought of many non-Western cultures. The question haunts any case that can be made for the beneficial qualities of past societies less sophisticated than our own. At this point we argue that agrarian societies, particularly in their models of life span progression for each sex, provided widespread potentialities for beneficial respect that deserve more careful examination than they have received. The costs of these agrarian systems appear to have been borne by women, slaves and pariah groups who helped others realize their potentials for social respect without gaining an equivalent measure of respect for themselves. (There is also the special problem of child labor which needs more treatment than given here.) We return to these arguments and the issues they raise in Chapter 8.

Continuity is a strong point of agrarian societies: it represents a clear subjective benefit that is much less attainable in societies recently transformed by mass urbanization and other forms of social change. Perhaps it represents costs to society in the form of conservatism and parochialism as obstacles to economic development – this is a common viewpoint – but it would be hard to argue that it was a direct cause of individual suffering rather than a form of basic satisfaction which all adults seek.

To summarize: the life chances of agrarian societies were provided by their ligatures, i.e., their local groups and networks of reciprocity, their code of fertility and filial loyalty and the interpersonal support, normative structure and motivating ideals of their local age-sex hierarchies. Potentials were conceptualized and experienced as inherent in relationships rather than in choices and freedom of action. The question of benefits and costs in the social ties of agrarian societies is a topic for further research. At this point, however, it is possible to state that there were benefits – experienced in the security, respect and sense of continuity provided by agrarian social structures and symbol systems – and that there were costs, experienced through the limits of small communities in controlling the threat of external violence and through forms of hierarchy that seemed to deny respect to certain categories of people.

At the unresolved center of agrarian life chances as a problem for cost-benefit assessment is the sense of self: can we believe that individual persons in agrarian societies so identified with their local reference groups and roles based on kinship, neighborhood and clientage that they experienced benefits to the group or patron as benefits to the self? Is it possible that the costs which we have pointed to were not experienced as diminished well-being due to such close identification of persons with others? Is our difficulty in accepting such strong forms of identification as valid due to our assumption of a minimal personal autonomy that seems universal but is in fact culture-bound? This is the challenge for further inquiry into this problem: to achieve a more adequate conception of the self in diverse cultures through examination of empirical evidence that bears on these questions.

3

REVOLUTION IN PARENTHOOD

During the past 200 years, the conditions of child development in much of the world have changed more drastically than they had in millennia – perhaps since the spread of agrarian conditions after 7000 BC. The history of this recent change can be traced numerically, with school enrollments rising and infant mortality rates falling, when countries industrialized, populations moved to the city and families reduced their fertility. It can be told as a moral tale, with the elimination of child labor and illiteracy, when parents and public policy-makers alike recognized the rights and expanded the opportunities of children. It can be, and often is, looked upon as a struggle for the welfare of children which is not yet won, particularly since many of the conditions abolished in the industrial countries, e.g. high infant mortality, illiteracy and child labor, still exist in the Third World.

However one regards this shift, it represents a fundamental change not only in the means by which children are raised but in the reasons for which they are brought into the world and the goals which they pursue during their lives. It is a change we are only beginning to understand in terms of its history, its causes and its contemporary directions. This chapter provides an overview of its major elements, particularly in the West, and considers its implications for the comparative analysis of parenthood and child development.

The social changes we review have undermined the agrarian conceptions of the life span described in the previous chapter, particularly the centrality of fertility and filial loyalty in the social identities of men and women. This shift has occurred in the industrial countries of the West, Eastern Europe and Japan. It has been occurring, and continues, in certain countries of the Third World, though not uniformly within those countries. That the shift deserves to be called 'revolutionary' can hardly be disputed; the question is whether it should be thought of as one revolution or many. Are all the socio-economic, demographic, educational and ideological changes involved but different aspects of one comprehensive process of social transformation (e.g., 'modernization') or separable processes that happen to be linked in particular historical cases? Are the sequences and outcomes of recent change – particularly in Japan and the Third World – replicating those of the past, particularly of nineteenth-century Europe and the United States?

This question, even in specific regard to family life, has concerned sociologists for a long time, but many of them chose to resolve it by positing a unitary process, driving history in a single direction – in advance of strong empirical evidence. In retrospect, theories of global modernization, like the classical Marxist stages of history, seem examples of what Hirschman (1971) has called 'paradigms as a hindrance to understanding': they prevented taking diversity seriously enough, until evidence of diversity overwhelmed the very theories that had denied their importance. Fortunately, social scientists have brought a wealth of new evidence to bear on questions of historical change in family life and the conditions of child development in social and cultural settings throughout the world. This evidence points to a history of the family changing in response to specific local conditions rather than moving in one preordained direction.

The abandonment of unilinear evolution as a conceptual framework for analyzing social change in family life does not mean the denial of recurrent trends that can be documented and are clearly significant. On the contrary, those broad trends must be the starting point for our inquiry. We begin with a brief consideration of the radically diverse perspectives from which children are viewed in the contemporary world, both in the private contexts of family life and the public contexts of national and international policy. Then we ask: How did it come to be this way? How did human societies develop such differing perspectives on children? In our view, this amounts to asking how – given a world with primarily agrarian perspectives only two centuries ago, did some societies move so far from these perspectives?

52

In this chapter we explore this transformation as it first occurred in the West, drawing upon some new evidence concerning economic, demographic, educational and ideological trends. In the next chapter we examine the transformation of schooling from its pre-industrial forms and premises in Western and non-Western societies to the mass phenomenon it has become throughout the world. Chapter 5 begins consideration of similar changes in non-Western societies, with a particular focus on Japan as a country that adopted the goal of educational mobilization from the West but achieved it – with unique success – in its own way, self-consciously departing from Western precedents. Chapter 6 continues the examination of non-Western change in the context of contemporary Chinese society, which represents the most extreme deviation from Western ends as well as means. In Chapter 7 we examine, in overview, the Third World societies, where new combinations of Western and indigenous models have emerged.

THE MEANINGS OF CHILDREN: DIFFERENCES AND SIMILARITIES IN THE CONTEMPORARY WORLD

In contrast with agrarian values, the cultures of industrialized countries, particularly their middle-class subcultures, tend to value parent-child relationships which provide unilateral support – economic, emotional and social – from parents to their children, with parents not expected to receive anything tangible in return. The period of such support in Western societies has been lengthening, from childhood through adolescence into adulthood, and the proportion of family resources devoted to children increasing.

The current state of the evidence has been summarized by Hoffman and Manis (1979, p. 590):

> [The] economic value of children is particularly salient among rural parents and in countries where the economy is primarily rural. In addition, children are often seen as important for security in old age. Children are valued for this function, particularly where there is no official, trusted, and acceptable provision for the care of the aged and disabled.
>
> In a highly industrialized country like the United States, however, with a government-sponsored social security system,

children are less likely to have economic utility. Even their utility in rural areas might be lessened because of rural mechanization and the greater availability of hired help. And, since the cost of raising children is higher in the more urban and industrially advanced countries, children are not likely to be seen as an economic asset.

When a national sample of Americans was asked about the advantages of having children, only 3.1 per cent of the white mothers with more than twelve years of schooling gave answers involving economic utility (Hoffman and Manis, 1979, p. 585). The rest of that sub-sample mentioned a variety of social, emotional and moral benefits. The responses of East Asian mothers to this question help to place the American figure in a global context:

Table 3.1
Advantages of Having Children: Per Cent Mentioning
Economic Utility

	Urban Middle Class	Rural
Japan	2	11
Taiwan	3	36
Philippines	30	60

Source: Arnold, 1975, Table 4.4

In the industrial countries, Japan and Taiwan, the proportion of urban middle-class respondents mentioning the economic utility of children is virtually identical to the more educated white mothers in the United States, despite differences in culture. In the Phillipines, a largely agrarian country, the proportion of the urban middle class perceiving economic benefits in children is ten times higher. Within each of the three Asian countries, with national policies of old-age assistance held constant, the rural proportion is at least twice as high as that of the urban middle class. While such figures from one limited question are only suggestive, they show the magnitude of the differences in attitudes and their powerful association with agrarian life both within and between contemporary countries.

The fact that the majority of middle-class parents in industrial countries expect no tangible return from children is paradoxical, not only from the perspective of utilitarian economics, which assumes that substantial investment must be motivated by the expectation of material return, but also from the viewpoint of agrarian cultures, in which reciprocity between the generations is a basic principle of social life. It does not seem paradoxical to most Westerners, who take it for granted that the parent-child relationship is exempted from ideas of material return and long-term reciprocation.

Indeed, the Western notion that the welfare of children should represent the highest priority for society as well as parents and that children should be unstintingly supported without calculation of reward – a revolutionary idea in world history – has established itself as an unchallengeable principle of international morality. The most fervent support for the idea, however, continues to come from northwestern Europe and the United States, where the public defense of children is an established cultural tradition, religious and secular, generating symbols used to arouse intense emotions, mobilize voluntary activity and subsidize programs of action.

What is most remarkable about this basically Western ideology that has been accepted in international forums as a universal moral code is that it entails a passionate concern with the welfare of *other people's children*. In other words, it presumes that the current well-being and future development of children are the concern and responsibility not only of their parents but of a community – local, national and international – that is not based on kinship. Westerners are proud, for example, of the long and ultimately successful campaign against child labor waged by reformers in their own countries, but their ideology requires that such benefits be extended to all children everywhere. In some Western countries such as Sweden, the Netherlands and Canada, there is more concern with, and activity on behalf of, poor children in Third World societies than there is among the privileged segments of the latter societies. This gap in cultural values belies the apparent consensus embodied in UN declarations and points to the radical disagreement about practices such as child labor that would emerge if Western reformers tried harder to implement their ideals as global programs of action. How did the West acquire its contemporary cultural ideals concerning parent-child relationships and other people's children? That is the question to be explored in this chapter, in terms of four topics: a) the shift from agrarian to urban-industrial institutions, b) the demographic transition, c) mass schooling, and d) the rise of a public interest in children.

THE SHIFT FROM AGRARIAN TO URBAN-INDUSTRIAL INSTITUTIONS

The industrialization of Europe and North America made its primary impact on the family through the rise of wage labor and bureaucratic employment as alternatives to agricultural and craft production, the consequent separation of the workplace from the home and of occupational from kin-based roles and relationships, the migration from rural villages to concentrated settlements where jobs were available, and the penetration of labor market values into parental decisions regarding the future of children. Each of these channels needs to be analyzed in terms of how it operated to alter the assumptions on which agrarian parents had based their conceptions of childhood.

The rise of wage labor and bureaucratic employment meant in the first instance that an increasing number of children would make their future living through jobs that were unfamiliar to their parents and which the latter therefore could not teach them. This was in itself a break with the agrarian tradition in which the work roles of one generation largely replicated those of its forebears: if a parent had not himself mastered the skills his child would live by, he had kin, neighbors or friends who had. Under the new conditions, however, increasing numbers of parents would have to acknowledge that they lacked not only the specific competencies required by their children for future work, but also the social connections with others who had the skills.

This decline in the parental capacity to provide training for subsistence was accompanied by a loss of supervisory control, as children and adults worked in factories, shops and offices under other supervisors. The dual role of the agrarian parents as nurturers and supervisors of their immature and adult children working at home – a role they could transfer to foster parents through apprenticeship in domestically organized craft workshops – was not possible when employers and foremen had no social ties with the parents of their laborers. This set the stage for the abuses of child labor that led ultimately to its abolition.

56

Equally significant, however, was the 'liberation' of adult workers from parental supervision in domestic production, even as they were exploited by industrial employers. Industrialism in the West cast off the kinship model of relationships that had prevailed in craft production in favor of a rationalistic and contractual model of work relationships we now think of as 'bureaucratic'. Industrial paternalism was not unknown, but the polarization of work *v.* family roles and relationships rose with increasing mass production, labor migration and the creation of a heterogeneous work force that lacked pre-existing social ties or common origins. The workplace required of employees not only skills but conformity to a new code of social behavior not foreshadowed in the domestic group; it re-socialized workers and gave them new identities distinct from those of birth and marriage. But since work for a particular firm was often not permanent, identification with it as an object of loyalty and idealization was the exception rather than the rule. Industrial employment was contractual, and the social identities of workers came to incorporate this sense of contractual distance from the firm. Sprung loose from the permanence of agrarian kin and community affiliations and from the parental control involved in domestic production, the more mobile industrial workers found new identities in religious sects, nationalism, voluntary associations – and in the ideals of organizations like trade unions and professional associations that were organized by occupation but offered membership more permanent than employment with any firm was likely to be. Whether one views this trend as facilitating personal autonomy or promoting anomie and social disintegration, it meant the greater salience of models of behavior that were not based on domestic relationships. It meant also a decline in parental control as an expectable concomitant of work roles.

Large-scale industrialization draws people from the countryside into concentrated settlements, either large cities with many functions or specialized industrial communities such as mining and mill towns, and this relocation is likely to have a great impact on the family. This does not mean the break-up of family and kin networks, for social historians and anthropologists have shown how resourceful rural migrants were and are in preserving these ties after moving to the city. But urbanization eroded many of the premises on which agrarian family values rested. The availability of residential housing, wild game and assistance from neighbors, for example, was taken for granted in many rural areas, but the migrant to the city found such resources to be commodities that had to be purchased, and at a steep price. Many more consumer goods were available in urban centers, and material aspirations quickly rose, but migrants had to develop a new awareness of what things cost in relation to their limited incomes. Thus urbanization encouraged families to examine the choices in their lives in explicitly economic terms.

The family's recognition of having moved from country to city in order to better its economic position through employment is another important factor. In the rural areas it was possible to see one's residence, occupation and social position as simply inherited together from the past and therefore fixed, but the knowledge of having moved to where the jobs were inevitably gave subjective priority to occupation and earnings as the source of the family's position, and it encouraged the younger generation to think of improving their lives through maximizing their incomes.

In the cities and increasingly even outside them, the influence of the labor market on parental thinking and family decision-making grew. Childhood was seen as a time for acquiring whatever skills would enhance their future employability in a competitive labor market where workers outnumbered jobs. The uncertainties inherent in this situation brought new anxieties to parents. In the agrarian past, the future position and livelihood of a son was pre-ordained through inheritance of land and an inherited role in domestic production, that of a daughter through marriage. Parents helped their children marry and start a household but (except where primogeniture was the rule) did not have to find occupations for their sons. The rise of industrial employment eroded the predictability inherent in this agrarian situation, forced parents to concern themselves more broadly with what would become of their children once they grew up, and offered hope for success in the future labor market only through adequate preparation in childhood. The domestic group, once the setting for the entire life cycle in its productive as well as relational dimensions, became a temporary nest for the nurturance of fledglings who would leave to wrest a living from an uncertain and competitive outside world. Parent-child relations, once conceived as a lifelong structure of reciprocity, were increasingly thought of as existing between adults and their immature offspring, leaving the future ambiguous.

By moving to cities, European families in the nineteenth century were moving closer to expanding urban school systems and enhancing the likelihood that their children would become enrolled. As the population of each country became more concentrated through urbanization, the difficulties of distributing formal education were reduced and literacy grew. Urban populations were generally more exposed than rural ones to the laws and programs of increasingly active and bureaucratized national governments, and schooling provided children contact with the symbols and doctrines of the national state.

Urbanization became a mass phenonemon in the nineteenth century as European villagers migrated to cities and towns in Europe, North and South America, Australia and New Zealand – and have continued to do so throughout the present century. In 1800, 7.3 per cent of the population of all these regions (in South America, only Argentina, Chile and Uruguay) lived in settlements of at least 5000 people; by 1900, it was 26.1 per cent and in 1980 70.2 per cent. Western Europe urbanized earliest and most heavily. Great Britain had by 1850 become the first major country with more than half of its population residing in cities; by 1900, 77 per cent of the British were urban residents and by 1980, 91 per cent. The major industrial cities of England and Germany grew to ten times their size and those of France grew by five times, in the course of the nineteenth century alone (United Nations, 1980). These figures suggest the massive increase in the proportion of the population affected by the impact of industrial employment on family life. Urban migrants did not necessarily lose their kin ties nor the significance of kinship in their lives, but their livelihoods and those of their children depended on the labor market. This was an irreversible change, and it reached out into the countryside, commercializing work relationships in agriculture and inducing even rural parents to regard wage labor as a major alternative path of life for their children.

Thus industrialization and urbanization changed the economic basis of family life (i.e., the role of the family as a productive unit) and replaced the local age-sex hierarachy of rural communities with new social identities and sources of motivation centered on the urban occupational structure. This trend has long been known in general terms, but it is only in recent decades that social historians have investigated whether and how particular Western countries fit into the general picture. Did they all start at the same place? Did they change in the same ways in terms of sequence and intensity? Did they arrive at the same outcomes in terms of resultant patterns of family life and child development? While the evidence is far from complete, the answer to all these questions is 'No'.

It has been shown, for example, that contractualism in property relations within and outside the family, as well as the independence of adolescent and pre-adolescent children from their parents, has a much longer history in England than on the Continent, and Mac-Farlane (1977) argues that these patterns antedate even England's pre-industrial economic development, representing a cultural tradition that sets England off from the rest of Europe. While his cultural argument is subject to controversy, there is no dispute concerning English primacy in industrial development and urbanization and in the utilitarian ideology of market relationships that social scientists have seen as an integral part of the urban-industrial transformation. In other words, England, along with its American colonies and the Calvinist communities of the Netherlands, Geneva and Scotland, may in the seventeenth century have had many of the social and psychological characteristics that the rest of Europe did not acquire until the urban-industrial transformation of the mid-nineteenth century.

Similarly, the pre-industrial family structures of the Western countries were far from identical, and some of them can plausibly be seen as preparing rural families for urban life under industrial conditions. Wherever the rules of inheritance did not permit the division of family land, for example, the 'stem family' in rural populations assured only heirs of a future on the parental land and created for the other sons something closer to the uncertainty of the industrial labor market. This situation in Sweden and Ireland was a factor in early (i.e., pre-nineteenth century) migration of rural labor to urban markets at home and abroad. The United States, with its lack of a feudal tradition and expanding rural as well as urban settlements, provided more opportunities for migration into newly established communities less dominated by inherited kinship and status relationships. Thus the Western countries, far from being homogeneous in culture and family structure before major industrial and urban development, were significantly varied in ways that bore directly on how they would enter and experience that historical transition.

It is equally clear that the processes of industrial and urban development were not the same throughout the West. France, for example, never became urbanized to the extent that England did. A much larger proportion of Frenchmen remained in rural villages participating in agriculture. In Italy and the United States, urban growth and industrialization were heavily concentrated in their northern regions, leaving the south rural and 'underdeveloped' down to the present, but this was not the case in smaller and more densely populated countries like the Netherlands. Thus the suddenness of the shift from agrarian to urban-industrial conditions, the proportions of the population who were uprooted from rural areas and absorbed in the urban labor force, the continuity of urban centers with a pre-industrial culture – all of these and many other factors were variable among (and within) the Western countries and are highly relevant to family life and the raising of children.

Do such historical variations make a difference in terms of late twentieth century outcomes? Not if outcomes are measured only by economic indicators such as gross national product per capita and demographic indicators such as birth and death rates for all the countries of the contemporary world. In these comparisons the Western countries stand out (with Japan) at the high end economically and the low end demographically – particularly in contrast with the Third World. There are major differences among the Western countries, however, in the results of industrial and urban development, especially in regard to the quality of life and the options and ligatures of Dahrendorf's framework. Indeed, he sees Britain and Germany as contrasting sharply in these terms.

The contrast between the United States and virtually all of Europe in residential mobility, for example, is enormous and of great significance in how occupational identities and local ties affect childhood and adult experience. Divorce, female participation in the work force and the extent of government welfare entitlements are other widely varying quantitative factors that affect both life chances and family life among the Western countries. On the qualitative side, the salience of social class divisions, trade union affiliations and religious participation represent other variables that create differing contexts for life experience in the several countries of the West.

It is clear, then, on the basis of available evidence that industrial and urban development has not simply homogenized Western countries as social environments for the development of children.

They did not enter the transition from agrarian life at the same places, they did not undergo quite the same historical experiences, and they did not arrive at identical destinations in terms of the conditions of family life and childhood. Their similarities in the urban-industrial transition are well established, particularly in comparison with other parts of the world, but neither the process nor the outcome of the transition should be considered uniform.

THE DEMOGRAPHIC TRANSITION

Between the late eighteenth and mid-twentieth centuries, Western birth and death rates declined drastically, eliminating the agrarian expectations of natural fertility and a relatively short life as normal features of the human condition. The impact on family life was as great as that of the more or less concomitant decline in domestic production and child labor. So many conditions affecting the family were changing during that time, however, that the connections between socio-economic and demographic change are matters of theoretical controversy rather than straightforward fact. 'Demographic transition theory' (Caldwell, 1982, pp. 117–33) includes all historical formulations that assume the inevitability and irreversibility of declining birth and death rates and the coupling of those declines to each other and to other socio-economic trends, regardless of which factors they claim to be driving the change. From our perspective, demographic transition theory is interesting not only because it attempts to make sense of secular trends affecting parents but because it explicitly proposes parallels between nineteenth-century Europe and the contemporary Third World. Recent research in historical demography enables us to make comparisons between what happened in the West and Japan and what is now happening in the rest of the world.

The basic facts have been succinctly summarized by van de Walle and Knodel (1980, p. 5):

In the first half of the 19th century, there were two general levels of birth rates in Europe. West of an imaginary line running from the Adriatic to the Baltic Sea, birth rates were under 40 per 1,000 persons per year – the result of late marriage and widespread celibacy – and death rates were in the 20's. East of the line, universal and early marriage made for birth rates above 40 per 1,000 – not unlike those in much of Asia and Africa today – while death rates were in the 30's. Now, at the end of the transition, most birth rates are under 15 per 1,000 in Western Europe and only a little higher in Eastern Europe. And death rates on both sides of the line are down to about 10 per 1,000.

The magnitude of these shifts, particularly if one considers them irreversible, deserves to be emphasized: Contemporary Europeans bear only one-third as many children and have a death rate only half as high as Europeans in the early nineteenth century. The decline in infant mortality was even more precipitous, from early nineteenth-century rates of about 200 infant deaths of every 1,000 births to about ten at present; contemporary Europeans thus lose only 1/20th as many infants as their forebears in 1800. Similar changes occurred at roughly the same time in North America and Australia.

The timing, sequence and socio-economic concomitants of these shifts are important to an understanding of how they might have affected, and been affected by, parental attitudes. Crude death rates, though not infant mortality, dropped moderately and gradually throughout the nineteenth century, then more steeply after 1900. The onset of mortality decline, probably in the late eighteenth century, was well in advance of improvements in medicine and has been attributed by McKeown (1976) to the greater availability of potatoes and maize, which improved the diet of ordinary people and made them more resistant to infection. Fertility, having increased in the late eighteenth century, began to decline around 1880 (much earlier in France, Switzerland and the United States), had dropped substantially by 1920, and continued its decline in the mid-twentieth century. Infant mortality declined little in the nineteenth century, except in Sweden, but dropped precipitously between 1900 and 1920, probably due to the pasteurization of milk, continuing its decline thereafter.

When European parents started to limit the number of their children, they had not yet experienced the enhanced probability of infant survival that came with the twentieth century. Thus the *onset* of fertility decline cannot be attributed to the greater parental confidence in child survival that follows reduced infant mortality. Whatever their reasons for limiting births (which are still a matter of speculation), they accomplished it through abstinence and withdrawal – methods theoretically available to all humans – rather than through advances in contraceptive technology. Parents in the nineteenth century were healthier on the average and lived longer than their forebears and they had large families that were less likely to be disrupted by the death of a parent during the reproductive years. The drop in infant mortality that followed the onset of fertility decline probably strengthened the trend but could not have instigated it.

Deliberate birth limitation on the scale that occurred in Europe and North America in the late nineteenth and early twentieth centuries was unprecedented in human history and seems to have marked a turning point in concepts and conditions of child development. The small-family ideal that emerged represented a departure from agrarian values toward a view of parent-child relations attuned to an urban-industrial economy, one in which each child signified increased costs and reduced contributions.

The relations of fertility decline to the urban-industrial transition and the spread of schooling are discussed below. At this point it should be noted that each of the major demographic trends of the nineteenth and twentieth centuries seem to have been instigated by changes in socio-economic conditions and subsequently amplified by use of new medical technologies rather than the other way round. Thus the decline in crude death rates around 1800 may have resulted from improved nutrition due to the more abundant food supply of early capitalistic economies, though the trend was certainly strengthened later on by better medical care. Fertility decline began because married couples decided to limit births and used existing techniques, though their efforts were later facilitated by the availability of contraceptive technology. Infant mortality may have begun to decline after fertility due to better parental care for each of fewer children, though the trend was powerfully strengthened by the pasteurization of milk, immunization and more effective drugs. In other words, demographic transition should not be seen as the simple result of changes in biotechnology but rather as the outcome of parental responses to changing socio-economic conditions.

The West, Eastern Europe and Japan arrived at roughly the same demographic destination by the last quarter of the twentieth century, with only a few exceptions. Their birth and death rates are low and vary within a narrow range. They did not begin the demographic transition at the same place, however, and did not move along identical pathways to their present positions. In other words, it would be a mistake to conclude that their current similarities in comparison with Third World societies are the outcomes of the same historical process or represent a shared historical background. This is particularly important to bear in mind when attempting to generalize from their past patterns of change in order to forecast what is possible and probable for the Third World.

As historical demography is pursued in greater depth, more country-specific patterns – including features of the pre-transitional social order – are identified as having been crucial to the process of demographic transition. Wrigley (1983), for example, argues that household formation in England from the seventeenth century was sensitive to the cost of living. Couples postponed marriage – and therefore child-bearing – when prices were high, thus reducing the birth rate. The customary practices by which families regulated the establishment of reproductive unions in response to economic conditions constitute a type of influence on fertility prior to the industrial revolution that might have facilitated the English fertility transition at a later date.

In France and the United States, the secular decline in birth rates began before 1800 – perhaps a century before the rest of Europe – and probably for different reasons. In both countries, however, the decline was initiated before industrialization and urbanization. This is particularly noteworthy because both France and the United States did not become as urban in the proportions of their populations living in cities as England and some of the other industrial countries. In other words, the forefront of fertility decline in the nineteenth century occurred in settings characterized by agrarian, or at least predominantly agricultural, conditions. This should provide a note of caution for those who see contemporary fertility decline as inexorably linked to urbanization.

A recent comparison of fertility decline in Japan and Sweden also emphasizes the influence of country-specific pre-transitional characteristics, in this case the patriarchal stem family, which is shared by those two countries but not by others in their respective regions (Mosk, 1983). Here again the evidence points to the conclusion that the demographic transition encompasses varied trajectories to the same destinations.

MASS SCHOOLING

There were schools in Europe from ancient times, but until the nineteenth century a relatively small proportion of children attended them. In the fifty years between 1840 and 1890 primary school attendance was enormously broadened and became compulsory in Western Europe, North America and Australia. This marks one of the most radical shifts in the parent-child relationship in human history. Mass schooling must be seen as both a reflection of powerful antecedent trends in social, political and economic conditions and a determinant of subsequent changes in reproduction and family life. The extension of schooling in the individual life span and its expansion across the globe have proved to be irresistible and apparently irreversible tendencies, fundamentally altering the way we think about children.

How did mass schooling affect the parent–child relationship? First, it kept children out of full-time productive work and minimized their economic contributions to the family. It furthermore established in a public and unavoidable way that childhood was dedicated to preparation for an uncertain future. It gave children a certain kind of power *vis à vis* their parents, either because the latter saw their better educated children as bearers of potentially higher social status or because the children themselves, having gained access to a new world of valuable skills and information, asserted themselves more within the family. Assertive, school-going children cost more than compliant children who work under parental supervision in domestic production; they required a larger share of family resources for their clothes, for space in which to study and for the satisfaction of the consumer tastes they acquired outside the home. Their demands, implicit and actual, were strongly supported by the wider society, particularly after compulsory school legislation, which had the effect of informing parents that the State had officially determined how their offspring should spend their time during childhood.

The parental response to this revolutionary change was first to minimize its impact, then to devise strategies to maximize the advantages it offered. At first, children enrolled in school were frequently kept home when their work was needed, as daily attendance figures show. In 1869–70, for example, although 57 per cent of the United States population aged five to seventeen was enrolled in school, only 35 per cent attended daily (Fine, 1983). Even those children who did attend daily were probably required to perform chores at home and to 'make themselves useful' to their parents. Caldwell (1982, pp. 117–31) has argued that so long as this was the case, parents could realistically consider numerous offspring advantageous even though they were not directly involved in domestic production. Eventually, however, the advantages of children in performing household chores must have been outweighed by their rising costs to the family, particularly if parents could not count on sharing their future wages, thus creating an economic incentive for birth control. According to Caldwell's theory, however, this shifting cost-contribution ratio was subjectively experienced in terms of parental ideology rather than economic calculation.

A new model of parenthood arose, with the goal of optimizing life chances for each of a few children through extended education and a measure of adult attention that had formerly been reserved for heirs to the throne. Thus did 'quality' replace 'quantity' as the focus of child rearing efforts, first in the middle classes but with a rapid spread into other classes.

The new model was effective as a strategy for optimizing the competitive position of offspring in a labor market that increasingly favored more education and personal autonomy, but what did it do for parents? Not very much in material terms, for economic 'returns' to parents were usually unfavorable. The code of filial reciprocity which had prevailed in agrarian communities was no longer binding on adult children, at least to a dependable degree. But something happened which cannot be accounted for in strictly economic terms, viz., parents came to identify with the children in whom they had invested so much of themselves as well as their resources, and they were able to derive subjective satisfaction from the economic and reproductive careers of their children even in the absence of material support. The ideological sources of this subjective satisfaction are considered in the following section.

The history of schooling in the West varied from one country to another. Before 1800, schooling (often limited to literacy acquisition) was widespread in England, Scotland, the United States, the Netherlands and Prussia. In these countries, at least half of the entire male population attended school, if only for a few years, and became literate. In the rest of Europe, smaller proportions ever attended school or became literate (Craig, 1981, p. 70). Thus the nineteenth century opened with major differences in educational development among the countries of Europe.

Policies of mass schooling were implemented through diverse forms of organization. Prussia pioneered the development of a governmentally planned and hierarchically organized school system, and France also built a centrally controlled national network of schools. England, on the other hand, had a wide and unregulated variety of religious and private schools, many of them of poor quality, until late in the nineteenth century, and never imposed the bureaucratic controls found in France. In the United States, schools were built and managed under state and local control (and financing), with a degree of decentralization unknown in Europe. These institutional variations affected long-range outcomes, for variability in school quality by social class in England and by locality (which is correlated with social class) in the United States have remained strong into present times. Hence the relations of schools to the central government and to the national system of social status have varied widely across Western countries.

THE RISE OF PUBLIC INTEREST IN CHILDREN

There can be no doubt that European attitudes toward children changed radically during the nineteenth century, but the changes had so many expressions and concomitants that they are not simple to describe or explain. Furthermore, ideas spread more quickly from one country to another than economic, demographic and institutional patterns and are harder to isolate for analysis. Most of the revolutionary ideas of the nineteenth century had been formulated in earlier centuries, and questions remain as to when their impact was fully felt. Stone (1977) and Plumb (1980) trace some of these ideas to the second half of the seventeenth century in England. On the Continent, the ideas formulated by Rousseau in *Emile* early in the eighteenth century were basic to the changing concepts of child development and education a century and more later. Pestalozzi, the eighteenth-century Swiss educator, spread these concepts to Prussia before 1800.

This complex intellectual and social history is still being

investigated by historians and remains an area of controversy. From a comparative perspective, however, its outlines are clear. Western conceptions of childhood after 1500 reflected a growing and changing debate over freedom, individualism and authority. At first this debate was conducted in religious terms and was associated with the rise of Protestant Christianity. Calvinism conceptualized the child as born with a will of its own, but viewed this as symptomatic of original sin, to be subdued by parental authority in the interests of moral virtue and divinely sanctioned moral order. Later, philosophers such as Locke and Rousseau proposed the natural goodness of the child and an acceptance of the child's playful impulses as beneficial for educational and individual development. Such ideas grew in influence during the eighteenth century, particularly in the arts (e.g. the poetry of William Blake) and in philosophical discourse on education (e.g. Pestalozzi). During the same period liberal political theory – emphasizing individual freedom rather than obedience to authority – not only developed but was dramatically implemented in the American and French revolutions. In the nineteenth century, literary and artistic romanticism established an emotional climate on which the struggle for children's rights as a form of political liberation could draw. It was during the nineteenth century, then, that the sentimental idealization of childhood combined with the liberal notion that children had rights to be publically enforced, in such cultural phenomena as the novels of Charles Dickens and the legislative struggle against child labor.

Much of the complexity of this history derives from the fact that the debate over freedom *v.* constraint in childhood has not led to a final resolution but continues even today, in issues specific to contemporary contexts. Furthermore, the Western countries represent a variety of experiences with this debate in terms of the particular sequences of intellectual discourse, public policy and effects on family life. What distinguishes the Western ideology as a whole from that of many non-Western cultures is not so much the preference for freedom, even for children, as the definition of freedom as liberation from authority – a polarity that pits options against ligatures in the struggle for a better life. This struggle, this morality play on behalf of children, provided the basic terms in which the modern European conceptions of the child emerged during the nineteenth century.

The new ideas were hostile to agrarian models of obedience and reciprocity. Focusing on childhood as a distinct and valuable phase of life, they emphasized autonomy, the child's development as a separate and equal human being, supported and protected by loving parents as he developed his capacities to make free and intelligent choices. In philosophy, literature and the arts, these ideas were advanced and elaborated. In psychology and child study they were justified on scientific grounds. In politics they inspired legislation to defend children against exploitation in factories and to restrict parental control. And in the family they inspired an emotional commitment that knew no precedent except in the rearing of royal princes.

The relation of these ideas to the socio-economic trends reviewed above and to the larger cultural ideologies from which they were derived deserves more intensive research. It is clear that these ideas were important in forming the emotional attitudes of parents and policy-makers alike and thus had an important impact. It also seems true, however, that the emotional component, and particularly the sense of a struggle for children against those who do them harm, was stronger in some countries than in others. In some European countries, then, the cause of children gained a political constituency of reformers, crusading against evil, while in others reforms were enacted, perhaps somewhat later, as the necessary steps required of a civilized society but without overt conflict.

All of these trends focused more public and private attention on childhood and the development of children than had previously been the case in European societies and in agrarian societies generally. Children were as never before depicted as valuable, lovable, innocent but intelligent individuals, to be cherished, protected, defended and developed. Public and private poles of this general tendency might seem to have been in conflict, for the public laws prohibiting child labor and compelling school attendance embodied the assumption that the citizenry bore a collective responsibility for other people's children in addition to their own offspring, while romantic sentimentalism promoted an intensification of the parent-offspring bond in the most private and exclusive terms. Both poles, however, were based on the notion that every individual child was uniquely valuable, to his own parents *and* to the wider society – an idea compatible with Western traditions but newly applied to children in the context of a secular national state.

The ideological complementarity of these two poles can be seen in the presumption that parents who cherished their own children would be able to support the public cause of all children through a process of identification, i.e. by imagining how they would feel if their own children were the victims of neglect or exploitation. Similarly, the argument that the development of children represented a national resource for public investment was expected to evoke in parents a complementary 'investment' in the educational and occupational aspirations of their own offspring. In the larger cultural ideology that emerged, then, the potential conflict between public and private interests in children was not only conceptually reconciled but embedded in the idea of their convergence to the benefit of children.

CONCLUSIONS

All of the trends reviewed above favor the bearing of *fewer* children receiving *more* attention (and other resources) over a *longer* period of their lives than was typical in agrarian societies. Changing economic, demographic and structural conditions led Western parents in the late nineteenth century to perceive the allocation of greater resources to each child as enhancing the future advantage of the child in an increasingly competitive environment. Changing ideological conditions motivated their willingness to commit resources to each child without expecting a material return. Similar trends have been observed in Japan and in some Third World countries as they have moved from agrarian to urban-industrial conditions.

This brief overview has also indicated differences among Western countries in the conditions of family life and child development before 1800, in the processes and sequences of change during the nineteenth and twentieth centuries and in the outcomes as of the present time. European countries were not homogeneous to begin with and are not homogeneous today, however much they contrast with other countries in the world. Moreover, their advances in formal education and the regulation of birth and death were not achieved by taking the same steps in the same order but through various pathways reflecting the diversity of their socio-economic and cultural conditions. This historical record as we now know it suggests that family change will continue to reflect the diversity of settings in which it occurs. Those who formulate policy will have to pay close attention to the unique resources and limits of each setting rather than assuming a universal series of prerequisites for replicating progress.

In attempting to explain how the West was transformed from its agrarian condition, it is not only diversity in local settings that must be taken into account but temporal diversity in the circumstances under which each major change occurred in a given country. Each secular trend showed at least two surges, often 80 or 100 years apart. Fertility began its major decline in the nineteenth century, but fell sharply after World War I. Infant mortality dropped after 1900 but continued to decline thereafter until it reached present levels. The spread of primary schooling was a nineteenth century phenomenon, but secondary schooling as a mass process did not occur until the twentieth century. New concepts of the child and education arose between the mid-seventeenth and early nineteenth centuries but did not have their major institutional impact until a good deal later. In each case the socio-economic and ideological conditions affecting the consciousness of parents were different by the time the later surge occurred, and different social forces were mobilized to advance the trend. This makes it possible for largely economic factors to have determined the first surge and largely ideological factors the second, or vice versa. It means that secular trends cannot be treated as single historical events and that the telescoping of historical process that seems to occur in 'late developing countries' cannot be treated as replicating a trend that took centuries in Europe.

4

REVOLUTION IN SCHOOLING[1]

Long before the advent of mass schooling in forms resembling our own, there were schools in the more complex agrarian societies of China, Japan, India, the Islamic world and medieval Europe, as well as those of indigenous Mesoamerica and Peru. As institutionalized arrangements of people, places and activities dedicated to the transmission of socially valued knowledge, these schools were precursors of formal education as we know it today. Their forms and functions, however, reflected the agrarian social and cultural contexts in which they developed and exemplify how agrarian models of the life span – and of life chances – differ from those of contemporary industrial societies. Understanding how the meanings of education have changed is central to our analysis of change in cultural conceptions of potential and the social means of its realization.

A world survey of formal education in AD 1500 would have found schools in all the major civilizations of Eurasia, distributed from the British Isles to Japan, largely associated with their religious and philosophical traditions. In Europe, there were both Christian and Jewish schools, and Christian universities several hundred years old. North Africa and the Middle East had Muslim schools and universities. India had Hindu, Buddhist and Muslim schools. In China and Japan there were both Buddhist and Confucian schools; and in Southeast Asia Theravada Buddhist temple schools. The Koranic School spread down into West Africa but was still largely confined to the Sahel. To the south, at the western end of the West African rain forest, however, there were 'bush schools' focused on the transmission of social and cultural lore in connection with initiation into society, among the peoples of the region later called Senegambia, Liberia and Sierra Leone. Finally, there were schools – at that time still undiscovered by Europeans – among the ruling Aztecs of the Valley of Mexico and in the Inca empire of Peru.

Schools did not exist in most of indigenous North and South America, sub-saharan Africa and the Pacific. Within the Americas, the Aztecs and Incas were as exceptional in having schools as in their degree of socio-political and cultural complexity. The 'bush schools' of Liberia, Senegambia and Sierra Leone – largely organized by secret societies – were equally exceptional in the sub-saharan region. Elsewhere in Africa, complex market economies and far-flung empires emerged without schooling or literacy, except where Islam prevailed. Many of the nomadic and semi-nomadic peoples of continental Asia had no tradition of schooling until influenced by Islam.

Schooling throughout the agrarian world was associated with greater complexity – in technology, the economy, socio-political organization, religion – singly or in combination. With the possible exception of sub-saharan Africa, agrarian societies with schools were generally those with urban centers of occupational specialization, long-distance trade, large-scale political organization, translocal religions and literacy. Isolated 'tribal' peoples lacking these aspects of societal complexity were more likely to lack schools. Thus schooling was for agrarian societies, particularly in Eurasia, Mesoamerica and Andean South America before 1500, a hallmark of 'advancement' and dominance, as it has been – though in a different way – in our own time.

Agrarian schooling was limited in scope and usually involved a small and socially elite part of the population, though in some communities all children (or all male children) were involved for a short period of time. For most pupils in most places, schooling bore little or no relationship to their future productive activities, being more closely tied to religion and the study of sacred texts. Its goal was the enhancement of virtue or piety rather than the acquisition of useful skills. The valued skills that were acquired drew their meanings from particular cultural and religious traditions. Despite the diversity of those traditions, agrarian patterns of schooling were broadly similar, particularly in comparison with later forms of

74

education. Their common features are summarized below.

AGRARIAN SCHOOLING: THE ACQUISITION OF VIRTUE

The agrarian school, as an institutional form common to a wide variety of complex but non-industrial societies in Eurasia, North Africa and the Americas, was characterized by the following features (Hussein, 1981):

1   The cultural context of learning was largely religious. The school was located at or near a place of worship or at the home of a religious functionary. The purposes of education, teachers' and pupils' roles, and curriculum were defined in religious terms, i.e. in terms of a religious or cosmological doctrine such as Buddhism, Hinduism, Islam, Judaism or Christianity.

2   The social context of learning centered on the hierarchical relationship between teacher and pupil, which included parent-like authority and responsibility. The pupil owed the teacher both respect and unquestioning obedience, and teachers were expected to use corporal punishment and other severe disciplinary measures whenever they saw fit. On the other hand, the pupil often lived with the teacher as a member of his household, receiving food and lodging and contributing labor. The same type of hierarchical learning relationship characterized master craftsmen and their apprentices in the same societies, i.e. young boys were sent as apprentices to learn a craft by living under the protection and authority of a master while learning from him. The master was *in loco parentis* in terms of both care and discipline and was often expected to punish more severely than parents in order to foster learning and production. In essence, the father-son, master craftsman-apprentice and teacher-pupil relationships involved closely related models of learning based on the age-hierarchy of domestic production.

3   Mastery of sacred texts was the central task of schooling, and this did not necessarily mean that literacy was acquired. The chanting of scriptures came first, and many pupils learned enough only to be able to read words in a liturgical language (Sanskrit, Pali, Arabic, Hebrew, Latin) they could not fully

understand. This degree of mastery, and the memorization and chanting of text, was highly valued in itself as an act of religious devotion.

4   Some pupils went beyond the first stages of mastery to acquire functional literacy for religious and other purposes. Their progress was based on appropriately deferential behavior and other signs of moral virtue as well as on competence in memorizing texts. These select few were true apprentices to the teacher and might become the disciples of more renowned teachers or join schools for the training of priests or other religious functionaries in which literate skills were cultivated. For this small but important group, school *was* linked to a vocation. The rest would gain their livelihoods in traditional agrarian roles. School for them involved acquisition of the meanings of sacred symbols and of respect for religious authority rather than of useful skills; it led to piety and virtue in the eyes of the community but not to a means of making a living.

5   School values were consistent with the local age-sex hierarchies of these agrarian societies, and they reinforced with translocal imagery the age and gender distinctions underlying local conceptions of the life span. Women were usually excluded from school, as they were from full participation in most of the religions. Their lives were defined by domestic and kinship roles under the protection of male kin who would not have tolerated their dominance by an unrelated teacher even if it were not ruled out on religious grounds. The embodiments of virtue and piety who served as ideal models for schoolboys were men advanced in their years for whom devotion, experience and reflection had matured into wisdom and purity. In many of the complex agrarian societies, men could as elders withdraw from participation in other activities and continue the religious learning and devotion begun many years before in school, thus enhancing virtue prior to death. Such elders were highly respected, and their public example reinforced a hierarchical social order in which status was differentially distributed by age and gender.

6   The organization of learning was looser and more variable in almost all aspects that became standardized and regulated in schooling as it later developed. Based on a relationship with a

particular master teacher, agrarian schooling could and often did operate without a fixed location, without segregation into groups graded by age or level of attainment, without group-administered examination procedures. Though organizational features varied widely across the agrarian world, these schools were largely disengaged not only from economic production, as mentioned above, but also from such competition for wealth, status and power as was socially organized in agrarian societies. With the exception of Imperial China, schooling did not serve as a means of publicly evaluating individual performance. Those who stopped attending usually did so because their labor was needed; they were neither labeled as failures in any general sense nor diminished in their future life chances.

This generalized picture of the agrarian school and its place in society does not fit all cases equally well and is not an accurate guide to any specific case. Much of the variation is due to the nature of religious belief and organization in agrarian societies ranging from Confucian China to medieval Europe. China not only had competitive examinations for powerful and lucrative positions in the imperial bureaucracy but less specifically religious organization than implied in the above account. Medieval Christianity not only had an elaborate ecclesiastical hierarchy but more female participation (e.g. nuns) and more formal schools – at least for monks, priests and canon lawyers – than the general picture suggests. Our point has been that schools in agrarian societies were based on agrarian socio-economic conditions and cultural premises, including their models of the life span as outlined in Chapter 2. Hierarchical relationships based on age and mastery of sacred texts, and a notion of acquiring moral virtue, were common characteristics. But schooling occurred and changed within a specific tradition to which no overview can do justice. We turn now to a brief examination of schooling in the Islamic tradition.

An Example of Agrarian Schooling: The Qu'ranic School

Islam's wide spread across the globe, and cultural dominance in places as diverse as Casablanca and Djakarta, as well as its significance as the major living example of a system and ideology of pre-modern education, make it the most accessible and interesting model for agrarian schooling. The Qu'ranic school exhibits the characteristics presented in our generalized model of pre-modern schooling, but a closer examination also reveals elements, contributing perhaps to its persistence, which correspond to persisting agrarian goals and means in the educationally mobilized, modern contexts of Japan and the People's Republic of China, to be discussed in the following two chapters.

> It is a pleasant and instructive scene to watch a grey, reverend-looking marabout surrounded by boys, listening attentively to his teaching, or all joining in and chanting a repetition of the lessons he gives them from the Koran, or busily engaged under his supervision in practising their writing lessons on boards. The discipline maintained by the marabouts in their schools presents an example of order and attention not to be excelled . . .
> (Mitchinson 1881: quoted in Sanneh, 1979)

The early morning chanting of the Qu'ran is common to Islamic schools everywhere: In Indonesia, Morocco and Senegambia young boys are taught to listen and repeat, to accumulate verses by memory, to write the words of the sacred text. The memoirs of Taha Hussein, a contemporary Egyptian, and the observations of nineteenth-century European travellers, as well as the ancient texts themselves, reveal a continuity in the practice and experience of Islamic schools[2].

While continuity in the texts and to some extent in teaching methods does exist across the vastly dispersed Islamic societies in the world it must be noted that no one locus is 'typical' of Islam. Egyptian Islam is Egyptian; Indonesian practise has evolved differently. The description that follows is composed of 'most typical' elements drawn from several cultural settings. While some characteristics such as the age of the child at entry into school, vary more than others, this picture of the experience of the school would be familiar to all who have attended Qu'ranic schools.

The acquisition of sacred knowledge was emphasized by Mohammed himself, and literacy was so highly esteemed that traditionally those who can read and write are given the title *Kamil*, or 'perfect'. Parents are the first teachers: the sacred is not reserved for the school, and parental involvement in the child's progress is strong. It is said that learning begins when the child first speaks. At this point, he is taught the Islamic article of faith, *La ilaha'ill Allah*, 'There is no God but Allah'. After this the child learns a verse from the Qu'ran, 'Exalted is Allah, the king in truth, there is no God but him, the Lord of the stately throne of Heaven' and others. It is believed that parents who teach their children in this way will not be brought to judgment by God. Salvation can thus be earned by properly educating one's children, conferring a double advantage and blessing.

Formal education usually begins at the age of seven with systematic instruction in the Qu'ran. When the child is admitted to the Qu'ranic school, his head is shaved to indicate his initiated status, and the verse which begins the Qu'ran is written on his palms. He is then told to lick his hands, and a ball of grain is placed in each palm. He is instructed in the call to prayer and in the ablutions. The school day is marked by the cleansing of the tablets. The water used for cleaning them is said to have magical powers and can be used medicinally, and even the rag with which they are wiped should be wrung out with care, lest the water that drips from it be profaned.

Qu'ranic education emphasizes, with great detail, the proper demeanor of the teacher toward his students, as well as the proper way to organize and conduct the school. It is believed that on the Day of Judgment, God will subject the teacher to an interrogation as to whether or not he maintained strict impartiality between his students. Punishment is also considered to be a necessity. There is one story that relates a beating so severe that the student's arm was black and blue. The student, a young prince, complained to his father, and showed him the injured arm. The father, who was pleased, invited the teacher to a banquet dinner, commenting: 'You are at liberty even to kill him: it were better that he die than remain a fool.'

The teacher of the Qu'ran (Spratt and Wagner, 1985) is, ideally, influential and powerful and is believed to have many secrets at his command. Parents believe that his glance has the power to correct wayward children. His authority is not to be questioned or doubted. The teacher traditionally was thought to be an embodiment of divine knowledge: 'The teacher's acceptance is the nearest thing to divine acceptance, and represents it as far as it can . . . the disciple must honour the teacher deeply. Therein lies his hope.' The teacher was to lead the disciple to eternal salvation by means of the devotion offered to him by the disciple, who, at the beginning of his studies, states: 'I submit my body and soul to you. Whatever you command I shall do, and whatever you forbid me I shall refrain from.'

The teacher is always an object of intense attention, whether or not he corresponds to the ideal. His most human failings, his personal quirks, his every gesture are observed and learned by the student. Taha Hussein's teacher in Egypt was a hypocrite and a swindler, who favored the students from rich families and reported more progress to their parents than students were making. Lamin Sanneh's teacher in Senegambia was

. . . a sphinx-like presence. He regarded us as God's mud bricks and himself as the divinely appointed mason. He was a small man, scanty alike in spirit and in physique, with bony cheeks and cold but deliberate eyes, with an authoritative and precise face. I never saw him smile once in all my years at the school. He was not by any means a cruel man. He was merely devoted to his job with a singleminded determination. He never lavished praise on any one though he was quick to reprimand at the slightest sign of slackness. With a cane in hand and the sacred words of the Qu'ran on his lips, sometimes accompanied by a deep, reverential hum, teacher rose to superhuman heights, the tiny frame of the man heaving him like a bridge being swayed on steel girders . . . His mind would be filled with the lavish picture the Holy Book paints of Paradise: the cool somnolent gardens watered by the blessed fountains, the beautiful fragrance that rose and laced the air, the colonnades and porticos that commanded the entrance to Paradise, all fashioned to perfect proportions by the Great Geometrician Himself, the vast emerald arches that held the entire scene in enchanted suspension, with the elect of god bathed in the rejuvenating light of eternity, their youth restored and their sins washed away. Then there was the bubbling stream of heavenly wine which flowed in full spate to refresh and restore, couches decked out in finest brocade and attended by angels of delight, and rooms flowing with sumptuous fruit . . . All this, teacher would think to himself, the just reward of those who strove to fulfil the law. In the appropriate setting of the Qu'ran school and the cane, teacher would sometimes recall this picture. It was worth all the clobbering he could give . . . (Sanneh, 1982)

The word Qu'ran means 'recitation'; this was, and still is, the central pedagogical tool of Qu'ranic education. In order to recite properly, students are taught to memorize as much of the Qu'ran as possible (Wagner and Lofti, 1980). This is a challenge of considerable magnitude, and the average student spends six to eight years of full-time study on this goal. There are basically four steps in the process. In the elementary school, the *kuttab*, the student learns the alphabet by chanting the letters. The second step is writing the letters. This is usually accompanied by the memorization of a few short suras or chapters of the Qu'ran. At this level, students can memorize what is written, but cannot read for comprehension. The third stage, the intermediate level, involves writing and reciting, and mastery of one section after another of the Qu'ran. The last stage is when the student is able to write from dictation. Most students, however, do not go beyond the first two stages. Whatever is ultimately attained in memorization, it is felt that the experience of recitation itself produces an ingrained response and that this is an important outcome: '. . . provided they learn in their childhood to respond to the music of Arabic consonants and vowels, and to the rhythms of the Qu'ran they will continue throughout their lives to have an emotional attachment to it' (Husain and Ashraf, 1979).

Many students leave the school after the second stage of mastery has been reached. If this happens, a 'passing out' ceremony is organized, and the parents are expected to give a monetary payment to redeem their children. In traditional times, the parents gave the teacher a slave, or the price of one, to get their sons back. If the parents had no money, the student remained the property of the teacher until he could work hard enough to earn his way to freedom. The implication here is that the student was a valuable resource or worker for the teacher, just as in a craft apprenticeship.

Qu'ranic education seems to embody both fixed and adaptive elements: the uniform text, stages in learning and the individualized progress along the path to knowledge: and the recognition that while the roles of teacher and student, and their relationship, were prescribed, there are in fact many variations in character, practise, and experience. Islamic schooling is thus not ultimately rigid, but instead provides a predictable model within which a wide range of abilities and paths are accommodated.

THE TRANSFORMATION OF SCHOOLING

Agrarian schools as we have described them still exist, not only in the Islamic world but also in India and Southeast Asia, though usually as religious supplements to a school system the form of which was imported from the West. The bureaucratized form of schooling developed in Western countries by the middle of the nineteenth century has spread almost everywhere, often in advance of industrial development and even significant urbanization, and has continued to expand, among Western and non-Western populations, in the proportions of children enrolled in school and the length of time they spend there. This has been closely connected to political and economic change, as the national state and the modern type of occupational structure have become the dominant forms of social organization. The bureaucratic hierarchy of occupations has partly or totally superseded the local age-sex hierarchy and other agrarian forms of social stratification (based on feudal, caste, and patron-client relationships) as a source of models for social identities that inspire personal ambition and public service. In this context, the meaning of education has been drastically altered.

The ways in which schooling changed from its agrarian forms, in those societies that had schools, to its recent global form, can be considered in terms of four trends: 1) the internal reorganization of schooling, 2) the growth of external links to a superordinate administration and to the economy, 3) the re-definition of schooling as an instrument of public policy, and 4) the extension of school enrollment to social categories formerly excluded – women, the poor, rural residents – and the expansion of school systems at all levels. Documenting these trends in particular societies is a central task of the history of education.

The history is a lengthy one in Europe, where internal reorganization took place gradually over a period of some 700 years (1100–1800 AD), with the other three changes occurring rapidly during the following century. By internal reorganization we mean the transition from the apprenticeship or master-disciple model of learning to the more formal, impersonal arrangement of contemporary education. Aries (1962, pp. 137ff.) has described this transition in France, indicating its different course in England, Italy and the German states due to their prior educational traditions (e.g.

the greater continuity with Hellenistic schooling in Italy) which nevertheless influenced each other to some degree. In all of these countries, by the seventeenth or eighteenth centuries learning came to take place in age-graded classes, situated in a permanent school building, where subjects were taught in a preordained sequence by level of difficulty. Concomitant with the development of this format, the teacher became less the 'master' in charge of the boy's life as well as learning and more the transmitter of a planned curriculum in the classroom. The emergence of an explicit and standard format for teaching, in terms of both content and setting, must be seen as facilitating the school expansion and administrative reorganization of later centuries.

As schooling developed, so did its administration. The hierarchical relationship of master and pupil was superseded by a wider hierarchy extending far beyond the school in which the teacher was at the lowest level. Though the church, which sponsored most early schooling in Europe, had its own hierarchy, organizational forms for school administration were borrowed from the army (especially in Napoleonic France), commercial firms and the government, which in due course became the principal sponsor of school expansion. Teachers served under headmasters or principals, who were responsible to superintendents and school boards and who were supervised by inspectors. Thus school systems came into existence as bureaucracies like other bureaucracies except for the activities of their component units, the schools themselves.

The links of schools to the economy grew with the development of the urban-industrial occupational structure. While most boys in medieval Europe had received no more than a 'choir-school education' typical of the more complex agrarian societies, there had been schools that prepared boys for clerical specialties such as theology and canon law. The idea of schooling as preparation for economically specialized occupations, however, was slower in coming. Dore (1976) has described the evolution of educational qualifications for the professions and other occupations in nineteenth-century England. The justifications that were offered, drawing upon the educational concepts of that time, were moral as well as technical. The 'learned professions' of law and medicine, like other occupations for which professional status was sought, were conceived of as bearing moral virtue and responsibility rather than simply technical skill. Education was still seen as developing virtue, along with skills, in young men. Economic outcomes nevertheless entered into consideration to an increasing degree. Professions attempted to restrict the numbers entering their ranks by raising the educational requirements. Employers in the industrializing United States supported public education as a means of creating a pool of literate workers who adapted more easily to bureaucratic regulations and would be more productive (Carnoy, 1974; Graff, 1975). But the economic rationalization of education as 'manpower development', emphasizing the relations of schooling at all levels to labor market demands in capitalist countries and state production requirements in socialist ones, is a development of twentieth-century economic discourse.

There is controversy among historians of education about the degree to which educational expansion in the nineteenth-century West was economically motivated. There can be no doubt, however, that the result of educational and economic change was an occupational hierarchy in which status positions corresponded to a significant degree with levels of school attainment. This was a major contrast with the place of schooling in the medieval social order.

The re-definition of schooling as an instrument of public policy was another important part of this transition. When schooling was a church function, it involved religious socialization, recruitment into the ecclesiastical hierarchy, and the training of record-keepers, scribes and literate men on whom the state depended. In the Protestant countries, the idea that everyone should be able to read the Bible was an impetus for more widespread schooling. But it was only in the eighteenth century that Enlightenment doctrines of rationality and perfectibility suggested that mass schooling at the national level was a condition of human progress independent of religious salvation, and outside of Prussia this was not translated into state policy until after 1800. Then schooling became the final common pathway for a multiplicity of national aspirations: civilization, military power, industrial development, democracy, equality, the building of a patriotic citizenry and a skilled labor force. Education in school became identified as an obvious good, to be promoted and expanded by every enlightened ruler, regardless of political and economic ideology. Each type of system, democratic or authoritarian, capitalist or socialist, identified schooling as a means to its end as well as a benefit to the public.

School expansion can be seen as the natural outcome of these ideas operating through state policy as well as private initiatives. It is noteworthy, however, that expansion did not stop when most males and females in the industrialized countries had a primary education; rather, it has continued in this century at the secondary and post-secondary levels, even as primary schools were being built for the first time in non-Western areas.

When activities become bureaucratized, they can be diffused from one society to another without repeating the earlier steps involved in the original development. The borrowers adopt the product of that development, an explicit prototype to be learned as a series of scripts within an overall plan. In so far as the results turn out to be different from the original, it is because in implementing the borrowed plan the borrowers must, at least to begin with, find a way to integrate it into their own institutional structure and assimilate it to their own cultural meanings. Dore's (1976, p. 44ff.) concept of the 'late development effect' recognizes this phenomenon and its significance for the comparative understanding of educational history. Thus the non-Western societies that borrowed Western models of schooling did not replicate the history of the West, or even that of previous borrowing societies. To illustrate some of the distinctive patterns of educational development, and the importance of pre-existing educational conditions, we shall consider India and Japan in the early nineteenth century.

INDIA AND JAPAN BEFORE 1850

Schooling for large numbers of rural and urban children, across all social strata, was available in parts of India before the importation of British schools and in Japan before a centralized and universal school system was established in 1872 (Di Bona, 1982; Dore, 1965a). Surveys carried out in India in the early nineteenth century by William Adam, Thomas Munro and G.L. Prendergast, revealed that almost every village in Bengal and Bihar had a school, and students came from over ninety castes, ranging from Brahmin to the low Chandal and 'untouchable' Dom castes. Brahmins were in fact in the minority in these elementary schools while they dominated enrollment lists of specialized and high-caste schools. There was a decline in enrollment in all except Brahmin schools as the British schools began to dominate, schools which for a long time attracted only those expecting to enter their sons into the state bureaucracy. The numbers of children of peasants in *any* school began to decline as the indigenous village school fell into disuse. However, before British schools spread their influence, these secular schools were widespread and derived their support locally, through parents' and local officials' stipends to teachers. Vernacular schools persisted in some areas, supported by local governments such as that of Bombay, where in 1840 120 schools served 7,000 pupils, funded through the board of education (Chatterjee, 1976).

The schools were diverse: each had its own curriculum, but they all provided basic literacy, numeracy, and even commercial and agricultural accounting for children in the context of moral training. Indeed even later, when high-caste families with intentions of placing sons in the civil service encouraged their children to do well in school, they invoked the role of education to 'civilize' rather than just to impart knowledge. 'Civilization' meant the imparting of culturally valued virtues. Nirad Chaudhuri's father, in the late nineteenth century in Bengal was such an advocate of the virtuous purposes of learning:

> There was emotional fervour in his attitude, so that we got a sense that by educating ourselves we should be acquiring, not simply the means to do something else, but some all-round and absolute goodness which was not mere skill but something desirable in itself . . . What he had assumed was that worldly success would attend us as a corollary to our better education without being made its primary purpose. He was not disposed to treat education as the means to an end or as vocational training (Chaudhuri, pp. 142–3).

The chief aims of Hindu education were to infuse the student with piety, assist in the formation of character and personality, and promote social and civic duties, the 'all-round and absolute goodness' which was the goal of much agrarian schooling. Because the development of moral feeling and character was the primary goal of education, intellectual achievements were secondary.[3]

The education available to the villager, as apart from the Vedic education received by high-caste boys in a *gurukula*, was a moral, if not strictly scriptural, education. The rules of behavior in the gurukula included those appropriate to the relationship of the student and teacher. These were also applicable in the village school. The student was to help the teacher, never offend him, observe proper posture when sitting, eating or speaking with him, and cover his ears or leave if the teacher was falsely defamed. The student was expected to show the teacher the utmost respect and reverence, even more than to his parents. In fact, the teacher was designated as the spiritual and intellectual father of the student. No education could be possible without the guidance of the teacher.

On the other hand, the teacher was expected to be patient and impartial. The teacher was also held morally responsible for the behavior of his students. Education was primarily oral, and noise was encouraged. It was often thought that a master's energy and skill could be measured from the volume of sound proceeding from the school. Recitation was preferred to writing, lest the sacred text be profaned by imperfect transcription. Thus attention was placed on accurate memorization. The average student could not afford a copy of a text-book and the desire to possess one was a sign of indolence. Rhyme and parable were used as aids in memorization. Every student received individual attention and was taught in a direct and personal manner.

To summarize our understanding of the pre-modern, indigenous educational system in Bengal and Bihar we would like to emphasize the following. First, that such schooling was open to children of non-Brahmin castes. Second, that basic cognitive skills (reading, writing and computation) were imparted and that children were often taught in the vernacular rather than exclusively in the context of Sanskrit religious texts. Brahmin higher schools might teach Hindu law and theology, in the context of Vedic texts, but even such schools were not seen as religious schools leading to the priesthood. Indian schooling for basic literacy was thus diverse in curricular and constituencies, secular, and supported by the community and governmental structures. At least in Bengal and Bihar, Indian development of schooling can be seen to have antedated the arrival of the modern educational system.

During the Tokugawa Period (1600–1868) in Japan basic literacy and numeracy were taught to children of commoner classes in *terakoya*, or 'parish schools.' It is estimated (Dore, p. 317) that at the end of the Tokugawa period, approximately 43 per cent of boys, and 10 per cent of girls of school age (six to fifteen) had had some schooling and were literate. These figures compare favorably with those of European countries at that time, and are far ahead of many

Third World countries today. Like the traditional Indian village schools, *terakoya* were supported locally, and were not nationally organized. Terakoya were based on older temple schools where Buddhist priests had taught children to read and write. The temple as the source of literacy was so prominent that the word *terako* ('temple child') had become synonymous with 'student'. By the end of the nineteenth century, the school shifted from the temple to the family house of the teacher as the otherworldly Buddhist teachings gave way to a more Confucian 'social religion' taught by lay teachers. In contrast to samurai education which was theoretical and idealistic, the content of *terakoya* education was focused on practical vocational ends. The training that children received prepared them to succeed their parents in their hereditary occupations. Lessons focused on basic Japanese reading and writing, arithmetic and the use of the abacus. The latter was proscribed for samurai youth since it was seen as 'the tool of merchants.' Teachers came from diverse backgrounds: village headmen, retired merchants, doctors, lordless samurai and handicapped people. Unmarried or widowed women often opened schools and as many as one-third of the teachers in Edo (Tokyo) by the mid-nineteenth century were women. Gradually, a common 'national' curriculum was informally disseminated and occasionally officials were sent to inspect schools.

Thus, in spite of limitations in curriculum, a lack of standardized qualifications for teachers and restrictions on the wide use of schools to those who could afford the fees, both Japan and India had surprisingly high levels of peasant participation in formal education before the advent of modern schooling. Parents saw schooling as providing enhancement for the child as well as status for the family but did not necessarily tie skills learned in school to an increase in the child's chances for economic success. Schooling did not provide a child with a kit of marketable skills or attributes but rather, moral and social 'goodness'.

No adequate history of education in India or Japan could ignore the existence of these pre-modern patterns of schooling or fail to explore their impact on the succeeding importation of Western educational models. That importation changed the life chances available in both countries by establishing educational career paths leading to bureaucratic employment in government and industry. The concept of schooling for virtue was overshadowed not only by schooling as skill development but, even more important, by

88

schooling as a competitive struggle for lifelong personal advancement. Their earlier development of schooling no doubt facilitated the modern educational performance of both Indians and Japanese even though the new meanings of schooling differed from the old.

In another respect, however, Indian and Japanese conditions for modern educational development represented a striking contrast. India was under the domination of Britain, and its educational policy was set by Christian Europeans until 1947, while Japan was an autonomous nation whose educators made their own decisions concerning the adaptation of Western education. The consequences of this situation for schooling and life chances in Japan are described in the following chapter.

II: Schooling and Social Change: Life Chances and Cultural Diversity

Our Country must move from its third-class position to second class, and from second class to first, and ultimately to the leading position among all countries of the world. The best way to do this is (by laying) the foundations of elementary education.

Mori Arinori, Japanese Minister of Education, 1885.

Students are taught that it is important to build the country by their own hands and to create a spirit of self-reliance; students learn from books but they also learn to criticize the bourgeoisie and to love physical labor.

Teacher at Peking Middle School 31.

5

EDUCATIONAL MOBILIZATION: THE CASE OF JAPAN

INTRODUCTION

Between 1850 and 1900, newly industrialized societies – first in Western Europe, then elsewhere – began to mobilize on a nation-wide basis for education as nations had previously mobilized only for war. In Europe and Japan, the extension of formal schooling was not only analogous to wartime mobilization in the degree to which it harnessed the resources of the country and the energies of its population toward a single end, but it was also part of a program of military-industrial preparedness which each country found necessary amidst the intense nationalistic and imperialistic competition of the period. In the United States, educational mobilization resulted from local efforts carried out in the context of an expanding and increasingly industrial economy.

Three processes were involved:

1   Policy-makers re-defined education, both general and specialized, as an essential element in the quest for national power, thereby legitimizing subsequent decisions to commit public funds to its expansion and maintenance. In other words, those who were in a position to set governmental priorities ranked schooling high in its claim on the state's resources.

2   Government educational bureaucracies were established at the national (or in the United States, state) level to expand the schools, administer them on a more centralized basis than before, train teachers and evaluate the performance of pupils, teachers and schools.

3   Parents were motivated, and motivated themselves, to match the public commitment to school programs with their own commitment to the educational careers of their children. This voluntary contribution of domestic resources was vital to the implementation of State educational policies.

Operating in concert, these three processes brought about dramatic educational change throughout the industrialized world in about one century. In each country, compulsory schooling was extended to adolescence, so that by 1980 large proportions of all age groups between six and twenty-three were enrolled in school: more than 90 per cent between six and eleven, more than 80 per cent between twelve and seventeen, and more than 25 per cent between eighteen and twenty-five. Furthermore, a high level of public expenditure on schooling became institutionalized, so that as of 1980 the industrial countries spent fifty times more on each primary school pupil than did the thirty-six poorest countries in the world (Heyneman and Loxley, 1983). Finally, the structure of society, particularly its occupational structure, was permanently altered. A multi-tiered educational system was established and connected with the labor market through a hierarchy of occupational specialties ranked by prestige according to the amount of schooling required to alter them (Treiman, 1977).

This is the legal, economic and structural situation (as of 1980), representing an enormous public commitment to education. The private commitment is equally important: families are kept deliberately small, with typically no more than three children, all of whom survive infancy and are provided with good nutrition and pediatric care. Family income is high (roughly ten times that of the poorest countries) and children have access to substantial material resources from the start. Parents are influenced by cultural ideologies that prescribe sharing domestic resources with children and devoting time and attention to their care and training. A majority of families live in urban areas, and parents are aware of the relationships between academic performance and the urban labor market/occupational prestige system of a capitalist society. In a variety of ways, depending on the country-specific cultural styles of parental commitment, parents attend to the educational careers of their children until they become employed. This private contribution to education affects the academic performance of students in all highly industrialized societies.

When international comparisons are made of academic perform-ance, cognitive skills, and intellectual achievement, children from the industrial societies score much higher on the average than children from other societies (Husen, 1967). This is an outcome of the processes outlined above, i.e. the political will, the economic investment and the parental commitment, operating in collabor-ation to foster the realization of academic potential through formal schooling.[1] The cultural basis for educational development, that is, the beliefs and practices which form a consensus in a society, plays a critical, and largely unrecognized, role in making this collaboration possible, as illustrated in the rest of this chapter.

Mobilization for education began in the West (see Chapter 3), but some of the most striking contemporary examples are in Asia: Japan, followed more recently by Taiwan, Hong Kong, Singapore and South Korea.[2] A deeper look at the context and quality of learning in one of these non-Western examples of mobilization, that of Japan, will give us a clearer picture of the role of culture in determining educational outcomes for children and societies.

This chapter reviews the evidence on contemporary Japanese educational performance and the history of Japanese schooling, showing the uniquely important contribution of Japanese cultural premises to educational processes in schools, families, and other settings.

SCHOOLING AND SOCIAL TRANSFORMATION

Japan was an agrarian society that mobilized itself on a national basis in the late nineteenth century for industrial production and educational achievement, without serious social dislocation and without wholesale adoption of the Western organizational and cultural modes which had accompanied these changes elsewhere. The Western tension between modern options and agrarian liga-tures had and has little relevance in Japan. Drastic reforms were carried out without destroying agrarian kinship and village ties or the social identities defined and motivated by agrarian models of communal and interpersonal behavior. An emphasis on social continuity and cohesion throughout the transition also influenced the way in which institutional models were borrowed, particularly for education.

Before describing the transition to modern schooling, we need first to discuss the nature and interpretation of 'modernization' in Japan at this period. The case of Japan has provoked much controversy among scholars in terms of defining modernization, and the Japanese themselves have spent more than a century considering its meaning. In fact, the indigenization of the *concept* of modernization has paralleled the selective adaptation of those Western institutions, ideologies and technologies which the Japanese call 'modern'.

In the early Meiji period, from 1868 to the turn of the century, the phrase *bummei kaika* ('civilization and enlightenment') represented the goals of a modern society for reformers. This phrase epitomized Japanese concern with cultural and moral aspects of change, a concern which persisted throughout the process of industrialization and increasing military and material expansion. A second phrase which embodied another aspect of modernization was *fukoku kyohei*, or 'enrich the nation; strengthen arms'. As Shively (1965) points out the first phrase represents a general outlook, the second, the way in which modernization was actually carried out, through centralization and the development of a strong military, as the basis for industrialization. Modernization, in both its Meiji period sense and in the contemporary translation, *kindaika*, has in Japan always borne more than an emphasis on the mechanical process of institutional and economic change, but has involved also a constant search for a national *moral* system whether rooted in Japanese pre-history, Confucian or 'democratic', which would provide a support for people as they experience these changes. Although it is hard to avoid the use of the word 'modernization' to describe social and economic transformation in Japan, we hope not to invoke only a Western formulation based on Western historical conditions and experiences, but to include the meanings and priorities the Japanese have attached to the process. Education is one of the clearest cases of an environment where the emphasis on a moral system, the need for centralization of a national institution, and the adaptation of Western models, was conveyed explicitly in the process of 'modernization'.

In 1853, the beginning of Japan's modern contact with the West,

Japan had no centralized or uniform national schooling. Pre-modern Japan was not seen as a potential major world power, or even as a future Asian leader. On the other hand India's colonial, educational and bureaucratic infrastructure and China's long contact with the West were seen as keys to their predicted development. Without this background, Japanese educators declared that Japan had a difficult, uphill struggle to become a modern state, and warned their countrymen that they must avoid evidence of backwardness and barbarism (Fukuzawa, p. 207). About a century later, however, Japan's achievements in mass education had exceeded those of most European countries, let alone those of their former colonies.

How was Japan's unpredicted success achieved, and how did agrarian cultural premises not only survive the transition to a modern society but, as it will be shown, provide the basis for Japan's modern economic successes? The importance of the role of education in Japan's social and economic development has been stressed both by Western observers and by Japanese national policy and ideology. It is in fact the clear priority given to learning and the agreement between institutional policy and popular attitudes in Japan, i.e. the complementarity between macrosocial priorities and the agrarian cultural premises underlying microsocial practices and experiences, which has produced both national educational achievement and national social and economic growth. In this context, Japanese educational and economic successes may be seen as the product of the congruity between two types of mobilization, 'popular' and 'bureaucratic'.

We will describe both forms of educational mobilization: the 'popular', in which an impetus for educational achievement is generated from agrarian microsocial values and practices, and the 'bureaucratic', in which a social consensus is given macrosocial expression through national policy and institutional development.

In our overview of Japanese educational mobilization, we will note that Japanese education is characterized by:

1 An historical continuity with pre-modern pedagogies and definitions of learning and development.
2 A consensus across society that childhood is important and that the education of children is the most important factor in developing society.
3 A functional adaptation and reinterpretation of Western

educational institutions and cognitive goals to Japanese cultural conditions.

4 Continuity and mutual support between parental interests for the child and those of the teachers and schools.

5 Pedagogies which integrate the effective, cognitive and behavioral development of the child and stress engagement, effort and commitment.

6 A functional separation between the goals of harmony. egalitarianism and homogeneity on the one hand and selective competition on the other, without severely straining the social fabric or diminishing the chance for individuals to develop skills, work creatively and activate personal ambitions.

The development of the educational environment noted by these characteristics will be examined in terms of pre-modern and modern cultural and institutional factors.

Japanese consensus: an agrarian heritage

The effects of Japan's 'natural' mobilization have encouraged a hindsight observation that Japan was, in the nineteenth century, an 'advantaged agrarian society', that in spite of limited natural resources and lack of continental or colonial influences there existed some preconditions for development which did not exist elsewhere. While some pre-capitalist conditions have been noted in nineteenth-century Japan as they were in pre-industrial England, Japan was not necessarily economically or politically better prepared for national transformation than China or India. What did set Japan apart, and what characterizes 'popular' mobilization, is an ideological predisposition for educational development. This predisposition, and the social organization in which it was generated, will be examined next.

Pre-modern Japan was characterized by its feudal social structure, and was largely rural. Even as late as 1912, 80 per cent of the population lived in rural areas. Village organization was based in cooperative relationships between families which involved sharing responsibility for and benefit from jointly owned agricultural equipment and irrigation facilities. Ceremonies and religious observances also helped the community to cohere and ritual gift-giving and sharing symbolized this cohesion. Marriages were arranged to bind families together in reciprocal relationships, and the continuity of these relationships over time was made explicit in the linkages to be inherited by each generation of the *dozoku* (lineage).

At any moment in time, the inhabitants of the *ie*, or 'house' were seen as obligated to the ancestors and responsible to future incumbents, and were not at liberty to endanger the prosperity of the house through self-seeking risk-taking. Nor could the property be broken up, except *in extremis*, since it did not belong to any one generation: it had to be passed intact from one to the next. Primogeniture was thus a feature of the Japanese stem family, in which eldest sons commonly inherited the ancestral home and land, while younger sons were established in separate houses, maintaining ritual and affective ties to the main house. During the modernization period, younger sons often went to urban areas to find non-agricultural employment, but maintained close ties to their rural kin. Without draining the resources of the main house, parents invested in younger sons' education, in the knowledge that educational experiences and credentials would both repay the main house and allow children to raise their own chances in life. It was more important, however, that the main house prosper than that primogeniture be strictly observed, and eldest sons, if less competent, were frequently passed over. Indeed, unrelated but promising young men were often adopted as heirs and married to a daughter to continue the line. Thus individual ability and potential, dedicated to the good of the family, were noted and rewarded even in the context of the transcendent ideal of household continuity.

The story of Ninomiya Sontoku (a Tokugawa period social philosopher) best exemplifies the agrarian values which prevailed in the rapid development of the Meiji period (1868–1912). Like the heroes of Horatio Alger in nineteenth century America, Ninomiya Sontoku's life became legendary and exemplary, known to every Japanese school child. As an orphaned child, he lived with his uncle and spent long hours in the fields, but, always aware that he must study to improve himself, he stayed up late at night to read Confucian texts. When his uncle complained of the waste of lamp oil, he raised his own crop of rape seeds and used oil pressed from them. He used his farming skills to reclaim wasteland and grow surplus crops by which he finally bought himself freedom to work and study on his father's lands. His statue, that of a boy carrying wood on his back while reading a book, remains in many schoolyards today. There are several elements in the story which appealed to the generation which modernized Japan and which have resonance even today.

While the model of the self-made man has yielded to the image of the establishment bureaucrat graduated from Tokyo University, the legendary attributes of Ninomiya Sontoku are still highly valued. What made him the exemplar of Japanese nineteenth-century morality were his self-discipline, industry and his drive to study for self-improvement. It is, however, interesting to note that he was highly independent and that his story does not include the values of cooperation and team work: the bootstrapping efforts of Meiji society, like those of the immediate post World War II era, allowed for more individuated (although not *individualistic*) activities and paths than were later to be supported by the mainstream consensus.

What is particularly of interest is the association of study with agricultural work. Study, for Ninomiya Sontoku, was not a means to 'rise above' labor in the fields, but rather a way in which to realize himself by improving his character and virtue. It should be noted that while this characterization of study of Confucian texts for virtue's sake also existed in China, the Chinese valued the life of scholarship (or of the bureaucracy which could be gained through study) significantly above that of manual agricultural labor, and the Japanese association of scholarly virtue with a strong value placed on manual hard work was a distinctly different pattern.

The association of study and work in the Ninomiya Sontoku story is evident also in an analysis of the cultural meanings of these activities. The words for 'work' (hataraku 働) and 'study' (benkyoo, 勉強 both involve the connotations of intense commitment of effort in order to become a better person, the active voluntary participation in a piece of study or work which leads to self-realization. This is not necessarily self-betterment in measurable terms: not, as in China, a source of upward mobility or even an explicit gauge of virtue. The only 'points' gained are those one can experience in the act of commitment itself. It is sufficient to learn what true *engagement* in the effort means: that is what study and work are (Kondo, 1984). In studies in a rural village in the early 1950s, George de Vos found that farmers felt that work is 'a positive opportunity to achieve success [rather than] . . . a burden thrust on them by circumstances . . .' (Beardsley, Hall and Ward, p.68). Everyone seeks out such opportunities: not to look for this challenge is seen as abnormal.

Ninomiya Sontoku represents agrarian virtues associated with the individual, but at the same time there has existed a strong communal orientation involving both obligation in hierarchically arrayed relationships and responsibility in the community. Communal consciousness and a priority placed on social linkages, along with *risshin-shusse* (improving one's place in life through struggle and endurance) are the keys to personal and social virtue. Work may be the path to fulfillment but there is less emphasis on private reward: maintenance of interdependence and harmony in relationships provide the setting for the enjoyment of fulfillment, as well as the ultimate proof of one's virtue.

The goal of this cultural model of potential may be summarized as personal success in service to both the hierarchical linkages and the wider horizontally-conceived group. During the early days of modernization, the Confucian vertical status linkages were more powerfully evoked, but gradually, exhortations to succeed for the greater good of the nation (sometimes personified as a family with the Emperor as father) broadened and flattened the points of reference providing meaning in people's lives. More broadly stated, the individual's moral duty in social relationships was congruent with his economic self-interest in the context of a society which was based on a reciprocal moral order, as we have shown in Chapter 2. The rejection of kin and community relationships was not seen to be in a person's self-interest and, in fact, throughout the process of economic and social transformation, the full realization of the self continued to be gained only through these relationships. In contrast, nineteenth-century Western patterns of change as described in Chapter 3, show trends toward weakening family ties, rural-urban discontinuity, reduction in fertility, an increasing separation of home and workplace, and the introduction of labor market values into parent-child relationships. Japan has shown a different pattern, one which preserved agrarian ways of life and pre-modern demographic characteristics far into the modern period. In brief, the early period of Japanese transformation was carried out in the context of low urbanization (Vogel, 1967), a rise in fertility (as in the West before 1880) (Hanley, 1974), and the maintenance of strong family-centered enterprises. The shift of large numbers of people from the fields to the factories did not shift their focus of identity from the farm, and those who did transplant to the city were strongly tied to their rural family base.

We have noted that Japanese modernization, at least initially, displayed a pattern rather different from that exhibited in the West, and maintained an agrarian focus on family and other social linkages as the appropriate recipient of the rewards earned by individual effort. While this effort, as in the West, was encouraged in the context of schools as a means of personal and social development, the benefits gained by the individual were experienced within the family and the group.

The resources with which individuals and families could improve their lives were scarce, and this scarcity itself may have contributed to cultural ideas of hard work and thrift to maximize success.[3] Japanese pre-modern cultural values, as embodied in the Ninomiya Sontoku story, interpreted constraints and obstacles as challenges to activity and achievement: overcoming handicaps through struggle and turning them into assets was a significant, culturally supported ability.

Finally, in the context of Dahrendorf's discussion of life chances, the pre-modern environment of Japan represents an anomalous case. No society exclusively values either options or ligatures but unlike the cultures of the industrial West Japanese culture does not involve a basic opposition between the two. The Western dualistic notion that one has to destroy ligatures in order to free the individual to pursue options efficiently did not, and does not, prevail in Japan. Obviously, the cultural meanings embodied in these concepts differ in Japan and the West: appropriate personal options in the West are different from those which motivate Japanese and, similarly, both in its structural characteristics (demands and delineations) and in the emotional experiences of social linkages, the Japanese context differs from that of the West.

Since 'family' has lost its earlier function and yet remains a powerful, though ambiguous, force in the individual's life, it may be that an American sees family as more of a constraint than a support. If its functions were more distinct, the areas of freedom would also be clearer from its demands, and there would perhaps be less tension over duties and benefits experienced by the individual.

It might be said that for the very reason that 'family' is a less well-defined area of responsibility and obligation in American culture, it is experienced as more of a threat to individual 'autonomy', just as it might be said that because one's options in Japan include self-realization through personal effort in service to the group, individual striving for fulfilment is not at odds with the ties that bind. These cultural definitions, the one involving separation of personal goals and group demands, the other emphasizing a consensus of ends and means, were an important part of the agrarian heritage which continues to shape modern experiences in Japan.

The cultural model for the motivation of individual effort is part of the ideological predisposition we described as important in the educational mobilization of Japan. The relationship described above between personal goals and social linkages does not completely describe the motivation for high performances which is the crucial factor in the efficacy of the model. The most significant aspect of the model is its stress on *motivation* itself: it is not innate ability which counts, but the creation of motivating environments in which one commits effort. As noted above, process and performance are stressed rather than product, with the understanding that highly-motivated performance will achieve high productivity. First, when effort is valued over ability, there is an egalitarian cast to the work environment: commit more hours, more sweat to the task, and your identity as a good worker will be ensured without reference to innate abilities or other personal distinctions. Second, building morale and motivation, not only measuring output, are the tasks and major functions of teachers and employers. While exhortatory rhetoric, company songs, extensive benefits and 'family style' management-worker relationships may seem like benevolent paternalism to Western observers, these are based in culturally-appropriate emphases on engagement and commitment.

Third, the cultural model emphasizes socialization into the motivating group: an individual is encouraged to see him or herself as part of a group – not '*just* part of a group' as Western perspectives would term it, but identified by self-enhancing membership which brings out the best of a person's potential. Thus Japanese cultural premises give a different conceptual frame to personal development and social identity from that which is presumed in the West to determine success.

The transition to a national educational system

As described in Chapter 4, in the pre-modern Tokugawa period (1603–1868) there was a variety of institutions and goals for learning and, although there was no central coordination and program, attitudes and aspirations conducive to the development of national educational and social mobilization, as well as significantly high levels of literacy, greatly antedated the creation of centralized institutions.

The changes in the power structure and social organization which were created in the Meiji Restoration (1868) were effected with little social upheaval, and were accompanied by a series of sweeping reforms, aimed at modernizing and centralizing Japan. The development of a national educational system was seen as crucial to economic and social modernization as well as important as a means for creating the coherence and consensus seen as necessary for a nation-state.

The key factor in the successful adoption of Western forms of schooling was an agreement throughout Japanese society, from parents (of all classes) to national planners, that education was important and that school was where the most important education takes place. Further, there was both 'popular' and 'bureaucratic' confidence that Japanese ligature-based goals were the appropriate basis for development. There was throughout the period of Tokugawa isolation from the rest of the world, a sense that while the West held out a tantalizing source of novelty and represented the future, Japan could not afford to join the world until political consolidation and the development of a strong cohesive national culture could protect her from imperialism. The cultural confidence which came out of this self-imposed seclusion allowed the Japanese of the Meiji period (1868–1912) to adapt Western models of schooling to suit the Japanese environment. Although the adaptations took time and although there were many false starts in experiments with school structure and curriculum, the criterion of appropriateness to Japanese society was always pre-eminent.

In the 1872 Fundamental Code of Education, the last vestiges of a class-based educational system were broken down, and schooling for all classes was integrated. Universal literacy was the goal, as stated in the Preamble to the Code: 'Learning is the key to success in life. . . . There shall, in the future, be no community with an illiterate family; nor a family with an illiterate person' (Passin, 1965). While the organization of the system was French, the curriculum was American and at first, translated and borrowed texts were used, until Japanese ones could be prepared.

Elementary education became compulsory and immediately primary schools were established throughout Japan. Indeed, by 1880 there already existed the same number of schools as exist today. Government scholarships were provided to encourage young people to attend the widespread normal school system, created to meet the sudden great need for primary school teachers. Further reforms in the 1880s and 1890s incorporated Prussian educational ideas, and by the end of the century, Japanese educational ideology fused Confucian ethics, evolving statism, and Western ideas about learning into a single model, summarized in the Imperial Rescript on Education of 1879 (Passin, 1965) as follows:

> The essence of education, our traditional national aim, and a
> watchword for all men, is to make clear the ways of
> benevolence, justice, loyalty and filial piety, and to master
> knowledge and skill and through these to pursue the Way of
> Man. (p. 227)

From German scholars and administrators, Japanese planners borrowed a rationale for an 'imperial' education, and from Western liberals, 'industrializing' progressive schooling.

What was *Japanese* in this mix was the experiment in adaptation itself and the optimistic insistence that there would emerge a modern, educated populace which was yet indisputably Japanese. From the beginning Japanese planners were alert to the intended and unintended cultural consequences of national development and 'industrial imperialism' and saw that if they themselves could control the importation of Western ideas and technology, in the world's most massive and dramatically swift development 'intervention', the goals of maintenance of cultural integrity and rapid transformation could both be achieved.

The Imperial Rescript on Education, which hung in every classroom from 1890 to 1945, emphasized the continuity of Japanese cultural integrity through education:

> Our Imperial Ancestors have founded our Empire on a basis
> broad and everlasting, and have deeply and firmly implanted
> virtue; Our subjects ever united in loyalty and filial piety have
> from generation to generation illustrated the beauty thereof;
> This is the glory of the fundamental character of Our Empire
> and herein also lies the source of our Education . . .

From 1872 to 1945 Japan's educational system developed as the central social institution in Japan, for several reasons which varied over time. First, and persisting to modern times, is the fact that Japanese cultural perceptions increasingly view personal skill acquisition and moral and civic socialization as the job of the school. Second, education is seen as the appropriate sector to turn to when issues of development, security, and resources become national priorities. Third, and related to both of the above, is the conviction that children's achievement in school is a source of national pride as well as an important national resource in itself.

There is a larger point to be made concerning the underlying premises of educational mobilization in Japan. We have mentioned that ('popular') cultural models for personal development complemented emerging ('bureaucratic') models for national development. This may be more strongly stated here: that leadership, based in a serious consideration of cultural norms, drew on folk models of personal achievement and interpersonal influence and motivation in devising and adapting a modern educational system to Japanese needs. The translation of folk models into national policy and practice, as noted above, is a product of both 'popular' and 'bureaucratic' adjustment. It is to be expected that a relatively homogeneous population will construct its institutions to be consonant with its cultural predilections. However, this 'natural' evolution was, in the case of Japan, supplemented by the conscious desire to develop institutions which would efficiently bring Japan into the modern world. This motivation facilitated the legitimacy of extending schooling to all children, and the development through schooling of national identification and unity. Whatever resistance there may have been to homogenization and equalization of opportunity, whatever opposition by interest groups there may have been, was overcome by the pre-existing consensus, deliberately made part of policy and incorporated in the institution of the school.

Finally, social and economic transformation took place supported by nearly uniform educational development in both rural and urban areas, to the importance of education – a condition not available elsewhere. This facilitated the relatively easy movement of rural people to the city both during the Meiji period and later, in post-war reconstruction, 'pre-adapted' as they were by a more or less uniform curriculum. Rural people, moving to the cities after World War II, had had good, and uniform, secondary school training, and so this pool of labor for factories was highly trained (Shibata, 1982). There was no sharp division between literate urbanites and illiterate country bumpkins, and both productivity and the sense of rural-urban unity were enhanced. Further, while children of farm families were, of course, seen as important contributors of labor, they were also seen as learners and as possessing a potential which would lend concrete value to the family.

American Models for Educating Japanese Children: 'Egalitarian Education'

Japanese educational planners in the immediate post-war period were faced with the need to adapt Occupation reforms to the pre-existing consensus surrounding educational goals and traditions. Post-war Japanese education was modelled on American ideas rather than on actual American practice. The key concept was 'democracy', understood for the most part in Japan as 'egalitarianism'. Japanese interpretations of democracy emphasized the provision of equal opportunity for all people, rather than equal entitlement and the encouragement of individualism. 'Democracy' was seen to be the antithesis of 'feudalism' (under which term all aspects of pre-war and wartime society and values were lumped), and yet, some pre-war cultural values could be incorporated in the vague new philosophy. Teachers and educational philosophers now found that the idealized traditional relationship between student and teacher could be re-created in the democratic society. The emphasis on affection and warmth in the classic relationship was given a modern context in Kojima Gunzo's (1959) phrase *kyoiku-ai* ('love in education') which he described as follows:

It is love in educational activities which generates the driving force of the teacher's action toward the learner in terms of personality and which gives vitality to guidance. [The first kind of love is] . . . the natural human love which is common in other aspects of human life and which the teacher always has in his heart as he . . . watches the sound growth of the immature and inexperienced pupil. . . . The second is a conscious love with which the teacher finds within the pupil the potentials for an ideal person, and endeavors for this fulfillment with sincere hope.

The 'democratic' relationship between student and teacher shows this love through discipline, respect and morality, all of which are seen as reciprocal and as evidence of the mutual love of student and teacher. This traditional 'vertical' relationship was thus seen as fully consonant with democracy: 'egalitarian' in this case does not refer to equality of status but to the two-way obligation which was to benefit both student and teacher, based on a kind of merging between them. In such discussions, one of the mechanisms of Japanese adaptation can be seen, in which emphasis is placed on pre-existing values and social structure which can support or complement an innovation. What is especially interesting in this example is not only the conversion of 'democracy' through 'love' to traditional 'respect' but also the idea that through love the teacher can analyze the student's abilities and, ideally, find a way to maximize them: 'love' in this context is a didactic device and a tool for the realization of human potential – one which has existed since pre-modern times in Japanese attitudes and practices surrounding the development of children. Similarly, the emphasis on the 'whole child' in post-war Japanese education, while derived from American and British models, was consonant with traditional Japanese child-rearing methods.

The 'second modernization' of the post-war years in Japan once again focused on education but emphasized egalitarian opportunity as well as the screening process implicit in the examination ladder. The post-war Constitution states that 'All people shall have the right to receive an equal education correspondent to their ability' (Article 26) (Passin, 1965, p. 287). The words in this statement which are key to the structural, pedagogical and ideological tensions in post-war Japanese education are 'equal' and 'ability'. Just as 'democracy' could, in a Japanese context, be meaningfully applied to the traditional respect in the relationship of teacher and student, so 'equality', can co-exist with a selection system for a hierarchically ranked occupational world. Of course, 'equality' – an American doctrine – has at least two applications in Japanese education: in one there is a deliberate de-emphasis on distinctions between children, and in the other, a stress on availability of equal opportunities for the demonstrations of differences in ability. These two meanings of equality, equally important to society's norms and practices, have produced a unique combination of homogeneous experience and fine-tuned ranking for Japanese children. The *Japanese* synthesis and conception of equality, while derived from a Western idea, produced a totally indigenous model and cultural practice. The importance of the stress on harmony and on the struggle to rise on the ladder of achievement will be discussed in the next section. What is significant for our discussion here is that both cultural priorities have been explicitly developed in institutional contexts, and form part of the consensus which produced Japan's educational mobilization.

Competition and Harmony: The Shape of the System Today

Japanese children generally achieve highly in school. Their test scores exceed those of children in the Western countries whose educational systems were models for Japanese development. The Japanese educational system scores high in terms of the numbers of children engaged in formal learning, the time they spend at it, the knowledge they achieve and the function of education in the child's success as an adult in the labor market. The children also, in greater numbers than elsewhere, report that they *like* school (Iwao, 1982).

Enrollment figures are high: 100 per cent of the age group is in primary school, 98 per cent of the appropriate group in high school (which is non-compulsory), and 41 per cent are in colleges or universities. Learning starts young and more than 70 per cent of three and four year olds are in nursery schools.

The richness of the curriculum is such that a high school diploma in Japan can be said to be the equivalent of a college diploma in the United States in terms of courses taken and material covered. In mathematics and science especially, Japanese children receive a broad and comprehensive education, and in recent comparisons with the United States, it has been shown that the lowest test scores in fifth grade classes in Japan are higher than the highest test scores in comparable American schools (Stevenson, 1983).

Significant also is the fact that there is less variation in performance across the population than in most other societies[4] (Comber and Keeves, 1973; Husen 1967). The gap between expectations and performances is small. A combination of high but realistic expectations, strong incentives, effective instruction, and parental support for learning has created this striking uniformity of achievement. In fact, it is a source of some wonder in Japan that children elsewhere do not perform as well and that standards and incentives in other advanced nations are so low. In Japan 'high achievement' has become a standard expectation.

The effects of this interest and achievement are seen beyond the years of schooling for widespread literacy[5] is accompanied by widespread readership and engagement in knowledge-enhancing activities across all sectors of the populations. There is a high level of cultural engagement as well – blue-collar workers submitting original 'classical' verse to newspapers; the assumption that everyone can read music; the use by national media of highly sophisticated technical vocabularies.

How are these outcomes, valued in the West as well as in Japan, achieved? A summary of the social conditions for these successes includes the following factors:

1   A high degree of parental involvement in and commitment to the education of children, and a society-wide consensus as to the appropriateness of this investment.
2   A basic eagerness to learn and positive attitude toward school on the part of children who, overall, show very low rates of disaffection, as manifested in juvenile delinquency and drop-out rates. In general, school is where children want to be.
3   High status for teachers and a strong commitment on their part to teaching and to involvement in their students' overall development.
4   The premise of egalitarian access to the rewards of successful learning. Government schools, and the national curriculum, have in general higher prestige than private schools, so economic status does not in itself provide an advantage, although parents do invest considerable sums in

tutoring and extra classes. These extra expenses are often covered by the mother's part-time work.

5   The assumption that it is effort rather than innate ability which yields rewards in schooling. The expression 'pass with four; fail with five' is an injunction to high schoolers studying for the college entrance examinations not to sleep more than four hours: if you log enough time studying, you'll pass. The selection of the fittest does not depend on innate capacity but on commitment and hard work. This is why mothers are encouraged to watch their children's morale and their diet during the 'examination hell': they are trainers of Olympic athletes, not parents of children whose god- or gene-given skills are about to be revealed through tests.

6   The fact that, as mentioned above, the occupational system values education (as credential and/or as substantive training and socialization) as appropriate preparation for work. This is both a condition for the consensus on the importance of schooling and an outcome, since the consensus depends on the production of a qualified labor force.

While the educational mobilization of Japan has been accompanied by problems, the intensity of concern about and the anticipation of future problems and needs has prevented major dislocations, inequities and crises. The ability of the national educational system to channel resources equitably and to attack problems effectively is supported by the microlevel consensus and practice: parental interest and willingness to be engaged in the process; teachers' alert and dedicated attention to children's needs and abilities.

The image of Japanese education in the Western media and, indeed, in the writing of many observers, emphasizes costs as well as benefits, both perceived in Western terms. Coloring these perceptions is an emphasis on the examinations to high school and college. 'Examination hell', the weeks (and years) of effort preceding the entrance exams, is central in most Western descriptions of Japanese schooling, but this phenomenon is far from being the central focus of the system, either for the great majority of children and parents, or for the planners and bureaucrats who establish institutional priorities.

While only about 10 per cent of the college-age group is engaged in the high-intensity effort to enroll in the high-status schools from which the most prestigious companies and ministries draw their future top managers and bureaucrats, the image of Japanese children uniformly engaged in a do-or-die struggle is the prevalent Western stereotype. This image is heightened by attention given to the annual juvenile suicide rate, to the incidence of school-phobia and psychosomatic illnesses among school children and to the prevalence of the 'education mama', overzealous for her children's success. And it is not only the Americans who seem to relish these 'atrocities'. The Japanese press, social commentators and other public figures emphasize violence in the classroom and at home, the prevalence of motorcycle gangs and the (highly organized) rock dancing by teenagers in a Tokyo street on Sundays. These are given as indications that the educational system has become a pressure cooker and that the struggle to get ahead has produced an over-competitive and demoralized generation.

It should be noted here that Japanese observers of their own society seem preoccupied with strains in the social fabric which to Americans would appear relatively unthreatening. Statistically, neither juvenile suicides nor violence and crime, seem to Americans to warrant the critical reaction they have received in Japan. When dyeing one's hair or lengthening a skirt can be counted as acts of 'school violence', it is clear that a different standard is being applied than that which is understood in the US. As an example of the need for a comparative view, the number of student assaults on teachers in New York City alone in the first semester of the 1974–5 school year was three times that of the total number of assaults in the entire 1976 school year in all of Japan (Rohlen, 1983). It is, however, exactly the attention and sensitivity given by Japanese to potential problems which has created the successes of the educational system. The Japanese feel they are living in a very precarious position, on a narrow margin, and their poverty in natural resources has produced an emphasis on human resources and potentials. To maximize these potentials, which are seen to be most realizable through education, there is naturally a great concern with the condition of childhood and a disposition to anticipate and attend to any problems which might arise.

A more useful focus on contemporary Japanese education is through the perspective that the system achieves its goals of maximizing children's abilities and performances through the collaboration of macrosocial and microsocial priorities and processes. The questions of how the schools stream and screen, how they achieve social cohesion while encouraging each child to work hard to achieve personal success, are best answered by an investigation of the consonance of goals and means in the home, school, and in policy-making institutions.

Japanese and outside observers agree that Japan's rapid development in the Meiji period and the post-war 'economic miracle' are closely related to the emphasis on education, both to raise the general level of skill in society and to give the especially talented a means for rising to influential positions.

The finely-honed system of selection for the most coveted jobs is seen as crucial to the continued stability of Japan. These jobs are not only high in status but are seen as highly demanding and requiring high levels of skill and effort. Success in school is seen as a good indicator of success in such jobs. To parents, the schools need to guarantee that their children will be given a chance at the ladder, as well as a high level of achievement, and appropriate social and individual development within the child's school career. In Japan, there are few opportunities to change paths or retool: the American idea that you can recreate yourself at any time in the life course, that the self-made person can get ahead is not viable in Japan, and the intensity of focus on the examinations is a product of both the need to restrict competition to one point in the life course and a result of a strong consensus on what the life course is and what its goals should be.[6]

In Japan, the importance of the modern educational system as a selector of talent for the benefit of society and the need to preserve harmony and homogeneity has produced a bifurcation in the educational system but one which seems composed of complementary rather than conflicting elements. The regular classroom is a place where the individual does not stick out and where active competition is not encouraged but where individual needs are met and goals are set. Children are not held back nor advanced by ability: the cohesion of the age group is said to be more important. Teachers focus on pulling up the slower learners, rather than streaming the class to suit different abilities. Teachers and the school system refuse for the most part to engage in examination preparation hysteria. Part of the reason for this is pressure from the Teachers' Union, a very large and powerful labor union which consistently resists any moves away from the egalitarian and undifferentiating mode of learning: turning teachers into drill instructors is said to be dehumanizing and the process of cramming a poor substitute for learning.

So where is the competitive selection principle served? It is in the *juku* or private after-school classes. Some *juku* are tough, highly competitive cramming classes, often large in scale with up to 500 in one lecture hall. The most prestigious are themselves very selective and there are examinations (and preparation courses for these) to enter the *juku*. Some *juku* specialize in particular universities' entrance exams, and they will boast their rate of admission into their universities. It is estimated that nation-wide, one third of all primary school students and one half of all lower secondary students attend *juku*, but in Tokyo the rate rises to 86 per cent of junior high school students. *Juku* are said to be necessary to bridge the gap between the fact of competition and the necessity to maintain 'egalitarian' values and methods in the classroom. The Ministry of Education's attitude towards this non-accredited alternative and complementary system seems to be to ignore or give window-dressing attention to the issues it raises, and to permit this functional bifurcation to take the pressure off the public schools. While there is considerable grumbling by parents and while it is clear that the tuition-charging *juku* introduce an inegalitarian element into the process of schooling, they do, by their separation from the regular school, permit the persistence of more traditional modes of learning. In any case, selection in education is focused on getting into a new school, or workplace, at a particular point in time, and doesn't focus on constant comparison and competition with peers throughout one's school life. What is won is a place in a new environment, not new status within the group to which one already belongs: the face to face relationships of everyday life are (relatively) unharmed. Moreover, what is said to make the difference between one student and another in the *juku* and elsewhere is *effort*, not innate ability or predisposition. Besides accumulated knowledge, what your grades in a *juku* show is your ability to apply yourself diligently, an ability theoretically available to everyone.

The relationship between the values of school and *juku* and the values of the workplace illustrates the symbiosis within the educational system. The white collar workplace exemplifies the values of harmony through minimal overt competition, and attempts to restrict arenas for distinctions between people in two ways: first, the promotional track is predetermined by the results of the examination which all white collar workers take at entrance which protects the internal structure of relationships from a basic source of competition. One's career in the company is restricted to the track into which one is placed at entrance. Second, seniority is the most common criterion for promotion, at least at the lower levels of the pyramid. The distinctions which are later invoked as the pyramid shrinks are made by means of careful long-term observations of an employee's skill, effort and commitment, enhanced by his ability to develop good relationships with relevant superiors as patrons or mentors (Hamaguchi, 1982). Competition is thus controlled by placing it in a long-term context, which gives the worker and the organization more predictability and leeway and allows the deleterious effects of direct and constant competition to be minimized through diffusion.

How, in such a supportive and non-competitive environment, is incentive for high productivity and performance maintained? American observers would doubt that the lifetime employment system, and the security of regular seniority-based promotions, could provide workers with motivation to exert themselves. Moreover, unlike the educational system, there is no external agent, such as the entrance examinations, to mobilize effort, and no 'side-line' system like the *juku* to train and focus commitment. Older explanations, such as Abegglen's analysis of benevolent paternalism and reciprocal loyalty in the Japanese factory (Abegglen, 1958), are insufficient to describe the complex relationship of the employee to his workplace. The fact is that Japanese see security as permitting people to exert themselves to the fullest extent. In the West, security is seen to reduce incentive, providing a reason not to commit energy, while in Japan it is seen as motivating more intense performances. The difference is perhaps explained by the differing *goals* for performance. In Japan, one's best efforts are given to working for *collective* success, and working for

115

advancement within a permanent reference group such as a company or other work team. In the West, such a collective environment is secondary to one's personal career path or recognition as a focus for commitment, and high job security is seen to deter ambition. Further, in Japan, competition exists *between* companies, not within them. These and other underlying cultural premises surrounding work, competition and commitment may be best approached through a closer look at the microsocial aspects of a child's experience of learning in Japan. Part Two of this chapter will examine early socialization and the school life of the child in an effort to analyze the role played by family and school in creating responsible, committed and high-achieving children and adults.

THE EXPERIENCE OF LEARNING IN JAPAN

Coordinated Commitment: School and Home Learning

The foundation of the successes (as well as of some of the excesses) of Japanese education is the relationship between mother and child. While observers of Japanese society have attributed the intensity of this relationship to a restriction on women's options and roles through the dissemination of a 'middle class' model of separation of male and female 'spheres' and through the diminution of household tasks through technological advances, the closeness and 'special' quality of the relationship seems to antedate significantly the urban nuclear family model and labor-saving devices. John Embree's work (1939) in rural Japan in the 1930s shows the special relationship of mother and child, and, much earlier than this, child-rearing books by educational reformers of the seventeenth century (Yanazumi and Nakae, 1976) point to the intimacy between mother and child, especially between the mother and first and last born children, as at once a contributor to the child's development and a possible threat to his maturation. In the mother-child relationship, a traditional cultural pattern has found a modern environment conducive to its perpetuation and utilization. The mother, in modern times having the chief responsibility for her child's development and having ample time to devote to child-related activities, as well

116

as herself having had extensive education, is encouraged in her preoccupation with her children's schooling by the demands of the educational system which relies on strong support from the home. Underlying these conditions is the long-standing idea that early childhood is the most important period for developing skills and attitudes necessary for success in adulthood, and the belief that a woman's primary and most valued role is that of mother, and that mothers are responsible for their children's development. The following portrait illustrates some dimensions of the relationship.

Mothering in the Middle Class

Ichiro and Keiko Watanabe married when he was twenty-seven and she was almost twenty-five. They had two children within the first four years of their marriage. When they were first married, they lived with his parents since he is the eldest son and will eventually inherit the family house, but are now living in a distant provincial city due to a company transfer. They live in a *danchi* (apartment complex) owned by the company, with one living room and two multi-purpose smaller tatami-matted rooms, kitchen and bath. Keiko worked for two years after completing a two year course in a women's college and before marriage, but has engaged in no formal economic or educational pursuits since then. Her only regular activity outside the home has been participation in a crafts club established by the company for the wives of employees.

Keiko's day is structured by the children's schedule. Her daughter is in the fifth grade and her son is in the third grade. After breakfast she helps them get ready, and sends them to school. Keiko airs the bedding on the tiny balcony, and cleans the house, while watching a nationally-televised soap opera. She may read for a while, usually a woman's magazine full of advice on the mother's role in her children's cognitive development.

Once a day Keiko does errands, usually in the neighborhood shops. She can find everything she needs within three hundred yards of her apartment and chooses this neighborhood cluster of shops, rather than the larger (sometimes cheaper) department stores a bus-ride away, as much for the intimacy and familiarity of her relationships with shopkeepers as for their convenience. She can accomplish errands and housework in a short space, at the most

117

three hours, but chooses to spread the tasks in a leisurely manner across the whole day.

The pace changes when the children return home, for while they are eating a snack, Keiko reads through their homework assignments and listens to their account of the day. They run out to play while Keiko prepares their home study desks and puts her daughter's after-school lesson notebooks in her schoolbag. She joins them outside with the bag and sends her daughter to *juku* while warning her son to begin his homework soon. She prepares dinner while her son starts his homework and then watches television. The two eat together followed by the daughter and *much* later, Ichiro, who returns after 9:00. The time between early dinner and the children's bedtime is spent in helping them with homework, using parents' guides and what Keiko can remember of her own schooling in math and social studies.

All family spending and planning, except for major expenditures, is decided by Keiko, and all concerns related to school and other activities of the children are hers. Her conversations with Ichiro usually focus on the children.

This pattern changes little as long as there are children at home, but as they approach high school and college age, the emphasis on study increases, and Keiko spends more time talking with teachers, reading materials designed to help her boost her children's capacity to do well in the examinations, and she may even attend a mothers' class to help them to be more effective coaches. She will stay up late with studying high-schoolers, to feed and encourage them and will later accompany them to the examination site.

Community and school expectations of mothering are consonant with Keiko's own perception of her role and she is very aware of both the constraints of her responsibility and the social value she will get from producing successful children. Her availability to the pressures of community and the educational system is rooted not only in the fact that she has no other options for self-enhancement or occupational identity, but perhaps more significantly in the fact that she receives such definite and positive reinforcement from the pervasive cultural norms prescribing the role of what was traditionally called a 'good wife and wise mother'.

What are the methods she uses as a wise mother (and as its modern version, an 'education coach')? The pedagogy she employs is both deeply sensitive to the child's own abilities and predilections and is also focused on goals outside the bounds of the mother-child relationship, towards which she exhorts the child to commit his/her effort.

The basic premises of Japanese maternal teaching strategies are:

1   That it is never too early to begin (traditionally, *taikyo* (womb-learning) was stressed as an important pre-birth enhancer of post-partum development).

2   That children are born with no particular innate abilities (or for that matter, disabilities) but all have a chance at developing them through environmental influences and the engagement of effort on their and their mother's part.

3   That it is impossible to impose direction, persuasion, incentive and discipline upon a child. Instead, the child's motivations and wishes must be first completely understood by the mother, and then he or she must be led to understand (and assimilate) the mother's objectives.

4   That what are translated into English as 'dependency' and 'indulgence' are proper and important attributes of the relationship between mother and child and through the 'indulgent' relationship a sense of empathy, responsibility and self-discipline are achieved in the child.

These premises will be examined in more detail, since they not only form the basis of maternal child-rearing 'folklore' but also provide an explicit background for early formal schooling.

The combination of 'indulgence' and early cognitive training in child-rearing seems as incongruous to a Westerner as the combination of lifetime job security with high productivity and self-improvement in the labor force. These pairs are in fact both internally compatible and strongly related to each other.

The enormous importance given to the mother as developer of her child's potential makes her role a crucial one. Children are seen to be born with no genetic or god-given propensities or special abilities, but their training can begin before birth. Beginning with injunctions to wrap her stomach and wear socks (to protect the baby from pre-natal physical harm), and continuing with traditional ideas concerning pre-natal 'cognitive training' and emotional development, pregnancy itself is considered a period in which the mother can influence her child's growth. The idea of pre-natal influence is not exclusive to Japan, but the vigor with which contemporary

Japanese women (pressured by the media and mothers-in-law) perpetuate the idea is notable.

Once a woman becomes a mother, her attention is to be focused on her children while her natal family, her home and her husband (let alone her friends, career, education or other interests she may have had) are lesser priorities. In periodic polls conducted by the Prime Minister's office, most Japanese women consider childcare to be the most important function of their lives. Moreover, urban women like Keiko above (over 80 per cent of the female population) living in nuclear households with less than full-time house-keeping tasks tend to focus on their children in lieu of other available people or activities and this is reinforced by the value they receive for being 'successful' mothers.

The mother's exclusive responsibility for raising her child in the context of an intimate and indulgent relationship has meant that there has not evolved, as in the West, the practice of babysitting by non-kin, and the use of pre-school daycare is limited to mothers who must work. Mothers of pre-school children rarely work and there is no institution of teenage babysitting. If a mother must occasionally be away from her child, she will travel relatively long distances to leave the child with her own mother or another close relative (Iwasa, 1983).

The mother's relationship with her children is framed by an intense reciprocal dependency: the mother needs to be sure of her child's affection and 'support', and so encourages the child to indulge *her* by exhibiting dependent behavior. This 'positively-valued dependency' or *amae* has been discussed in depth by Takeo Doi (1973) but has also a significant positive function in maternal pedagogy.

A closer look at the terms used to describe the culturally-valued 'dependent' relationship between mother and child will yield not only a fuller ethnographic description but will point out the differences between Western methods and perspectives on child-rearing and those salient in Japan – both aimed at least in part at similar outcomes in terms of children's cognitive development.

The first group of terms, those related to goals for children's growth, add up to a description of an *ii ko* (a good child). Usually included in the list of wished-for characteristics are words such as *otonashii* (mild, gentle), *sunao* (compliant, obedient, cooperative) *akarui*, (bright), *genki* (active, spirited, energetic) and *hakihaki* (brisk, prompt, clear). Such words describe valued qualities which may be produced in a child through appropriate socialization.

The second group of terms describe means towards achieving the valued qualities and both imply a pedagogical theory and describe the active 'teaching' relationship through which the theory is implemented. These words, such as *gambaru* (persist, endure), *amaeru/amayakasu* (depend, indulge) and *wakaraseru* (get the child to understand), to list only a few, involve strategies in nurturant and didactic relationships with children which overlap Western categories of affective, cognitive, and conative development. A look at these terms immediately suggests that there may be very different conceptions regarding the proper training of children which involve strategies which we have so loosely translated as 'indulgence' and 'patience', towards ends we have inaccurately called 'obedience' and 'submission'.

First, let us look at the word *sunao* which has frequently been translated as 'obedient'. It would be more appropriate to approach its usage through a cluster of meanings which mothers and teachers have given, such as 'open-minded', 'non-resistant', 'trustful', or as Kumagai (1981) says 'authentic in intent and cooperative in spirit' (p. 261). Murase (1974) says that '*Sunao* is almost impossible to translate into English. It contains such implications as naturalness, naivete, straightforwardness, simplicity, frankness, open-mindedness, mildness or gentleness and compliance . . . ' (1974: p. 440). One Japanese mother noted the range of meanings for *sunao* available to her by saying 'it means obedient if I see my child as bad; it means autonomous if he is good'. She said most mothers see their children as naturally good, needing only proper treatment to grow up 'straight'. Kumagai (1981) also points out that the English translation 'obedience' implies subordination and lack of self-determination, and says that *sunao* 'assumes cooperation to be an act of affirmation of the self' (p. 261). In this statement, by the way, Kumagai has already converted obedience/compliance to the more 'Japanese' meaning of cooperation, closer to *sunao*. A child who is *sunao* hasn't yielded his personal autonomy for the sake of cooperation: cooperation doesn't imply giving up the self, as it may in the West, but in fact implies that working with others is the appropriate setting for expressing and enhancing the self. How one develops a *sunao* child involves the technique of *wakaraseru* ('getting the child to understand').

121

As Ezra Vogel (1963) and Betty Lanham (1966) have described the process of *wakaraseru* or engaging the child in the mother's goals for him, the chief principle seems to be *never to go against the child*. Vogel points out that 'there is no distinction in the Japanese language between 'let a child do something' and 'make a child do something') (p. 245). Where an American might see this manipulation of the child through 'indulgence' as preventing him from having a strong will of his own, the Japanese mother sees long-term benefits of self-motivated cooperation and real commitment from her strategy of keeping the child happy and engaged.

A Western observer sees a paradox of contradiction between the use of *amayakasu* (translated as 'to indulge') as a technique of socialization and the goal of producing a child committed to and positively engaged in disciplined effort. As Lois Taniuchi (1982) has pointed out, there may be no contradiction between the device of 'indulgence' and the goal of 'effort' in Japanese childrearing. She describes the process through which intimacy and supportive attention to a child is used by the mother to teach the child the standards of the society which exists beyond the protection of their relationship, and the need to work hard to achieve and be valued in that society. 'Love-oriented' techniques, rather than 'power-assertive' methods in disciplining children are also cited in Conroy, Hess, Azuma and Kashiwagi (1980).

Along with the goals of creating a 'mild' or 'cooperative' child is the wish to encourage lively and 'engaged' commitment. *Hakihaki* describes an interesting cluster of desired qualities: brisk, active, quick and clear. It also implies that the child can speak forthrightly (and is usually used to describe boys, or with a slightly negative tinge, girls). There are other terms related to this one – *tekipaki* (brisk and positive), and *kichinto* (accurate and punctilious) among others. These words describe a child (or adult) confident and engaged in an endeavour. The style in which one does one's work indicates affective commitment and is considered almost as important as the product of the performance. A crisp, upbeat, cheerful demeanor is highly valued. Hakihaki, simply translated as brisk or active, seems to Western ears very superficial because it does not carry the Japanese sense either of the engagement of the child nor of the deeper significance given the 'style' of a performance. How this affective engagement as well as the incentive to achieve and conform to external expectations is encouraged in the context of an 'indulgent' relationship will be of great interest to those who are considering the problems and paradoxes of Western education which seems often to demand autonomy, independence and self-discipline within the context of a basically authoritarian framework. There are clearly many meanings and uses for dependency and discipline in the context of socialization and learning.

The caricature of the mother's over-investment portrays a woman who has totally identified with her child's success or failure. The media emphasize the negative aspects of this involvement with accounts of *kyoiku mama* ('education mothers') who suffer nervous breakdowns and a recent story of a murder by a mother of the next-door child for making too much noise while her child was studying. But the media also feed the mother's investment by exhorting her to prepare a good work environment for the studying child, to subscribe to special exam-preparation magazines, to hire tutors and to prepare a nutritious and exam-tension-appropriate diet. High-schoolers and middle-schoolers from outlying areas taking entrance exams in Tokyo come, often with their mothers, to stay in special rooms put aside by hotels – provided with special food, study rooms, counsellors, and tension-release rooms, all meant to supply home-care away from home. The home-study desk bought by most parents for their smaller children symbolizes the hovering care and intensity of the mother's involvement: all models have a high front and half-sides, cutting out distractions and enclosing the workspace in womb-like protection. There is a built-in study light, shelves, a clock, electric pencil sharpener and built-in calculator. The most popular recent model included a push button connecting to a buzzer in the kitchen to summon mother for help or for a snack. To summarize the role of the mother: the availability of the mother as a coach and comrade to her child, rather than a task-master, is based in a non-authoritarian relationship which motivates the child to high levels of effort and achievement. The child has learned to empathize with her feelings and experience them as his or her own. Japanese consider academic achievement to be the product of an interdependent network of cooperative effort between people, as well as of long-term planning.

Teachers in elementary schools, to varying degrees, employ techniques similar to that of the mother, especially in the first years. There is in the schools as well a recognition that attention to the child's affective relationship to his work, peers and teachers is necessary for learning, and that patient, observant 'getting the child to understand' will pay off not just in 'compliance' but in the child's cognitive development.

A look at a Japanese classroom will yield some concrete examples. While many Westerners believe that Japanese educational successes are due to an emphasis on rote learning and it is assumed that the classroom is rigidly disciplined, this is far from the reality. An American teacher walking into a fourth grade science class in Japan would be horrified: children all talking at once, leaping and calling for the teacher's attention – the American's response is to wonder 'who's in control of this room?' But the lively chatter, and all the noise and movement is focused on the work itself – children are shouting out answers, suggesting other methods, exclaiming in excitement over results – not gossiping, teasing or planning games for recess. The teacher is not concerned over the noise, as long as it is the result of this engagement, and in fact may measure his or her success by such manifestations. It has been estimated that American teachers spend about 60 per cent of class time in organizing, controlling and disciplining the class while Japanese teachers spend only 20 per cent in control-related tasks (Bloom, cited in Cummings, 1980, p. 111).

A description of a fifth grade math class will reveal some elements of this pedagogy. The class was presented with a general statement about cubing. Before any concrete facts, formulae or even drawings were displayed, the teacher asked the class to take out their math diaries and spend a few minutes writing down their feelings and anticipations over this new concept. (It is hard to imagine an American math teacher beginning a lesson with an exhortation to examine one's emotional predispositions about cubing.)

After that, the teacher asked for conjectures from the children about the surface and volume of a cube and asked for some ideas about formulae for calculation. The teacher asked the class to cluster into its component *han* or workgroups of four or five children each, and gave out a wide variety of materials for measurement and construction. One group left the room with large pieces of cardboard, to construct a model of a cubic meter. The groups internally worked on solutions to problems set by the teacher and competed with each other to finish first. After a while, the cubic meter group returned, groaning under the bulk of their model, and everyone gasped over its size – there are many comments and guesses as to how many children could fit inside. The teacher now set the whole class a very challenging problem, well over their heads, and gave them the rest of the class time to work on it. The class ended without a solution but the teacher has made no particular effort to get or give an answer, although she exhorted them to be energetic. (It might be several days before the class gets the answer – there is no deadline – but the excitement doesn't flag.)

It is clear that Japanese teachers recognize the role of affect in learning and stress the emotional as well as the intellectual aspects of engagement. Japanese pedagogy (and maternal socialization) is based on the idea that effort is the most important factor in achievement and so the job of the teacher is to get the child to commit him or herself to a positive and energetic engagement in hard work. This emphasis is most explicit in elementary school but persists as a very strong subcurrent later and as a prerequisite for the self-discipline and effort children employ in high school.

By the end of junior high school many parents and children in urban areas especially are conscious of the building pressure to anticipate the college entrance examinations by gaining entrance (through exams) to prestigious high schools. This may look like competition of the fiercest sort to Westerners. It is, however, necessary to note the differences in the context and meaning of competition in Japan and the West. Competition for the scarce places in the most valued schools does, of course, exist but competition between individuals is not valued in itself as a pedagogical tool or adjunct to personal development. Competition in Japan is compartmentalized, restricted to a single moment in the life course, and buffered by an emphasis on harmony and homogeneity, by at least a partial separation of the individual's most salient social identity from the success or failure of the enterprise of exam-taking, by the support of the mother who joins the fight on the side of the student 'against' the exam (Vogel, 1963), and by the acceptance of a range of options for a satisfying life.

We have seen how competition is negotiated by means of the *han* in the elementary school classroom. The educational system as a whole has similarly bifurcated to accommodate both the ideology of harmony and the socio-cultural interest in hierarchy and ranking. The introduction of graded competitive Western modes of education into a society where a strong value is placed on minimizing differences between people often has produced personal anxiety and interpersonal conflict, as in Africa and other parts of the Third World. In Japan, the importance of the modern educational system as a selector of talent for the benefit of society and the need to preserve harmony and homogeneity has produced a bifurcation in the educational system but one which seems composed of complementary rather than conflicting elements.

Conclusion

Japan's modern development has fascinated observers (and competitors) because of the apparently successful combination of traditional (what we in this book have called agrarian) practices and values and perspectives with modern goals of bureaucratic efficiency and productivity. Japanese educational practices and values confound and challenge Western conceptions and models in two ways: first, because they achieve what we have aspired to by different means, and second, because their means incorporate what we have called 'culture', left out or regarded as an obstacle by Western educational planners in considering educational development. What that 'culture' consists in and how the anticipations embedded in Western development planning are not met in the case of Japan will be outlined below.

It is appropriate here to return to the work of Albert Hirschman cited first in Chapter 1 of this book. Elsewhere (1971) Hirschman refers to the significance of 'obstacles' which turn into assets in economic development. Factors which social and economic theorists consider antithetical to growth and the improvement of the human condition may instead, given broad enough conceptions of the 'good' toward which societies are said to strive, and the means by which it might be achieved, actually be positive factors, even prerequisites for development, in certain cultural settings. Looking at such 'obstacles' in the case of Japan combines our discussion of diverse paths and the importance of culture in educational development.

Japan's modernization illustrates very well how what Western theorists might consider insurmountable problems might either be themselves incentives to development or exist in a climate conducive to development in spite of the obstacle. Japan's large population and limited land with few natural resources might have predicted a low development level, and high dependency on imported resources leading to impoverishment and lack of power in the world political order. Instead, as has been seen since the turn of the century, this scarcity has provided a powerful incentive to manage well what exists, to control overseas sources of necessities instead of being controlled by them, and to bring to a pan-societal level the domestic virtues of thrift and hard work. Both industrial and agricultural development have exceeded greatly the levels which might have been predicted from measurable resources alone.

Similarly, Western predictions on the basis of our human development experiences and the theories they have generated do not describe the outcomes of Japanese educational development and the psycho-social environment of modernization. What observers have called the persistence of 'groupism', 'familism' and the 'situational ethic' in Japan are seen as antagonistic to the individual autonomy 'required' for an industrial society. Social structural concerns such as the value placed on hierarchy and seniority in Japan over horizontal equality of opportunity as well as the supports and buffers provided for the individual by the group in exchange for commitment and loyalty to the group's goals and priorities are seen as diminishing incentive and opportunities for individual achievement and options on which, from a Western point of view, life chances depend. In education, too, Japanese avoidance of overt competition and concern with interpersonal harmony are seen as antithetical to individual achievement in school.

As we have shown, however, the implied Western correlations between individual autonomy and competition and personal achievement and life satisfactions do not hold for the Japanese case; nor do theories of successful development based on abundant resources and a favorable population/land ratio. The latter assumptions based on Western social science thinking have been for some time understood not to hold true for Japan and specialists *have* considered alternative models, or described the Japanese case as 'unique'. In the case of educational development, this realization is just beginning and its implications go beyond education *per se* to broader questions of cultural conditions and definitions of the psychology of learning and personal and societal development.

6

SCHOOLING IN CHINA: MOBILIZING FOR VIRTUE

PROLOGUE

The People's Republic of China represents one of history's great experiments in planned social change, re-structuring education, the family and the possibilities for individual development. As the largest attempt by far to build an uncompromisingly collectivist society, it requires close examination by the student of educational development. In the past as at present, China has served as a prototype for an entire class of societies, while at the same time constituting the greatest exception. In the nineteenth century, China was the classic example of agrarian social structure, with its patriarchal extended family, corporate descent groups, ancestor cults, ideology of filial piety, oppressive landlords and poor peasants and a remote dynastic monarchy. Though many of these characteristics were widespread in Asia and Africa and among the rural inhabitants of Latin America, China's traditions also included an urban bureaucracy, a literate elite, and a linkage between schooling and personal advancement – characteristic of what came to be known as modern societies. After 1949, China joined the company of revolutionary Marxist societies, but once again proved exceptional in its ideology and organization – particularly as concerns the linkage between schooling and personal advancement. While the Soviet Union and most other socialist countries eventually adopted an occupational hierarchy based on educational qualification not very different from that of the Western capitalist countries, China experimented with more radical egalitarian arrangements, with results described in this chapter. Thus, though China can be seen as a largely agrarian society that has undergone a Marxist revolution, neither of these broad categories account for its distinctive recent history or the life chances of its population.

> The nation's educational policy must enable everyone who receives an education to develop morally, intellectually and physically and to become a worker with both socialist consciousness and culture. (Mao Xedong, 'On the Correct Handling of Contradictions Among the People, 1957)

In the massive restructuring of political, economic and social priorities which took place in the creation of a socialist state in China, there were some consistencies with the prerevolutionary past as well, and it is these, in the service of new goals, which give contemporary Chinese education its special importance as a man-ifestation of an 'alternative' to the Western model for mass educa-tion. John Fairbank has called these consistencies with the agrarian past 'residual attitudes', including the assumptions 'that brain and brawn are naturally separate, that learning is to serve society through the state, and that orthodoxy is essential to order' (Fair-bank, 1982).

In the traditional class structure, and in Confucian teachings, intellectual powers and statuses are ranked higher than manual ones, and the work of the scholar-official is seen as more worthy than that of the peasant. While these assumptions are no longer overtly approved, 'brain' and 'brawn' are still separated, but their values *reversed*. Labor is now (or at least until the most recent modernization campaign) more virtuous than knowledge. Learning remains a route to national development, and education *not* re-levant to such development is devalued. Finally, orthodoxy, a single 'right way' of doing things, needing approval and indeed genera-tion, from the central authority, governs China's social and political structures. Overriding all of these assumptions is that which states that it is the *moral* rather than the intellectual development of the person which comes first. One of the key differences between Chinese universal schooling and that of Western systems is, as in the above quotation, in the emphasis placed on morality, or, rather, in Chinese willingness to subordinate skill development to virtue. It is as if the success of the enormous social experiment were based on the maintenance of each citizen's virtue, a virtue unascribed and hard-won, and constantly subject to measurement.

The nature of this virtue and the moral system which underlies it has been remarkably consistent since 1949. First, in China the locus of virtue to be developed is in the individual rather than in the group for whose benefit he or she works. The mass of people does not have to be measured in virtue or to justify itself: it *is* the good and deserves to be served. Virtue is a testable quality and it is through acquiring and possessing virtue that the individual can live within society harmoniously. It is rare, for example, to find revolutionary exemplary tales criticizing a whole work team or commune: 'bad elements' (in the present) are always individuals or pairs, although in the past they could be whole classes of persons, such as landlords.

David Wong (1984) discusses the differences between societies based on 'virtue-centered' moralities and those based on 'rights-centered' moralities. The first type includes cultures which emphasize the following:

a good common to all members . . . (which) is partially constituted by a shared life, defined by a system of roles specifying the contribution of each member of the community to the sustenance of that life. Virtues are the qualities necessary for the role performance and for successful contribution to the common good. (p. 121)

The second type stresses the individual's entitlement to claim from others his or her rights, such as freedom, property and well-being. Wong's analysis provides models of morality congruent with Dahrendorf's analysis of societies based on 'ligatures' and 'options'. There is, of course, a range of virtue-centered moralities among agrarian societies in which life chances are based more on ligatures than on options (in ideology and reality) Wong's own description of Confucian Chinese values is only one *Chinese* model, ignoring the diversity represented by other non-Western or historical virtue-based value systems.

In the last chapter, we discussed the basis for Japanese educational development and stressed the importance of relationships in group-oriented motivation for personal achievement. Japanese 'virtues' include interpersonal sensitivity and other behaviors enhancing group solidarity, as does Confucian Chinese morality. However, the social context of Japanese virtues differs from that of China. In both societies hierarchical values and practices have persisted through major social transformations. Japanese post-war egalitarian premises however, are based in a traditional aversion to ascription and a reluctance to view people's potentials as innately fixed. Hierarchical status can be earned and everyone, ideally, can aspire to a position on the ladder, to be gained through the exertion of effort supported in relationships. There has thus been continuity from earlier agrarian models to contemporary times in this aspect of the social structure, and this is linked closely to the perpetuation of ligature-based virtue.

In the case of socialist China, however, one must look more deeply to discover such continuity. While both traditional Chinese and socialist value systems stress 'virtue', in Wong's terms, they are rather different from each other and from the Japanese case. Since 1949, 'virtue' has had many meanings in China but the symbolic place of virtue itself in the moral orientation of Chinese society has not diminished – if anything, with political exhortation as reinforcement, its significance has increased. In all of its manifestations, moreover, 'virtue' has continued to serve to unite 'brain and brawn', to integrate and mobilize efforts for personal and social development.

THE COMMUNITY OF VIRTUE

The society served by the individual before Liberation was composed of kin, clan and villages on the one hand, and, remote from the masses, the empire and its loose but far-flung ties, while today the relevant society ranges from the work group to the whole nation. Although in the past there might have been contradictions between the levels and units of allegiance, now all are said to be ranged in widening concentric circles all partaking of the same values and focused on the same goals. Therefore, caring conscientiously for children in a collective nursery is seen or at least extolled as serving the people of China. There is an interesting tension nonetheless between what is perceived as necessary or appropriate to the individual's development and what is seen as the greater good of the group: as one professor of education at Guangzhou Teachers' College said, 'Society is developed through the efforts of individuals; the extent of the development of the society depends on the abilities of the persons themselves . . . ' (Professor Y, Research Institute of Education, Guangzhou, May, 1982) and more strongly, another teacher noted, 'China needs more exhortations to be communal rather than to fragment because of its greater inherent individualism' (Dr Z, Peking, May 12, 1982).

Morality then, lies in the proper balance between the individual and the group. At different times in recent Chinese history this balance has been interpreted differently, and the center of gravity has shifted from what might be seen as virtue in service to personal development to what might be seen as virtue in service to the perpetuation of a revolutionary mass society, and back again. Virtue (or 'politics', often an equivalent term) is always 'in command'. 'Virtuocracy', a term coined by Susan Shirk to describe the political-moral structure of the Cultural Revolution, captures the inner contradiction of a rule by virtue: the qualities valued in the person are both those which emphasize that he or she is an important political unit as an individual and those which promote self-effacement and self-sacrifice. As noted above, the person is the unit of virtue which is measured and yet it is his or her 'redness' or political consciousness as a member of society which is at the core of this virtue. It is not quite true, as William Kessen (1985) wrote, that ' . . . The only approved individualism is the individualism of self-sacrifice' (p. 44). There is great potential for personal success in China, as long as it comes through virtuous actions and motivations.

The emphasis on virtue in Chinese society must be seen in the context of the ongoing dialectic which shapes it, and which antedates the advent of modern socialism. The Chinese model of the relationship of the individual to society with respect to considerations of tensions surrounding virtue may be best seen in the context of the stress on opposition between 'brain' and 'brawn', 'virtue' and 'vice'. But while the Japanese have chosen resolution, through an emphasis on *work* (and the development of a 'work ethic' which gives priority to positive models of harmony over competitive struggle), the Chinese seem to have chosen continuing tension between the polarities of virtue and vice. In this, Chinese culture seems more similar to medieval Europe, to wrestling with devils and to unending Crusades against the forces of evil, than it does to its East Asian neighbor. Socialism, with its Marxist basis in permanent revolution, could take hold in such an environment, while Japan's rapid industrialization seems to be based in a more unitary, positivistic world view. The history of the development of education in China must be seen in the context of this dramatization of basic polarities.

A correlate to the general tension between the perception of the benefit to the individual and the benefit to the State is the set of contradictions which have provided a focus for national debate on education in the PRC. These may be summarized as: equality and access versus quality and legitimacy (Colletta, 1982). Since 1949, and indeed since the Yenan discussions and experiments in revolutionary education of the 1930s, there has been agreement at all levels of Chinese society and among all policy-makers that the success of the Revolution would depend on the successful implementation of universal education. There have been, however, many different positions taken over the past thirty-five years as to the appropriate emphasis in education, both in terms of curricular content and societal and personal development, and these cluster around the issues of 'access' and 'legitimacy'.

Since the establishment of the People's Republic, education has been seen as the key to building a socialist state: through the creation of a centralized uniform system of socializing children; through the creation of a literate population and the development of better communication; through the preparation of people able to implement technological modernization; through the promotion of egalitarian socialist values across the population and through the creation of socialist virtues in children. How to provide access to primary and secondary education across the vast and highly differentiated population, as well as what sort of education is appropriate to a 'worker-peasant' society have been major issues. In a situation of limited resources in terms of qualified teachers, schools and equipment, in a time when national priorities focused on broadening the base and reducing the urban-rural distinction, as well as maintaining continuity with the agrarian values on which the Revolution was based, the problems of fulfilling the major national goals through education are many. To reach the greatest number of people, and to provide them with a relevant education, an educational system was established which rejected the Western occupational prestige hierarchy and its labor market, and substituted a concept of life chances different from those of the West,

133

even of the socialist West. Thus what Dore calls 'credentialling' was de-emphasized in favor of equality of access to schooling, and the function of schools became the creation of a morally sound, motivated population. This interpretation of the role of education, and of the population it is to serve, is continuous with what we have described as an 'agrarian' pattern, but the scale of this manifestation is vastly greater than that of previous agrarian societies. Moreover, the centralized planning associated with Chinese educational policy has produced an anomalous blend of 'peasant' goals and values and 'modern' national implementation. The role of political 'virtue' has been to organize agrarian purposes and environments of learning in a context far beyond the family and village which gave meaning to personal development in the past. How the system which has been based in this apparent contradiction has evolved is of some interest here.

REVOLUTIONARY LEARNING: THE CREATION OF A SOCIALIST EDUCATION

Two thousand years ago, in the Han Dynasty, a centralized bureaucratic government was established with all the supporting structures common to bureaucracies in the modern world: a hierarchy of positions with an accepted promotion pattern and fixed criteria for advancement; civil service examinations for admission to the ranks; a system of communication (paper and printing were invented in this period) to tie together the empire; and schools to prepare potential civil servants. The examinations became central to the governing of the nation and created status hierarchies of their own of those who prepared them, administered them, and took them.

The examinations and the administrative systems which supported them were not static and continuous from the period of the Han Dynasty. For several centuries after the fall of the Han, the system broke down, and during the T'ang and Sung dynasties they underwent changes and refinements. There was also a 'counter-industry' of scholarly and policy attacks on the exams, beginning with Wang An-Shih in the eleventh century, focused on the potential for elitism, and the basically inegalitarian nature of the 'meritocracy' (Miyazaki, 1976). Education was geared to the examinations, and led to a curriculum which '. . . rewarded literary skill, orthodox thinking and conservative morality if not bigotry, while offering little chance for technical specialization' (Fairbank, 1982, p. 13). The examinations were finally abolished, and a 'universal' primary school system begun, in 1905.

Before the twentieth century, and especially before 1949, schooling was far from a universal experience in China (Rawski, 1979). The class system, decentralized responsibility for schooling and great regional differences all contributed to a very uneven distribution of educational opportunities. Moreover, rural families were less interested in prolonged literacy and numeracy training for their children than in training them for lives as farmers and in receiving the benefits of their labor in the fields. Because learning was not expected or valued by peasants and because the responsibility for organizing schools in any case was left to the family, clan or village, most children (more accurately, most *boys*) received no more than four years of schooling, if that, and this was often subject to the needs and schedules of an agrarian calendar. In rich homes, a tutor might be hired to give children an elite classical education and merchant families ensured that children could read and write and perform competently on the abacus. While the gentry and its ambitions for its children provided a model for even lower merchant class families, there was no class-appropriate formal education for peasants and little incentive in a feudal society to prolong years of schooling for peasant children.

In spite of twentieth-century reforms in education, in 1949 the People's Republic inherited a vastly unequal school system with great differences between regions, and between urban and rural areas. The population of five hundred million was 85 per cent illiterate (Arnove, 1984), and only one school-age child in four was enrolled in primary school (Pepper, 1978). (As elsewhere, enroll-ment figures exceeded actual attendance rates, but the national rates for the latter are lacking.)

The first priorities of the reorganization of the system were: to expand facilities to reach all children; to 'secularize' the schools, removing explicit Confucian or Buddhist teachings; to put all schools under direct centralized control by the State; and to revise the curriculum, making it more practical as well as introducing modern scientific and technological material. Underlying all these changes was, of course, the importance of inculcating socialist principles, in every part of the curriculum and organization of schooling.

To encourage children of workers and peasants to attend school, the schools had to be attractive to parents, not penalize those without intellectual backgrounds and positively reward manual labor and value agrarian goals; and provide graduates with skills and incentives appropriate to their occupational opportunities. While the rate of enrollment of 'worker-peasant' students increased from about 20 per cent in 1952 to 84.7 per cent in 1966, the eve of the Cultural Revolution, there was still a preponderance of urban over rural attendance in this group (Colleta, 1982).

The efforts to bring in more worker/peasant students included the shortening of the school 'ladder', the institutionalization of a work-study program and the adjustment of rural school schedules to fit planting and harvesting demands, the use of simpler texts and the reduction of requirements for entrance to and completion of the course of study. Criteria for entrance into university stressed family class background and political behavior over academic performance (but not as stringently as these would later be emphasized during the Cultural Revolution) to give the advantage to those whose background was seen as virtuous and deprived or victimized.

There were many types of schools in the period prior to the Cultural Revolution, and while the diversity was associated with inequalities, the incentive to provide *some* form of schooling to all, keeping the needs of workers and peasants in the foreground, motivated the inclusion of a range of schools. Regular full-time schools were mostly found in the cities and part-time schools of various kinds dominated rural education. There were many kinds of these, some state-run, some organized by communes and production brigades. There were technical schools, girls' schools and many adult literacy classes. Most rural schools were arranged on a work-study basis. In both countryside and city, there were 'keypoint' schools, at both primary and middle levels, admission to which was by examination, interview and recommendations based on the student's political activism. These keypoint schools existed in every district and attracted more state funds, and the best teachers, as well as having the best facilities. They were themselves ranked by the numbers of their graduates who were admitted to universities.

The pressure on the universities began to grow, as more (especially urban) youths were educated and sought admission. In the 1950s, the problem of the unemployed graduate was anticipated and at least temporarily resolved by the 'enrollment plus job assignment' system (Pepper, 1978) in which enrollment meant that a job assignment would be made available to the graduate. Superfluous urban graduates were also sent to the countryside in 'voluntary' groups for at least temporary relocation. By 1966, however, the numbers of graduates exceeded the urban jobs available and the population of potentially disaffected youth began to grow.

Virtue in Command

From about 1962 until the Cultural Revolution, the Socialist Education Movement, a precursor to the Cultural Revolution, was developed by Mao to create a higher level of political consciousness and give incentive for better performance among Party cadres, especially in rural areas.

The Cultural Revolution (1966–76) represented, among other things, a purification and revitalization of revolutionary goals and morality. Whether it is to be seen as the conflict between 'virtuocracy' and 'meritocracy' as Susan Shirk (1982) terms it, or the ' . . . inevitable conflict between the . . . ruler's customary need for ideological loyalty and the modernizer's need for special skills' as Fairbank (1982) states (p. 13), the political, social and educational environment of the period can only be called chaotic.

In June of 1966, university classes were suspended 'for six months' (a closure which extended in some places until 1972), to allow time to revise curricula, restructure enrollment policy and procedures, and develop new guidelines for teachers. This dramatic move was part of a transformation occurring in all sectors of society, which was to bring aggressively egalitarian politics into every aspect of life. The trickles of earlier criticisms of education as elitist were now full rushing streams of critical struggles and, at the height of this period, anyone or anything connected with learning was seen as backward, or even anti-revolutionary.

Primary and secondary schools were in great confusion and many of them, too, were closed. High and junior high school students roamed the country, riding free on trains and buses, and provided an army of supporters for Mao's attacks on 'capitalist roaders'. They acted out of patriotic fervor and idealism as well as out of dissatisfaction with the severity and competition of the 'elitist' educational system. The destruction and confusion of this period was especially focused on schools and on the meaning of credentials and advantage gained through education. Thus, along with this upheaval, were some significant debates on the nature of education in a socialist state. These were focused on the perennial questions of equality versus legitimacy, 'redness' versus 'expertise'.

By 1966, there was a significant population of educated youth with less than adequate occupational opportunities, a growing disparity in educational facilities between the rural and urban areas, and an increase in elite 'ascription' amounting almost to hereditary positions among a class of higher cadres. A clear need was seen to expand opportunities at the bottom of the scale and reduce elite privilege. All changes, ideally, were to be produced through the process of 'struggle-criticism-transformation' in which basic contradictions (previously seen as tolerable and inevitable tensions which kept revolutionary sensibility alert), must be now resolved in favor of the side of virtue or redness.

Urban students and youths were sent in vast numbers to the countryside, to help raise agricultural production, not as a 'Peace Corps' effort for a limited term, but as a permanent migration, to bring technological expertise and modern ways of organizing work to rural areas, to redistribute the population of potentially disaffected young people, and to focus policy on peasants and associate virtue with manual labor. These huge displacements, amounting over the ten-year period to seventeen million people, involved dramatic changes in the expectations and life chances of young people. In Canton, alone, most of one generation, three-quarters of the secondary school population, were sent to the countryside in the winter of 1968–69 (Unger, 1982).

All schools were to provide opportunities for productive labor: from kindergarten work units assembling radio parts to middle school teams working in large machine shops, a significant part of each week was devoted to production. In the rural areas, children had always worked in productive labor, but urban children were seen as removed from work and unable to appreciate the social meaning of labor. Besides workshop activities, older students worked for several weeks on communes or in factories every year. Many schools had their own vegetable gardens as well, worked by the students. While Western educational theory might encourage such work in schools as part of basic education, helping children to improve their dexterity, master other skills, and understand relevant abstractions, Chinese interests focused on inculcating in children a sense of the importance of labor in society (Davis-Friedmann, 1980).

Primary school was reduced to five years, and the schedule and curriculum of the schools were greatly changed at this time. The full-day schools in rural areas became part-time to accommodate working children, both on a daily basis and in conformity with the cycle of agricultural activities. Older children, when acting as caretakers, were permitted to bring their pre-school younger siblings. Children with poor performance records or high levels of absenteeism were not to be penalized or held back, and the curriculum and texts were simplified. On average, about 60 per cent of course materials focused on general knowledge and practical training and about 40 per cent on politics. These changes were made to encourage families to place and keep their children in school, and to give explicit value to manual labor and morality over academic achievement.

Teachers were 're-educated' or, in extreme cases, were weeded out, but as there was a great shortage of teachers, most who were suspect politically were retained and simply relocated to remote areas. Grades were used only as guidelines and academic competition was strongly discouraged. Each class was divided into sub-units and each unit into so-called 'Red Pairs' of children. Each pair was composed of an 'advanced' and a 'slower' child who would work together. The criteria for determining the pairs were political, not academic: as in the use of model workers and other emulation campaigns, the 'advanced' child was supposed to act as a role model in virtue for the less advanced.

While there was still great inconsistency across the country, by 1977 nearly universal schooling (95 per cent) at primary levels was achieved. Education, however, could not keep pace with schooling, and literacy rates are said to have dropped as enrollment rose:

the range of experiences in schools was great and the 'open-door' policy as well as the bias against academic achievement lowered the possibility that teachers could teach and students learn in basic cognitive skill areas. Nonetheless, the goals of egalitarian access, of reducing the population of jobless middle school graduates and the exaltation of the status of the worker/peasant had been achieved.

What was missing was a structure within which to apply the discipline and virtue stressed by the political morality which was 'in command'. Since all pre-existing social and educational structure had become suspect in the near-anarchy of the Cultural Revolution, practical application or the current (and ever-shifting) concept of virtue in such institutions was problematic. At the height of the influence of the Gang of Four, a resolution of the dialectic between political purity and social realities was forced and virtue itself became both subject and object of political and social action and influence and became itself imbued with destructive contradictions.

Susan Shirk's (1982b) analysis of the problems of 'virtue in command' reveal some of the reasons for the collapse of the programs and rhetorical stances of the Cultural Revolution. Shirk says, drawing on Weber and Walzer, that societies which reward the morally virtuous, based on a charismatic mode of validation, by giving them better life chances, are inherently unstable. While it might be better in this case to say that the reward of *virtue only* produces instability, it is clear that the programs of the Cultural Revolution, by not emphasizing *both* morality and science, (called 'Walking on Two Legs') both past and present, actually weakened the legitimacy of the moral structure of the revolution. A virtuocracy, Shirk says, because of the natural vagueness and subjectivity of standards of moral worth, produces opportunism, sycophancy, patronage, alienation and mutual suspicion. Eventually, the activist zealots are mistrusted, just as those who *don't* exhibit outward signs of moral probity: one's worth is based on the judgment of peers and, in the situation of limited opportunities, all are in competition with all in a zero-sum game. At worst, competitors in this system can only make themselves look good by making others look bad.

It was not even clear what constituted 'looking good'. There were some factors without which no one could be 'virtuous', and chief among these was a 'good' class background, meaning, in an inversion of traditional conceptions, that of the poor peasant or worker. But there was confusion even over these 'ascribed' characteristics as, for example, when a youth of urban origins, having spent two years on a rural commune, received the benefits of enrollment in a university as a 'poor peasant'. Shirk notes that the qualities valued in the person in the Cultural Revolution simply continued the very uncertain, constantly changing pattern of earlier years: in 1960, it was political and academic achievement; in 1963 it was class background; in 1965 it was achievement again and the waffling continued in the Cultural Revolution. As Shirk says, the uncertainty engendered by the confusion over and emphasis on virtue made participation in public activities problematic and encouraged privatism. Ultimately, however, there was dissatisfaction with the forced retreat from the wider community, since communal identity and activities, and socialist goals, are deeply valued.

Competition and Communal Goals: The Four Modernizations and Human Talent

By the early 1970s, it was clear that the excesses of the Cultural Revolution were past, and the focus on the Gang of Four as the culprits behind radical left-wing policies producing the excesses signalled the end of the campaign. With the announcement of a new emphasis on modernization in 1976 came a shift in educational policy towards the development of human resources through schooling, towards specialized abilities and technological expertise, rather than the primary focus on the creation of moral revolutionary persons. The past eight years have seen as many diverse policy options as had the years previous, and many of the current guidelines seem to be remedial adjustments to counteract some of the effects of the Cultural Revolution, especially in education (Fei, 1981).

Western observers, Chinese officials and individuals interviewed in Hong Kong and China agree that 'a generation has been lost'. Those who were of higher secondary school and university age and who would have had access to these levels of education are said to have been sacrificed. Moreover, national economic development suffered setbacks through the loss of ten years of technological research and skill training.

In China, as in Japan, 'modernization' must be seen in historical context. For both countries, social and economic development has become a national concern in the context of perceived 'backwardness, *vis-à-vis* the Western world. In both, the need to catch up came as a sudden realization after a prolonged period of deliberate isolation from the rest of the world. Both moments of mobilization occurred at times when the level of development in advanced nations had rather precipitously 'taken off'. For Japan, Western nineteenth-century industrialization, and for China, the sophistication of Western arms, high technology, and the interconnectedness of the international economic order, provided a shock catalyzing a national need to modernize. But like Japan's, China's 'modernization' is the product of an indigenous cultural perspective on national development. Catching up was and is neither a matter of adoption and emulation, but of planning congruent with, for Japan, existing cultural models for personal and social behavior, and for China, persisting conceptions of value and moral-political priorities. The term 'modernization' in the People's Republic of China must be understood in this context.

The emphasis now on economic development, coupled with a need to recoup the losses of the recent past, has focused policy and resources again on mass education, but with an interest in quality as well as equality. A well-publicized movement of the late 1970s and early 1980s, called the Rencai (Human Talent) Movement, clarified the losses and provided a future direction for educational policy.

In the encouragement of rencai, political, innate and socially developed ability or 'talent' are considered to be equally important in the creation of high level performances by individuals. Specialization and expertise are not in themselves problematic, as they had been in the Cultural Revolution, and in fact should explicitly be developed to keep pace with the 'explosion of knowledge' (Lei and Wang, 1979). A talented person, however, must always think of *contributions* he or she can make to society, and his or her political orientation should be correct. Such a person 'must possess virtue, by which is meant morality and an idealistic world outlook, as well as will and devotion' (Mao, 1981).

Even without the emphasis on 'special talents' advocated by the Rencai group, the post-Gang of Four period has seen a return to several educational practices which have focused on individual academic achievement and, according to some, academic competitiveness in the early 1980s has surpassed that of the 1960s. The competitive school ladder and examinations were restored, making academic achievement again the primary criterion for admission to schools and universities. Keypoint schools were reinstituted in December 1977 and were provided with teaching and material resources beyond what they had received in the 1960s. Science and engineering have been given special attention and students have been allowed to specialize in these fields without interruption. Illustrating the renewed importance of the study of science, a 'We Love Science' campaign was launched throughout China in 1979, 'to make every boy and girl realize the importance of science in the nation's efforts to achieve the four modernizations, so that they will set high goals for themselves and study hard for the motherland' (Ruth Sidel, 1982, p. 79).

The return to achievement testing is hailed by some Chinese, who feel it is 'fairer' since political virtue can be faked (Shirk, 1982b). But a pure meritocracy began to look decadent by 1980 and there have recently been attempts to organize new, but more moderate, standards of virtue. Some of the virtues seem nearly Confucian: diligence, honesty, even filial support of aged parents accompany the call to 'serve the people'. But more individualistic goals are, as before, attacked as selfish or decadent. The return to these agrarian virtues involves a denial of individualism which is less political than that of the Gang of Four, and which is congruent with the agrarian emphasis on interdependence in the smaller community.

An example of the continuing campaign against self-seeking was in a newspaper story given prominence in the late spring of 1982, which associated such behavior implicitly with foreign influences. The story concerned a cadre who participated in the Revolution in the 1930s and who now encouraged one daughter to study abroad for her self-enhancement, and another daughter to become a concubine in Hong Kong. Chinese morality does not tolerate this kind of behavior and he was criticized in the press and held up to the entire country as a negative model (He, 1982).

Morality and correct political orientation are still the backbone of education, and broadening the base of literacy and basic skills in the population is still a high national priority. Balancing the elite keypoint schools are a diversity of schooling options which aim both at creating a skilled mass labor force and at relieving the pressure on the universities. 'Self-study' is one such option. This is part-time study for workers who have received permission from their work unit to take time off for independent study. Workers can get credit through credentials achieved through Ministry of Education testing and can receive job promotions by acquiring such 'degrees'. In May of 1982, there were newspaper stories lauding a seventy-four-year-old woman who, before Liberation, had been denied an education and had now put herself through such a course of study, and received a special award of encouragement. Others have taken equivalency examinations given by specific colleges and have earned diplomas from those institutions through self-study. Vocational training, television education (both formally organized and informally opted) and self-study without time off also provide post-primary learning.

The efforts of educational policy-makers since the Cultural Revolution have had first to focus on the damages done in the ten years prior to 1976, in terms of individual and national losses through the implementation of radical educational policies. Moreover, the Cultural Revolution could not achieve even its own goals of educational equality, due to the irregular schedules, resources and curriculum of the schools – if they were open at all. Children's ability to learn during this period was closely tied in many cases to their parents' ability to educate them at home, and many had no education at all. Dr Zhu, of East China Normal University, says that the academic level of children re-entering schools in 1977 was overall very poor, and that simply to organize the schools rationally children had to be sorted by their abilities in each subject rather than by age and grade level, but such organization obviously reflects a willingness to give priority to ability. This sorting lasted at least two years in most schools until remedial work had been accomplished.

Schools and Pedagogic Practices

We teach that children are not born clever or born slow. We teach them to have confidence in themselves. Differences among children are not so great (primary school teacher quoted in Stevenson, *et al.*, 1981, p. 5).

The efforts made to minimize differences between children in schools has contributed to what Dore (1976) has called a sophisticated understanding in China of 'society's need for useful fictions' – in this case the need to believe that all children are innately equal (p. 175). School policy and curricula emphasize that everyone can contribute to society and that, as in the case of rencai, *contribution* is more important than ability.

The difference between educational policy before 1976 and that of the present, lies in the interpretation of contribution: previously academic learning was explicitly subordinated to productive labor (P. Mauger *et al.*, 1974) but today intellectual contribution, through technical expertise, is equally legitimate.

The following brief descriptions of educational settings are drawn from current observations and represent a range of age groups and experiences. The 'normal' path for full-time schooling now includes five years of primary school and three of junior middle school. After this point, children are streamed, either into a two to four year terminal vocational school or into a three year senior middle school leading to university (four years) and, potentially, to graduate studies.

Moral Learning in Nursery and Primary Schools

When Chinese parents and teachers view a small child who is in their charge, they do not see a personality struggling to create meaning out of a multitude of fragmented experiences and sensations. Instead, they see a small, unformed, social organism for whom their first obligation is to cultivate appropriate social behavior. By virtue of their positions as parents or teachers it is their societal responsibility to develop a moral being acceptable to the . . . Chinese community. An individual matures only as a social being and maturation as a moral person is the primary human endeavor (Davis-Friedmann, 1980, p. 29).

Visiting East China Normal University's nursery school in May of 1982, we were struck by the following interaction. One of us approached a group of two-and-a-half-year-olds who were playing 'hospital' and, trying to start a conversation with the 'nurse', asked if she would look at a 'cut finger'. She became very stern and

145

unsmilingly said: 'Don't you know it's not your turn? These sick children are ahead of you, and *they* are patiently waiting.' This was a lesson in behavior and consciousness: we retreated in embarrassment and respect.

The nursery classroom is a very positive environment where, as Davis-Friedmann (1980) notes, positive behavior is reinforced and as far as possible negative feelings are not attended. Learning is through imitation and emulation of models, such as the recent campaign to learn from the virtuous acts of Lei Feng. In this atmosphere, a child receives a very optimistic view of human development: hard work and a cooperative spirit are all that are needed to succeed, and success itself is not the lonely goal of the individual but should be sought and shared in social units. Teachers feel that all the child needs in order to grow and learn are clear explanations for valued behavior and deliberate corrective actions: there is little interest in, and some overt denial of, the role of the unconscious (Davis-Friedmann, 1980).

Children are encouraged to help each other, and to work in groups. The earlier practice of employing 'Red Pairs' or working in twos to increase the moral virtue of the slower, has persisted but now consists in matching a child with strong intellectual skills with a slower child to bring up the academic performance of the latter (Interviews held at Ministry of Education, 1982).

The role of the teacher in nursery schools, as in later primary and secondary schools, is to act as a guide in virtue;

> If a student acts badly, the teacher does not punish him, but
> helps him to improve. The teacher tries to reason with the
> student and to help him gain consciousness of his own
> behavior. . . . The teacher acts not only as an instructor, but
> also as a model and as a 'psychologist'. His or her influence is
> conveyed not only through direct teaching but also through
> personal behavior and his or her thoughts. Thus the teacher acts
> as a model. (Interview with Professor Yuan, Department of
> Psychology, Guangzhou Teachers' College, May 4, 1982)

Teachers who focus on children's overall development and offer political instruction, acting themselves as models, are called *ban-zhuren*, or 'class monitor', meaning the teacher in charge of a class. These are not the academic instructors who teach specific subjects, but are responsible for the moral growth of their charges. A *banzhuren* is attached to a classroom, and moves up with his or her group of children through their school career.

Teaching varies widely across the country, in terms of its quality and depth. There is a wide range in schooling experiences between the better equipped urban keypoint schools and locally financed and run rural schools. Many primary school teachers in the countryside have themselves only finished junior middle school and have classes of up to eighty students to teach. The rural-urban differences of education form a focus for educational reform, since 80 per cent of the population continues to live in the countryside and the educational resource imbalance produces a 'dual structure' of life chances in China today.

Training and Work: Learning One's Job

Respect for work includes respect for experience and skill in the worker and in the descriptions of model workers in emulation campaigns, emphasis on their 'morality' in terms of selfless effort and personal involvement in their work is matched by praise for their great skill and ingenuity. Veteran workers are seen as teachers and in every work situation are expected to train new recruits. In fact, although there were many campaigns against the hierarchical structuring of the workplace and the arrogance of superiors who suppressed the talents of the young, the older worker is assumed to be an appropriate mentor to the young. The older worker, called a 'veteran' rather than a 'superior', is to be a talent scout and a trainer, and is also to provide a historical context for revolutionary morality. This last function is served by the older worker 're-living the bitterness' of the past, and although there are few in the labor force now who remember working under pre-Liberation conditions, there are many who suffered under the excesses of the Cultural Revolution, and their stories are used in the same way.

On-the-job learning is the preferred mode of training, since engagement in productive labor is more satisfactory as it combines learning both the technical aspects of the job and the social meaning of work. Spontaneous moments of instruction are encouraged at the workplace. When a machine malfunctions, a worker will assemble a group and will give a demonstration of how to fix it, or if he or she cannot, will ask for group consultation on possible solutions. When quality of the product, or the rate of production, slips, a study group will be formed to analyze the problem and to implement improvements. Learning is a positive lifelong activity, and people of all ages belong to workplace and neighborhood study groups.

Workers in many sectors are encouraged to improve their skills in formal training programs offered at the workplace or in technical training schools, such as the Maritime Academy in Guangzhou. This school provides specialized courses for sailors who are given three-month leaves to join these programs. These men will be eligible for a promotion examination at their return to work and most receive an advancement.[1] There are also students coming directly from secondary schools for four-year programs, and this track is considered more 'elite', in a reappearance of the old attribution of higher status to 'brain' over 'brawn'.

At the Shanghai Conservatory of Music, children with exceptional talent are trained in both academic subjects and music, as well as in moral and physical training. Morality here is in part defined as dedication, and the *banzhuren* monitors the child's self-discipline and incentive to work hard: logging too few hours in the practice rooms will yield black marks in the child's 'morality' record as well as obvious slippage in performance.

Competition in this environment is said to be inevitable, but children are rewarded for many kinds of achievement – from a full 'bachelor's degree' in music, to special certificates for various kinds of performance at several levels. Teachers noted that even before a child enters the Conservatory he or she has been subject to much special attention from parents and teachers, and with such background, 'individualism' is an inevitable problem, along with competition. 'Model students' at such a school are defined first by their prodigious musical abilities, second by their breadth and morality. Success stories included one who is now studying with Menuhin in London, and one who, entering at university level, showed both political soundness and musical skill and, after graduating, became head of the Shenyang Conservatory.

Social and Personal Development: A Note on the Contradiction in Education and Morality

The reintroduction of educational credentials as criteria for occupa-

148

tional selection has produced what some Chinese educators have termed a contradiction between the goals of society and those of personal development. The issue is seen to be one *created by* the system, not an inherent one, until now suppressed by egalitarian institutions and policies. In this analysis, examinations, which measure individuals by differences in acquired abilities, create competition which pits people against each other as individuals and teaches them to work individually. This competition, and the individualized sense of identity engendered by it is in opposition to the morality and identity demanded by the group or larger social context. But of course it is society itself which has created the competition, through its need for skills and expertise. The fear, at all levels of educational and occupational planning and policy, is that the internal contradiction of socialist modernization will result in the polarization between 'red' and 'expert' which occurred in the Cultural Revolution, and so on the one hand, the use of examinations is always tempered with work unit recommendations, and on the other, politics can now be less rigidly defined as a moral system advocating good citizenship and service to others rather than 'correct thinking'. The need to reconcile contradictions during the Cultural Revolution upset the balance and paralyzed economic and social development, but the recent return to balance (with a lean toward development) has not completely resolved the issue. The tension in educational policy 'between the principles of redistribution and developmental efficiency' (White, 1981) is perhaps unresolvable; it mirrors the tension, in the context of schooling, between social virtue and individual achievement.

FAMILY AND LIFE COURSE IN CHINA

Public statements of policy and ideology concerning the life chances of people, while implying an ideal uniformity of commitment and a consensus as to the greater social good, present a great variety of options for socially valued lives. In societies such as China and Japan, where there appear to be uniform models for 'the good life' and where there is a strong emphasis on consensus, there would appear also to be severe problems for those who are deviant. Together with an egalitarian premise that all lives are valuable, and that society needs a wide range of activities to function, there are problems for those who are seen to be off-track. While in China (unlike Japan), there is overt recognition of individual responsibility, individual choice is devalued. Those young people who, for example, have recently begun to turn down assignments to universities in favor of working for another year to do better in the entrance examinations so as to enter a university higher on their priority lists are seen to be improperly exercising choice for 'selfish' reasons. In both China and Japan there exists a single-track occupational ladder, although it seems that options and buffers protect the individual from failure and marginalization. The tension produced by these factors is in Japan 'resolved' through the system of *tatemae/honne*, the existence of permissable contradictions in a culturally approved contrast between 'appearance' and 'reality'. In China, the tensions produced are central to the revolutionary dialectic and form the basis for consciousness-raising struggle.

In the description of policies and environments related to education given above, we have described the tension created by the societal needs for an emphasis on a 'group' definition of potential and the seemingly contradictory need for the encouragement of personal development in order to fulfill this societal potential. In the following discussion of the life chances of Chinese people today, we will examine the realities and apparent contradictions in terms of the cultural priorities given to social bonds and ligatures in policy, in institutional settings and in the ordinary lives of individuals.

Pre-Liberation Bonds and Life Chances: Norms and Realities

The Chinese revolutionary dialectic is dependent on the deliberately maintained memory of a problematic past. In Chinese development it is also crucial to maintain the functions of certain social institutions such as the family while transforming value systems and standards of behavior, as well as loci of loyalty. The family is still perceived as an important institution but its function and meaning have been significantly changed.

The model for family in pre-Liberation China was a Confucian one, governed by priorities codified in the fifth century BC, in *The Doctrine of the Mean* (Munro, 1969). The Five Human Relationships which, properly observed, were said to order all of society included three that were specifically familial and hierarchical, the reciprocal obligations between father and son, elder brother and younger brother, and husband and wife. As a corollary, the 'Three Obediences of Women' were added: obedience to her father while she lives in her natal family, her husband in marriage and her sons in widowhood. The maintenance of a stable family through these prescriptions was not merely a private moral act but a civic duty as well.

Within the family, parental goals for children focused on health and strength, obedience and the capacity to support parents in their old age. Beyond this, the child was expected to be skilled in relationships with the wider community:

> They want a son who will not embarrass or impoverish them by his excesses, who will maintain if not increase their standing in the community, who will handle relations with outsiders skillfully but at the same time keep them at a polite distance (Wolf, 1978 p. 224).

Parents hoped to produce this exemplary child by early indulgence and warmth followed by pressures to conform (and greater distance from the father) which were imposed at the age of six (or entrance to school).

The constraints (and indulgences) were differently distributed and experienced by boys and girls. The fact that the latter most often left their natal homes at marriage and were not seen as continuing and future investments and assets for the family meant that mothers and fathers indulged their daughters, and mothers encouraged them to develop the skills and habits appropriate to becoming a daughter-in-law in a new household. Discipline for daughters was associated with their low rank on the hierarchy, and was appropriately manifested in proper humble behavior and obedience, while discipline for sons directed them to be hardworking, responsible future heads-of-household, who would continue the line by providing grandsons, supporting parents in their old age, giving them proper funerals and maintaining the family altar for the dead.

Cultural sanctions have traditionally had different effects on men and women in China. Male authority and power are sanctioned while women's is covertly achieved and only informally recognized. The best interests of the latter are served by developing informal affective ties with their children, especially with sons, which will ensure her comfort and position. Margery Wolf has noted how subtly women must work to create these linkages, and how superficially women's relationships and strategies are treated in ideological models for family. Wolf (1972) makes a distinction between the strictures and dictates of classical Confucian relationships and those relationships which characterize women's lives, informally arranged and strategized but critical to woman's identity and security:

> With a male focus we see the Chinese family as a line of descent, bulging to encompass all the members of a man's household and spreading out through his descendants. With a female focus, however, we see the Chinese family not as a continuous line stretching between the vague horizons of past and future, but as a contemporary group that comes into existence out of one woman's need and is held together insofar as she has the strength to do so, or, for that matter, the need to do so. (p. 37)

Viewed from a woman's perspective, the Chinese family looks very different from the classical patrilineal, patriarchal model: both value, and are governed by, relationships, but the distinction between relationships defined by the male hierarchy of authority and those worked out in the more *ad hoc* strategies of each woman's life must be observed in considering the role of ligatures in traditional and contemporary Chinese family life.

We have introduced the question of a gender perspective in terms of the definition of familial relationships as only one example of the diversity of meanings 'ligatures' can have, and as a caveat against simplistic treatments of 'traditional' cultures. Family was and is, a dominant force and institution in China but the life chances created by this environment, generally characterizable as 'ligatures', are in fact diverse in their nature and degree of impact on the individual.

The Range of Experience and Opportunities: Age and Gender

Relationships as classically modelled in the family and currently experienced in the People's Republic of China must be seen within a range of demographic qualifiers and in considering how people's lives are charted and explained in terms of Chinese ideas of human development, it is necessary to look at the contemporary population in contemporary terms: that is, by some of the categories established in cross-cultural or international investigations of human development – chiefly, by age and gender. We will see that some of the distinctions creating diversity in life chances in a traditional population continue to influence them today.

In China today, the most significant aspect of the category of age is *generation*. One's life chances, in terms of occupation, education, geographical location and general standard of living, depend on one's historical experiences which currently can be summed up in the question, 'What happened to you in the Cultural Revolution?', and what happened was most strikingly determined by how old you were when the Red Guards were most active. The oldest, unless they were 'privileged' or had 'bad class background' and were in powerful positions, were not the most affected, nor were 'poor peasant' families in the rural areas, except by the advent of (sometimes trouble-making, sometimes merely burdensome) youth sent down from the cities. The generation most touched is that upon which the Rencai Movement has focused, those in their thirties, and among those, those whose education was interrupted or totally foreclosed.

Gender as a determinant of one's life chances has waxed and waned in the past forty years. Before Liberation, to be born female was a distinct liability to one's family and offered very limited possibilities. With the advent of the Revolution, the statement 'women hold up half the sky' offered the potential for paying attention to women's roles and lives. Theoretically, since 1949 women have had access to all the opportunities open to men. However, in several key areas, the realities have shown great differences. In terms of educational levels, while 100 per cent of primary-school-age males are in school, 79 per cent of females attend, and 52 per cent of males attend secondary schools compared to only 35 per cent of females. In higher education, the percentage of those in the twenty to twenty-four-year-old group attending university is 1.6 per cent for males, 0.5 per cent for females (UNESCO, 1982).

In terms of occupational possibilities and earning potential, women have a clear disadvantage, chiefly due to the fact that while all 'public' jobs are open to women, men have not filled in the gaps in the domestic duties demanded of women and women must attend to children and the household as well as to their jobs. In China this provides more of a problem than simply that of time and energy expended by the '200 per cent woman', for time spent in domestic chores is seen as 'private' and thus not politically valued. In rural communes women simply cannot earn as many workpoints as can men, and in fact are not allocated as many simply because it is not expected that they will receive them. Women in the cities have somewhat better opportunities if they have access to daycare facilities or the help of retired relatives in caring for small children and if they have helpful husbands.

Zhang Suwo, an executive of the All-China Women's Federation, which coordinates national programs on women's health care, maternal activities and working conditions, says that the problems women have are the same as those borne by the country as a whole: overpopulation and uneven distribution. Overpopulation results in reduced quality of education, and a lower standard of living for all people (Zhang, 1982). While Zhang concedes that women in the countryside have not received equal opportunities and benefits, her remarks in general conform to official public statements stating that women in China do not need to create their own revolution; their liberation is tied to the liberation of all people. The development of women's potential, however, is not subject to the same kind of basic paradoxical contradiction as is inherent in the 'Red' versus 'Expert' problem, for there is no basic cultural or political problem in seeing women as workers, wives and mothers in China.

It may be that Zhang's emphasis on overpopulation and the inequalities of distribution of institutions and resources is the correct one in considering the inequalities which exist for women in China. In the recent and on-going campaign to promote the 'one-child family', cases of female infanticide have been reported and condemned in the press, as families especially in rural areas are registering a preponderance of male births. Zhang's response to the apparent preference for sons again refers to scarcity of resources: the preference is 'backward' and was relevant in a time when women had less explicit roles in production; it will be naturally eradicated when there is greater equality of opportunity and resources.

However, sons are important also as a source of support for parents in their old age, and since patrilocal marriage persists and there continues to be a lack of State social security support or pensions for the aged, sons continue to be preferred.

Policy and Life Chances: The Debate over the One-Child Family

> Birth Control reduces the quantity of children and raises the quality of education for the one child. Parents will pay greater attention to the child both from the point of view of its care and its education; therefore we regard it as a positive thing. (Zhang 1982)

Family planning is not a new idea in China. In the agrarian family, natural child spacing was practiced, and although the early revolutionary policy encouraged childbearing, child spacing by various means continued. However, since the late 1960s, there has been an ongoing campaign to encourage parents to limit childbearing, and recent policy has requested that couples have only one child, that is, not even to reproduce themselves. By 1981, the campaign had been reinforced by economic disincentives to have children, in the form of a tax on 'extra' children and denial of benefits such as larger housing units or other resources. Further, local collectives monitor women's menstrual cycles and if they do not thus prevent pregnancies, abort them early. It should be noted that the policy stresses prevention of pregnancy, and that the psychological and other pressures for abortion are only a final alternative, not the standard practice. Whatever the correct view of the situation, the seriousness of the issue of population control is undoubted.

As in India, the gender of children is still a matter of cultural preference in China and presents problems in the one-child family campaign. Traditionally, raising a daughter was seen as a liability rather than an investment which would enhance the family. Boys were valued and among all classes and occupations, the more sons the better. Peasants needed field hands, and merchants and crafts people expanded their trade and production by employing their sons. Less directly, sons could enhance a family's status and standard of living by becoming educated and providing schooling for boys was considered important at all levels of society. Women carried amulets which were inscribed with the phrase, 'Five Sons Pass the Examinations', meaning that they hoped to bear five sons, who would all pass the examinations and become officials (Miyazaki, 1976). Families bore many children in order to ensure that enough would survive, both as producers and to guarantee the continuation of the family and, very importantly, the maintenance of the old parents and proper burial and ancestor rites.[2]

The traditional cultural conception of the family as primarily an historically continuous, productive unit shifted to a focus on family as producer of children with socialization appropriate to a socialist state and as haven for the elderly or incapacitated. In no other major sense is the family to be a significant unit. In the countryside, however, ambiguities arose with the decline of large-scale communes and the increase in the use of 'sidelines' and private plots. A family with more children can fulfill its collective responsibilities for labor and enhance its income by working its own plot. Urban families do not, of course, see such advantages in having many children since space is limited, and they lack household sidelines as labor opportunities; the one-child family policy has been easier to enforce in the cities.

Recently, the policy has been a subject for debate in public and private contexts, and the most prominent issues in the debate are those which concern the development of the child (Wu and Wu, 1983). Educators, policy-makers and psychologists have all expressed doubt that the family can properly raise a single child to conform with the needs of Chinese society. All recognize that family is a very powerful influence on the child, but anticipate that where there is only one child, that child will be subject to indulgence and will be the focus of privatistic, materialist ambitions. Moreover, the child will not be able to benefit from the natural cooperation and healthy competition assumed to develop among siblings. While, as stated above, the Ministry of Education officially advocates the one-child family, the same source also noted that '. . . we have found that if single children live only in their families and do not get a collective social living experience, they do not develop properly' (Interviews conducted at Ministry of Education, Beijing, May 13, 1982). The principal of Guangzhou Middle School Number 7 said that one solution would be to encourage parents in new modes of training: to get them to act as teachers, rather than as 'parents' in the home. Parents should also enroll their children as early as possible in nursery schools to allow them a collective experience. Parents who do not will be standing in the way of their child's success. He added that it is teachers who know best how to develop children; any problems in a child's progress are seen to be generated in the home (Interview, Guangzhou, 3 May 1982).

The relationship between a child's educational experiences and his moral development is emphasized over the effect of education on his personal productivity and individual 'life chances'. While it is obvious that schooling enhances a person's economic status and opportunities, this is officially played down. In the countryside, of course, agricultural activities do not demand educational credentials nor is academic knowledge seen as crucial to productivity. Schooling may even be seen as counter-productive since, at middle-school level particularly, it takes children out of productive activities at an age when they are capable of full participation in farming (Zeng, 1982).

The issues which have been raised in the campaign to promote the one-child family highlight major issues in the consideration of child development in the People's Republic today. First, the relationship of the child in the family to his or her future development and to the goals of the wider society is a focus of attention. Although the excesses of suspicion directed at the family during the Cultural Revolution are no longer evident, the home is still seen as a potentially bad influence on the child. The role of parents ideally is to prepare a child for collective life and to motivate the child to work hard and to be a moral person. Second, the tension between the image of the child as an individual with capabilities to be developed and tested and the role of the child as a member of a wider group where participation is more important than individual identity and abilities, is seen to be exacerbated by the conditions produced in a one-child family. The need for both competition and cooperation is currently stressed in discussions of child development and the one-child family is 'an environment where neither cooperation nor competition can be experienced by the child' (Interview with Dr Xia Shuzhang, Guangzhou, 2 May 1982).

And yet, the primary responsibility for the child's development falls on the family, however suspect the latter is as a good environment for children. The fact that academic achievement once again can be measured and once again serves to sort children, to some extent, combines with the fact of smaller families to focus parental anxiety on a child's performance in school. One informant discussed the problems of her fifteen-year-old grandson as follows:

> He's in the second grade of junior middle school and has no interest in study, doesn't obey his parents and cannot pass his tests at school. His parents are worried. His younger sister is

smart and does better than he does. If he falls behind in too many classes he will repeat a year. His teachers are too busy to help him much; his parents are worried but since they both work they can't spend much time with him. They get impatient and shout at him, which is entirely the wrong way to deal with him. He simply feels no reason to work hard and there are many like him. His parents think a boy his age should be self-motivated and independent, but I don't think so. Parents have to spend time, sacrifice something, to help their children to develop well.

Options and Life Chances: A Case History

As Shirk has pointed out, during the Cultural Revolution's 'virtuocracy' it was possible, at least in theory, to 'get ahead' by simply being more moral than thou: one could do well by doing good. However, it wasn't easy to be good, and moral competition was as fierce as any meritocratic battle. Even in times of less rigid definitions of 'goodness', the satisfactions of life have been gained more through virtue than through 'expertise'. The distinction itself, however, is inappropriate from the point of view of orthodoxy: morality is not separable from personal and social attributes or behavior, just as politics (itself a moral category) permeates every relationship and environment. It is thus not cynical to speak of a person's 'moral ability', morality as *means* as well as end, as long as it is not seen as a means to *self*-aggrandizement (again, a contradiction in terms but evident in the Cultural Revolution).

By what means, if not only through what we have narrowly termed 'morality', do people improve their life chances (seen in our terms as options for better personal, social and economic conditions, the availability of better futures for one's children and emotional security) in the People's Republic of China?

The life of a woman in Shanghai will reveal some contemporary considerations affecting 'life chances' in China. The traditional roles available to her mother and grandmother, the changing policies and practices surrounding women's roles since 1949 are still only a backdrop to what is more important, her access to a 'vision' of what her life *might* be, and her use of 'ligatures' in the sense of relationships which support and motivate her movement toward that vision.

Born in 1941, Wei Yu-lan[3] was eight years old at Liberation, the second daughter of a worker in a small tool shop in Shanghai. She finished junior middle school in 1956, and began to work in a factory not far from her parental home. Her maternal grandmother and two young cousins also shared their home, since her uncle and aunt were posted to factories in different areas.

Wei has seen a striking variety of women's lives in her forty-three years, and has herself experienced both variety and confusion in what we have called 'life chances'. When she was young, her mother cared for her and her sister and two brothers while working as a laundress in the foreign legation quarter. Her mother was always last to bed, first awake in the morning, as she was at that time still the 'young daughter-in-law' and had to perform many household tasks before going to work herself. Wei observed, too, her paternal grandmother (who died in 1947) as a watchful and demanding mother-in-law, and as an indulgent and loving grandmother.

After Liberation, her maternal grandmother moved in with them, and her mother's life became a little easier. Her mother no longer served as a laundress, and instead worked in a cottage industry run by housewives, producing socks. Neither her mother nor her grandmothers could read, but in 1953, her mother started to learn in literacy classes established by the neighborhood committee. Wei remembers helping her mother learn to read, and reading short stories in the newspaper with her.

In the Great Leap Forward of 1958–60, there were many campaigns related to the expansion of women's employment opportunities, and to changing the traditional view of women as housewives and mothers. Since Wei's family lived in an urban area, these campaigns had more impact on them than on rural families, and there was scarcely any family in their neighborhood whose women did not earn wages outside the home. Urban women had access to health care, childcare and other support for their wage-earning roles not available to rural women.

Wei went to work after middle school in a large factory, along with several of her female classmates. Her wish was to learn to drive and to be a bus-driver, or perhaps to work a crane at the port, loading and unloading ships. She wanted to get married and to have children, but not for a long time: the combination of her personal occupational ambitions and the heady excitement of 'working for the revolution' inspired in her through her workplace study group were more immediate. Her mother still saw work only as a means for greater family security and for acquiring material goods. Her grandmother was proud of Wei's accomplishments but not so subtly encouraged her to think of herself as preparing for marriage.

By the early 1960s, women were very evident in public occupations, in industry and government offices at all levels. In Shanghai, there were in 1965, three hundred female factory directors and two-thirds of the city's doctors and medical workers were women (Andors, p. 102). 'Men's jobs' were open to women, at least officially. Wei's wish to drive a bus or crane did, however, transcend popular conceptions of what women could do, and even though she persuaded her work unit to recommend her for a training program, and even though she excelled in this program, she was hired by the bus company only as an office employee. At first she was simply happy to have done so well in the program, to have received praise for her hard work, and she was content to do rather menial tasks. By 1965, however, she had engaged the help of a 'veteran worker', an older man, who helped her gain the position of dispatcher and it is this position she has maintained until now.

In 1965 she was married to a man whose family lived nearby. They met through introductions her grandmother arranged. Wei was at first reluctant, but with the guarantee that her work could continue and that maternity leaves were assured, she married and over five years bore two children. Her husband had finished senior middle school and came from an 'educated family'. In 1968, during the Cultural Revolution, he was sent to a factory in the north in Shensi Province, and could visit Wei only twice a year. Wei and her children remained in Shanghai and lived with her mother. Her husband was finally transferred back to Shanghai in 1974.

Wei's life has been affected by state policy, by politics and by 'virtue', as well as by the traditional cultural conceptions of women's roles. The development of universal schooling allowed her to finish middle school, campaigns to engage women in work outside the home permitted her to be a wage earner, and to think of herself as developing an 'occupational career'. Her 'virtue' gave her the chance, through the recommendation of her work unit, to develop her career and her husband's 'lack of virtue' (through his suspect background) caused their separation for several years.

What may be most interesting, however, is how what we have called 'ligatures' may have affected her path. As in the past, kin and colleagues are valued as resources and support. She actively sought the help of her work unit mates and the veteran worker (called in Chinese 'uncle'), to give her the chance she wanted. Her relationships with family and workmates are still the most important source of satisfactions. These are the 'new' ligatures: the traditional ones have been replaced by non-kin social linkages which serve some of the functions of support and motivation performed by family in the past. The satisfactions gained through these linkages are not 'recreational' or 'sideline' to the goals of life but are themselves the ends toward which people engage their efforts and by which they measure their successes. Although Wei has had what Westerners might consider 'personal' goals, the fulfillment of which was aided by kin and workmates, her life course should really be seen in the context of a wider circle than just that of an individual. As we have said earlier, in many non-Western societies the significant unit of 'chance' or 'potential' may be larger than the individual, and even to describe an individual's life as we have just done distorts the perspective and creates perhaps a false impression of individual life-charting in which we might assume that work and relationships are valued as they contribute to the life of the person being described. The embeddedness of the person in her ligatures makes such a description a non-indigenous exercise.

There is a larger contemporary question also to be asked about incentives and satisfactions in China today. In industrial societies ligatures of course remain, but, as we have suggested, they are either 'recreational' or residual, or are seen as *means* – as 'contacts', 'sponsors', or 'mentors' – to an individual's career or other goals and may not be reliable. Thus, as in Western academic disciplines, where social and behavioral studies are seen as 'soft' while the other sciences and technologies are 'hard', relationships are considered the 'soft' part of work and life, no matter how valuable individuals know they are.

We have noted that in agrarian societies, ligatures provide the contexts in which the *ends* of life are experienced. While we may see China today as vastly transformed from its pre-Liberation social structure and economy, we also see a society based on relationships, which are still considered to be the basis of life and work. The important question is, are these social linkages experienced as fundamentally rewarding for the individual? The nation depends on familial relationships to supply people's needs, even after the society becomes fully socialist, but is ambivalent about the effect of their influence on people. In several cases, as we have noted, families are seen as pernicious in their influence, especially as a source of selfish materialism. Do other structures, such as work teams and political study groups, provide meaningful benefits which resemble those of older ligatures? We cannot yet know how deeply assimilated and how thoroughly rewarding are the new socialist bonds; nor whether they will survive the tests of increasing material wealth with modernization and increasing 'individualism' in the one-child family.

The widening options for the educational and occupational development of women were achieved in China not as part of 'women's liberation' but as part of a society-wide revolution. To treat women as an especially oppressed group in China has been prolematic and approaches which aim at increasing women's personal 'freedoms' are seen as too individualistic. In the first case, women are not defined as a politically oppressed group, but rather tied by biological factors to certain oppressive traditional customs and roles. Biology is not 'political' and women like everyone else have to prove that their primary commitment is to the socialist society to which they belong.

There are in fact contradictions between women's 'equality' and the greater good of the society. The State has not had the resources for establishing sufficient institutions and facilities related to social welfare, such as nursing for convalescents and care for the aged. It has relied on the family (in fact, on its women) to continue its traditional functions as caretaker and support for infirm or aged relatives. Moreover, daycare facilities are still not adequate to the needs of families and especially in the countryside this has meant reliance on the family to take care of its own children. While 'family' has been accused of encouraging political backwardness, selfishness and materialism, it has also been seen as a necessary support and resource in a situation of scarcity and massive mobilization. For 'family' it is well to read 'women'; the contradictions in State policy regarding the role of family have the greatest effect on women's life chances.

SOCIAL MOBILIZATION AND ITS COSTS: CULTURAL MEASURES AND MEANING IN THE PEOPLE'S REPUBLIC OF CHINA

No models have existed in the world which Chinese leaders see as appropriate to the construction of their society. The mobilization of a mass society, in all its permutations since 1949, has obeyed the laws of its own growth alone, and one of these has been the deliberate incorporation or justification of 'contradictions'. We have described a few of these as they relate to education and the life chances of children and adults.

These contradictions, as we have shown, are not so much problems begging for solutions, or even impediments to the full realization of an achieved socialist society, but are in themselves important, motivating cultural forces. There are two kinds of contradictions: 'antagonistic' ones, leading to revolution, and 'non-antagonistic' ones, allowing reappraisal and return (Kraus, 1979). The latter are being emphasized and both the 'mass line' and the 'contradictions' form the 'culture' which we have called the 'mover' of development.

This is not to say that there are no problems, nor to say that no one suffers or loses. There are those who are caught by a contradiction, sacrificed to it, made into negative examples for the greater good of society, or who in other ways have been marginalized in the massive mobilization.

In order to look at such costs and losses, we will first recapitulate the basic principles of education and human development as they are discussed in China today. First, all children are equal, and equally educable: there are no innate differences, and the social environment provides the primary distinctions between people. These distinctions tend to be seen as based on moral differences. There are ancient and modern bases for this emphasis on equality, and for the distinctions based on virtue rather than on birth (Munro, 1969). Second, children should be educated in three equally important areas: to develop in morality, knowledge and physical strength and health. Third, the consciousness of, sensitivity to, and empathy with labor forms the base for one's own work and for one's commitment to the masses. Self-discipline is the personal quality needed and peer observation and teacher- or other model-emulation the pedagogic tools for learning. Since environment is the most important factor in the development of the person, and education is the most significant of environments, societal mobilization has, even in the absence of links to occupational ladders, focused on schools and the training of children.

The 'contradictions' which have emerged from this mobilization, particularly in the context of an explicit focus on modernization, are many. These include the fact that education is valued but that educational credentials are suspect, and that occupations are hierarchically ranged because of a need for specialization but that expertise is only awkwardly accommodated and legitimized. Knowledge is a scarce resource and thus promotes competition and its own value scale; the morality which is also valued is rewarded on another scale which seems to be in conflict with that of knowledge. The criteria on which people are judged and rewarded are in flux and subject to change. This appears to be necessary to the contradiction on which social development is based, and cannot disappear. The attempt to resolve this contradiction during the Cultural Revolution failed essentially because it cannot be resolved and in fact must remain unresolved.

For the individual, the uncertainty as to what traits and abilities (virtue or expertise; productivity (for whom?) or good class background) are valued creates great tension. We have seen that academic achievement in school is recognized but cannot contribute to a career; that family status is sometimes considered; that one's own political activities and general social consciousness are significant measures; that the recommendations of peers are important but that 'too much virtue' (activist or leftist) may make them shy away; and that becoming a high level official or powerful cadre may in fact make it difficult for one's own children to succeed later.

Non-official buffers, not recognized in policy or ideology, do exist to resolve informally the problems of confusion and potential disaffection. One such is the ability to transform a person who is intellectually a suitable candidate for higher education or responsible position but politically or morally less qualified, into a proper object for university training or occupational advancement by sending him or her to the countryside for moral 'laundering': after three years in the fields, the urban youth-turned-peasant is now able to enter the urban school or job with a new identity. This transformation, like other 'backdoor' dealings in all parts of official life, contributes to the cynicism many Chinese have towards social and economic structures and practices (Liang and Shapiro, 1983).

Who has 'lost' in the many balancing acts between palpable productivity and intangible morality? It depends, clearly, on the historical moment being considered. There are two major categories of persons who are seen to have suffered loss: the rural woman and the person who, in 1966, had intellectual promise but who was denied training and work appropriate to his or her potential – and who, in fact, was explicitly identified and punished for that potential. The rural woman is still underpaid, overworked – still has more children (and perhaps even less help in domestic chores than before collectivization) than her urban counterpart – and still has less education. She continues to bear the burden of supporting the productivity of others. What she has, of course, are the support and intrinsic rewards of ligatures: children, kin, and community reinforce and justify her work and life. The urban person who suffered in the Cultural Revolution from being denied an education and being separated from a fulfilling occupation may have lost more, since his life chances depended on his personal development and less on his ties to others.

Recent changes and unevenness in rural and urban development have also produced differentials in personal development. Because of the recently enacted system of 'responsibility', allowing rural people to contract land for sideline profit making, rural children are often called out of school or drop out to work this land. In the cities, high unemployment rates among youth have produced a new legitimated entrepreneurial class, active as wholesalers, street merchants, and self-employed in service industries. Policy changes permitting these novelties have also opened up options, while creating (and acknowledging) some confusion in the relationship of the socialist ideal to personal ambition and gain. There are others of course, who, not suffering simply from geographical, demographic or historical marginality, could be said not to be benefiting from the mobilization we have described. The Tibetan lama who cannot study his ancient texts, the late-bloomer whose musical talents were not spotted in time for entrance into a local conservatory, the couple whose widely separated job assignments make them like the legendary Chinese lovers who died of yearning and were changed into stars whose paths meet only once a year – these, too, cannot be said to have satisfying lives. What then has been gained, and what cultural conceptions of a good life, or virtues and vices which motivate and deter people along the path to that fulfilling life have supported those gains?

R.H. Tawney in 1932 said that the Chinese peasant is 'like a man standing permanently up to the neck in water' and leads a life so precarious that even a single ripple is sufficient to drown him (p. 77). Oppressed by landlords, subject to heavy taxes and vulnerable to crop-destroying climatic conditions, poor peasants lived at the edge of survival. But, as in pre-modern India, Egypt, and Japan, or anywhere where agrarian life, though precarious indeed, was supported by a system of beliefs and relationships giving meaning to that life, the Chinese peasant's life was shaped by more than his economic vulnerability and political powerlessness. Today, although subject, some critics argue, to pressures similar to those of the past but emanating today from party leaders and national production plans, these cultural motivators and meanings – some traditional, some new – still shape life. At the most basic level, using the economic and political measures stressed by international organizations, the People's Republic of China is serving the people: while life may seem spartan, no one is starving; the responsibility for caring for children, old people and the incapacitated may rest in the family but the State is also engaged; women have at least the legal potential to escape many traditional oppressions and to be productive; children are being educated. Moreover, these facts of post-Liberation life are not all there is to claim for the Revolution, or for the conditions of life for ordinary people.

In emphasizing political, ideological and economic factors in a 'satisfactory life', observers not only leave out areas of considerable importance, such as morality, but tend to distort the meaning of the factors they emphasize as problematic. The emphasis on lack of freedom of choice, on conformity, on the lack of individual mobility in China tends to hide the fact that these may have different meanings in China, meanings that may not have as much to do with personal life satisfactions as we would imagine. As Fei Xiaotong has said,

> To a Chinese, freedom is the lack of obstacles in the pursuit of a goal. As one gradually moves towards one's goal, one gradually liberates oneself by removing obstacles, and continually clarifying the goal. To Americans, freedom is the presence of

166

choices, and the right to make contractual agreements in choosing among them. . . . In truth, these choices are only fictional ones; American 'freedom' is limited by the number of choices the society offers, and the types of contracts the society recognizes. . . . Individual mobility and career advancement are so important to Americans that the social utilization of talent is seen chiefly in terms of the selection of bright young individuals. To the Chinese, each age and ability level has a role to play; the fate of bright young individuals is only a small aspect of the problem. . . . (1981)

However they may be seen by Western observers, the meanings of life for ordinary people must be seen in Chinese perspective. While there persist in China conflicting models of human development and of the realization of potential, the agrarian basis for these models remains the same. Agrarian ligatures, here seen in collectivism and social duty, personal virtue, respect for work, the importance of experience and learning, the mutuality and reciprocity implied in all relationships, are given meaning and dignity, and are positive forces in Chinese life.

7

LIFE CHANCES IN THE THIRD WORLD: THE LIMITS OF EDUCATIONAL MOBILIZATION

During the age of educational mobilization in Europe and North America (roughly 1850 to 1980), most non-Western peoples underwent neither the massive industrialization of Japan nor the socialist transformation of China. Their social changes, though exceptionally rapid after 1945, were less centrally controlled, less pervasive, more complex in direction, and more varied in the accommodations between indigenous agrarian cultures and imported institutional forms. Much of Asia, Africa and the Pacific was under European colonial rule until well after World War II; their difficulties in achieving national unity as newly created countries proved greater than anticipated. Latin American countries, though separate national units since the first half of the nineteenth century, also faced problems of national integration in their ethnically and economically divided populations and virtually feudal patterns of rural life. The political conditions for a unified national effort to transform the country and its people from agrarian to 'modern' ways have rarely been attained. Yet the spread of Western education and the academic-occupational hierarchy has been impressive.

At the present time, it is possible to read conditions in the 'Third World' as spelling either progress or disaster. The case for progress is based on increasing literacy and income and decreasing birth and death rates since 1945, combined in some countries with the Green Revolution in food production and the growth of industry. The spread of Western education, though instigated by the manpower requirements of government and commercial bureaucracies, has led to increased agricultural production (World Bank, August

1980), smaller families (Cochrane, 1979), and greater rural receptivity to adaptive innovations (Critchfield, 1981). It is possible to imagine on this basis that the future historical development of Third World countries will approximate the recent history of the West or Japan. The case for disaster, however, is supported by the increasing gap in income and infant mortality between the industrialized nations of the 'North' and the poor countries of the 'South'; the continuing population growth in Africa, Latin America, the Indian subcontinent and the Middle East; and the effects of oil prices, foreign debt and environmental degradation on the lives of people in the poorest countries. A view based on these data sees little chance of the Third World acquiring the economic and educational advantages currently characteristic of the North. Yet both of these perspectives are based on facts.

The inadequacy of these contradictory forecasts is due less to inaccurate interpretation of the economic and demographic evidence – figures aggregated at the national level – than to a failure to look beyond it. A deeper analysis of Third World conditions for human development must begin with recognition of the diversity, not only between countries but within each country, in the socio-economic and cultural patterns that determine the life chances of its population.

THE PROBLEM OF INTERNAL DIVERSITY

In the drive for national development of late nineteenth-century Europe, agrarian countries – those lacking industry, large cities and widespread literacy – were increasingly seen as 'backward' problem cases requiring reform or revolution. Progressive political theories, re-cast in 'scientific' form as evolutionary stages of human progress, provided the intellectual framework that enabled reformers and revolutionaries alike to adorn their plans with a powerful sense of historical inevitability. Independent nations that failed to embrace progressive change would be left behind in mankind's march toward prosperity and enlightenment and become vulnerable to the dominance of the most powerful Western states. Japan, as we have seen in Chapter 5, responded rapidly to this challenge; so, in its way, did each autonomous non-Western country.

Nineteenth-century Russia had been Europe's clearest example of a backward agrarian country, a feudal social order dominated by a conservative monarchy. By 1914, however, it had become something of an anomaly, for substantial industrial development had occurred and co-existed with the old social order without resulting in a nation-wide transformation. When that transformation was initiated by revolutionary violence in 1917, the anomaly deepened – at least for Marxist and other stage theories – for in skipping from a largely pre-capitalist social order to a socialist stage, Russia had defied theoretical prediction.

Trotsky's reflections on this anomaly years later are relevant to our consideration of the contemporary Third World:

> The laws of history have nothing in common with a pedantic schematism. Unevenness, the most general law of the historic process, reveals itself most sharply and complexly in the destiny of backward countries. Under the whip of external necessity their backward culture is compelled to make leaps. From the universal law of unevenness thus derived another law which, for the lack of a better name, we may call the law of combined development – by which we mean a drawing together of the different stages of the journey, a combining of separate steps, an amalgam of archaic with more contemporary forms. Without this law . . . it is impossible to understand the history of Russia and indeed of any country of the second, third or tenth cultural class (Trotsky, 1936, p.6).

Trotsky discusses what has more recently been called the 'late development effect':

> Historic backwardness . . . compels the adoption of whatever is ready in advance of any specified date, skipping a whole series of intermediate stages. Savages throw away their bows and arrows for rifles all at once, without traveling the road which lay between those two weapons in the past. The European colonists in America did not begin history all over again from the beginning. . . . [The] backward nation . . . not infrequently debases the achievements borrowed from the outside in the process of adapting them to its own more primitive culture (1936, p.4).

Despite his ethnocentric language, Trotsky's observations capture some evident historical truths better than the stage concepts he

170

is attempting to modify. His 'laws' constitute little more than a concession to historical particularism by a Marxist who was also a leading participant in the Russian Revolution. That revolution was, he recognized, less the outcome of a predictable process than a scheme for national development forcibly imposed on a largely agrarian population.

Contemporary Third World countries are at least as uneven as pre-revolutionary Russia. Differences between the urban middle class and the rural population in income, literacy and life expectancy can be as great – within India, for example – as those between the industrial countries of the West and the agrarian countries of Africa. Economists refer to the 'dual economy' characteristic of such situations, but this only touches the surface of complex socioeconomic and cultural realities.

The Third World manifests, for example, new forms of unevenness never experienced in Europe. In Latin America, urbanization runs far ahead of industrial development. In Africa, mass education runs far ahead of urbanization. Infant mortality declined throughout the Third World before the fertility transition began – the reverse of the sequence in historical Europe (see Chapter 3). Thus it cannot be assumed that the consequences of change for parents, children and families in contemporary Asia, Africa or Latin America resemble those of other times and places. The 'late development effect' applies to life experience in general as well as education in particular.

OBSTACLES TO EDUCATIONAL MOBILIZATION

Most Third World countries inherited Western schools and the academic-occupational hierarchy from their colonial past, when only a small proportion of their populations were directly affected by them. At independence, the national leaders of these new states adopted the Western model of educational mobilization as their goal, a means of gaining economic and political advantages already visible in the industrial countries. The expansion of schooling in the Third World since 1945 has been remarkable, changing the lives and aspirations of many millions of people. Yet the goal has not been achieved, and some major obstacles stand in the way. One is the simple lack of wealth to invest in schooling on the scale and intensity needed to approximate the educational performance of the industrial countries. Many Third World countries are already spending a larger proportion of their national budget on education than any industrial country.[1]

A second obstacle is population growth, which means there are more and more children in each school-aged cohort. Educating the same proportion of each cohort with the same per-pupil expenditures requires more and more facilities and teachers – and greater cost. 'Catching up' becomes a distant dream. A third obstacle is geography. The size and transport problems of many countries makes it difficult and costly to reach much of the population with schools. Finally, there is the social and cultural heterogeneity of many Third World countries. Strong identification with component ethnic groups and regions makes it harder to build a consensus for nation-wide educational programs, and social stratification blocks the kind of collaboration between parents and the state that facilitated educational mobilization in Japan. Thus economic, demographic, geographical and socio-cultural factors as they combine at the national level operate as severe constraints on the possibilities for educational mobilization in much of the Third World.

The political boundaries of the nation-state determine how these potentially constraining factors will affect possibilities for educational investment. Since each country operates as a separate economy, its capacity for implementing compulsory school attendance and its expenditures on primary schools – two of the three elements of educational mobilization, as outlined in Chapter 5 – are constrained by its GNP, the size of its population and the logistics of transportation involved in extending and maintaining a school system. Large, heterogeneous countries like India, Nigeria and Mexico face formidable difficulties not found in smaller and more homogeneous countries like Taiwan and Cuba. Indeed, countries coterminous with islands are strongly represented among the success stories of health, education and welfare in the Third World. The colonial decisions that gave them separate nationhood proved fortunate for their citizens, who live within easy reach of government services and do not have to share resources with a far-flung population of varying economic levels and cultural identities. But compactness and homogeneity alone are no guarantee of success, as some of the Caribbean countries other than Cuba suggest.

In many Third World countries, there is a multi-tiered system of educational institutions serving a relatively small proportion of the population, while the rest attend schools with inadequate facilities for only a few years. Education has become a factor maintaining the dual economies of these countries, with increasing division into 'modern' and 'traditional' populations, involving enormous disparities in lifestyles and economic advantages. Such societies are frequently deplored as cases of failure in educational development, but the question of what life chances they provide their members deserves closer attention.

LIFE CHANCES FOR THIRD WORLD PEOPLES

Few unqualified generalizations are possible concerning life chances across the diverse cultural contexts of the Third World, but there are some conspicuous common features that must be taken into account in any cultural analysis: limited employment, child labor, limited government welfare programs, and a problematic government bureaucracy.

First, the modern occupational sector of Third World economies cannot absorb a large proportion of the able-bodied adults with appropriate skills and/or credentials who are seeking employment or who would seek employment were it available. Thus there is a good deal of unemployment, underemployment (in which people work at jobs below their skill level), marginal employment (seasonal, occasional, low-paying, low-skill jobs) and self-employment (small shops and crafts, peddlers) – in addition to those who remain on the land as small farmers and agricultural laborers. It is important to bear in mind, however, that categories like 'self-employed' and 'underemployed' are Western economic concepts that draw their meanings from an implicit comparison with the economic position of a full-time worker in a bureaucratic organization.

The meanings are likely to be fundamentally different in the Third World. The self-employed person in the West is often an independent professional like a lawyer, doctor or accountant who practices on his own. But 'self-employment' in a Third World context is usually experienced in terms of continuities with the agrarian model of domestic agricultural and craft production. The family that worked together in the village to produce its own food or items for sale in the market now works together in the city to sell

173

from a shop or on the street, to repair manufactured goods such as cars and electrical appliances, or to engage in tailoring and other surviving handicrafts. While this business is normally the responsibility of the father, the mother or an adult child, other family members will contribute their labor for varying periods of time. If they have been to school or have been trained for other (higher status) occupations, such persons may be classified as 'underemployed', since they are working at lower-level jobs, or 'unemployed', since they may be receiving no regular wage. But from their point of view, the primary meaning of what they are doing is likely to be helping the family as any virtuous person would, fulfilling a moral obligation, reciprocating to a family that makes food, lodging, emergency assistance and long-term sponsorship permanently available without calculation of expenditure or specific expectation of return. This relational meaning of labor is not captured by the economic concepts of employment, unemployment or underemployment, yet it is fundamental to an understanding of life chances in Third World contexts.

Those who are not regularly employed in the modern sector do not lose their agrarian social identities, their claims to land (if they have any) or their ties with rural communities, no matter how much they want to obtain employment in the modern sense. For them, agrarian models of the life span offer unique pathways to security and esteem, through the reciprocities of kinship and local association. More surprisingly, perhaps – at least from an economic point of view – many of those who do have permanent employment in the city, with the security and esteem offered by the modern sector, also retain their agrarian social identities, and their attachments to the ends and means of life as defined by the rural communities in which they grew up. Thus a large part of the population remains agrarian in its outlook and values, even when living in the city, and even when aware that their outlook and values do not accord with those of the modern world. This is unlikely to change soon, since rural-urban migration continues, and population growth has increased the size of the potentially employable work force beyond any conceivable capacity of the economy to absorb it in modern occupations. The agrarian cultural models of such countries, then, must be regarded not as a disappearing inheritance from the past but as continuing sources of meaning and guidance for the populations of these countries.

174

A second, related common feature of Third World societies is child labor, i.e. the participation of children in economically valuable work. In keeping with the agrarian model of parent-child relationships, children are expected to help in the family enterprise, even when attending school. Indeed, it is often the case that domestic agriculture or craft production is dependent on child labor, either for the work itself or for household chores such as infant care that free the mother to work. As cities expand, so do such self-employed families seeking to sell to those in the modern sector. In the urban context, novel situations and less social support and regulation make it more likely that children will become wage laborers outside the home and suffer obvious exploitation and abuse.

In the industrial countries, child labor is socially unacceptable as well as legally prohibited, and the prohibition is enforced. In the Third World, on the other hand, it is socially acceptable and economically important; where there are legal prohibitions, they are not enforced. The use of child labor is likely to continue among peoples of the Third World because, as long as fertility is high and children are socialized to be compliant and loyal to their parents, it is an economic resource available to families with few other resources. If the family enterprise is their survival strategy, the use of child labor is an essential tactic.

In agrarian models of life, child labor at home is a virtuous activity, one part of a long-term reciprocal exchange between parent and child that constitutes the moral order of kin relationships. This exchange is by no means limited to economic goods and services but includes many symbolically significant forms of obligatory social and ritual actions. Child labor is seen as an expression in the work domain of this broader relational concept. Reducing it to its economic component is taking the child labor out of the indigenous context in which it is experienced by a large number, probably the majority, of Third World families.

The cultural, as opposed to narrowly economic, context of child labor is perhaps best seen in well-to-do merchant families of Third World regions such as Latin America or the Indian subcontinent. It is often expected that the children will work in the family firm during childhood and often in adulthood as well, even though it would be possible to hire others to do so. While this might be instigated by the parents in order to preserve and enlarge the family's existing economic advantage, the adult son's compliance in the face of alternative opportunities is frequently a function of filial loyalty rather than economic calculation. It is incontrovertible obligation, not merely pesos and rupees, that binds children to their parents in work relationships. Child labor must be understood in terms of the moral code that legitimizes it, not only the interests it serves.

Minimal government welfare programs represent another feature common to Third World countries. Old age assistance is usually absent; other welfare benefits such as unemployment compensation or aid to poor families are absent or limited to a small fraction of the population. The national budgets of Third World countries are strained to the limit in providing education and some health services to a young and growing population; the elderly still represent a tiny fraction of their citizenry; and more able-bodied adults are classifiable as unemployed than employed. Furthermore, the record-keeping necessary to determine who and how many would be eligible to receive benefits is usually missing.

From the viewpoint of the ordinary citizen, then, it is clear that unless one enters the employed elite, retirement pensions and bureaucratically organized protection against major financial disasters are simply unavailable. One must look to one's children and other kin and patrons for help in old age and at times of emergency. This means maintaining relationships one has inherited and cultivating new ones when one can, as a means of social security. To ignore the need for potential kin support is to risk living unprotected from the expectable dangers of life. Here, once again, is a pragmatic basis for acting in accordance with the agrarian models of one's forebears.

Finally, Third World families share the problems of dealing with government bureaucracies that range from neglectful to oppressive. Except for the hope of employment, the government civil service is seen by the average citizen as representing an environmental hazard rather than a source of protection, support or opportunity. The bureaucracies of Third World countries have been criticized as excessively large, badly run, inefficient and corrupt. Specifics vary, but in each case it amounts to the following:

1   Expectable services are not provided – police do not protect against crime, mail goes undelivered, telephones do not work, etc.
2   Personal contacts, available only through kin or close

friends, are required to obtain the official permissions or other documents regulating many activities, including property claims.
3   It is therefore essential to maintain and cultivate strategic relationships with kin and friends in the bureaucracy as a basic adaptation to one's social environment.

This means that people feel – and are – unprotected and insecure unless they have these strategic relationships, grounded in networks of kin and neighbors. The crime situation is illustrative. In many Third World communities, there is much homicide and other violent crime, as well as illegal land encroachment, fraud and burglary, in rural and urban areas. Police action to prevent crime and apprehend criminals is usually erratic at best, and rarely are investigations pursued at any length if the criminal has not been caught red-handed. More frequently, however, whatever the evidence available, police can be bribed so that indictments do not occur. In many countries, the police are believed by ordinary citizens to engage in crime themselves – robbing, raping and assaulting those with whom they come into contact, particularly the poor. The lack of police reliability is particularly felt where inter-group violence or the molestation of women is common. People are fearful due to the lack of public safety. Constant vigilance may be necessary for lengthy periods, with most people staying at home when it gets dark. People come to feel they can trust no one outside the circle of immediate kin and friendliest neighbors.

In such a situation, which is widespread in some parts of Asia, Africa and Latin America, the existence of a police bureaucracy does not make it possible for people to give up dependence on local ties for actual protection and a sense of safety. On the contrary, since the police are feared themselves as violent predators, they are helping to reinforce reliance on the adaptive strategies drawn from agrarian models. Deprived of the public safety promised by their government, parents need their own children and siblings to defend their interests as a family – a condition that endows the agrarian values of fertility and filial loyalty with a practical rationale of considerable urgency (Caldwell, 1982, 1983).

Thus the majority of Third World families cannot count on the labor market or the government for economic security or physical safety. Their strategies for survival in the face of poverty and danger cannot be limited to seeking employment or filing a claim for government benefits. They have to rely upon resources for protection and personal advantage available to them as parents and members of kin groups. Hence the continuing vitality of agrarian patterns of work such as child labor and agrarian patterns of mutual support through patronage based on kin and local ties. Advantages accessible through these relationships will not be foregone so long as equivalent advantages are not accessible through other means. Even when they are, in the case of job-holders with pensions and other fringe benefits, kin connections are not abandoned but used in new strategies for the pursuit of wealth and power.

The persistence of agrarian patterns, however, is not simply a matter of economics or even the rational pursuit of self-interest in a broader sense. The uneven pattern of change in Third World countries has left many agrarian organizations relatively intact, in towns as well as villages, where they continue to serve as reference groups and sources of social identity for a large proportion of the population. Prestige, even when acquired through activity in the modern sector, is often experienced only as translated into the traditional symbolism maintained by agrarian social organizations and as regulated by their standards. Traditional symbols continue to define virtue in the life course and in interpersonal relationships. Newly applied, frequently altered, they remain the ultimate sources of meaning. To dispense with the agrarian symbols would be to do without the sense of permanence, continuity and respect that they provide.

The popular cultures of Third World countries – their public representations of persons, places and relationships, real and imaginary, in song, story and ceremony – apply symbols inherited from the past to contemporary situations and current problems. They celebrate agrarian models of the life span adjusted to the changing contexts in which Third World people find themselves, providing images of life in which both traditional and modern goals can be pursued. They foster the formation of social identities that subordinate Western means – jobs, money, consumer goods – to indigenous ends, that is, the maintenance and expansion of locally defined social and spiritual relationships.

Folk religion is a major component of popular culture. It offers the ordinary person a transcendent context in which personal problems are publicly framed and shared, and processes such as healing, in which they can be resolved. Its moral code and affective-

178

ly charged imagery are both part of and above the social life of the community. Its meanings define the deepest potentials of life experienced by Third World peoples.

DISTINCTIVE CULTURES: LOCALITY AND NATIONALITY

Third World peoples face the problems described above with adaptive resources drawn from their distinctive agrarian traditions. The results in terms of personal well-being are dependent on both 'objective' conditions, i.e. options and ligatures assessed by external criteria and 'subjective' conditions, i.e. the cultural models through which options and ligatures are experienced by the individual. Both sets of conditions vary widely from one country to another.

Table 7.1 provides some quantitative information on the objective conditions in three diversely located Third World countries – India, Mexico and Nigeria – as well as Japan and the United States. The last two present the profile typical of 'developed countries',

Table 7.1   National Statistics on Five Countries in 1980

	India	Mexico	Nigeria	Japan	USA
SOCIO-ECONOMIC:					
Percentage urban	22	67	20	78	77
GNP per capita (US$)	240	2090	1010	9890	11360
DEMOGRAPHIC:					
Crude birth rate per 1000 population	36	37	50	13	16
Crude death rate per 1000 population	14	7	17	6	9
Infant mortality rate per 1000 live births	123	56	135	7	13
EDUCATIONAL:					
Percentage of adults literate	34	81	30	99	99
Percentage enrolled in secondary school	27	37	10	91	98

Sources: World Population, 1983. Washington, DC: US Bureau of the Census.
World Development Report, 1982. Washington, DC: The World Bank.
UNESCO Statistical Yearbook, 1982. New York: The United Nations.

i.e., they are high on the socio-economic and educational factors (urbanization, Gross National Product per capita, literacy and school enrollment) and low on the demographic factors (birth, death and infant mortality rates). If there were a single historical pathway through which countries developed, approximating the profiles of Japan and the United States, then one would expect a uniform ranking of the three 'developing' countries on these seven variables. The table shows, however, that Nigeria has a GNP per capita more than four times that of India, although on all other variables it is by far the 'least developed' country. This is, of course, because of Nigeria's rich oil resources, which were largely discovered in the 1960s and developed during the period of rapidly rising oil prices. Furthermore, India has a birth rate slightly lower than that of Mexico, reflecting massive government efforts to control population, although India is far 'behind' Mexico on every other indicator of development. Thus it is not inevitable that Third World countries will simply approximate the profile of Japan and the United States. Particular historical events such as the discovery of oil or a national campaign to lower the birth rate can deflect a country and set it on a different course the outcome of which remains unknown.

The figures on Table 7.1 conceal as much as they reveal about India, Mexico and Nigeria. These are all large, populous countries marked by internal diversity. India has a population more than three times as large as that of the United States. Some of its component states are highly industrialized and some have much higher levels of income, literacy and school enrollment than the national data indicate. Were they independent nations, they would rank much higher on economic and educational development than India as a whole does. Similarly, Nigerian educational development is heavily concentrated in its southern states. The historical events that made the Punjab part of India and the southern states part of Nigeria rather than separate countries are responsible for these national averages that fail to show the maximum developments that have occurred there.

The GNP per capita figures for Nigeria and Mexico (also the locus of an oil boom in the 1970s) are misleading if interpreted as indicators of what ordinary people in those countries received in income. In both countries, wealth is highly concentrated, with massive differences by region, urbanization and education level.

180

There is much poverty in the countryside, despite the national income from oil exports (and in the case of Mexico, from decades of industrial development). No automatic process translates wealth from national economic development into greater literacy and life expectancy – let alone enhanced life chances – for the majority; that translation is dependent on the operation of social and political processes in a particular country with a particular cultural tradition.

Each country embodies a differing set of subjective as well as objective conditions for the realization of potential. The subjective conditions are their indigenous cultural models of the life span, drawn from agrarian traditions and revised within the contexts of contemporary social life. With their dramatic representations of public virtue and personal well-being, these models formulate conceptions of lives worth living, goals worth seeking, potentials worth realizing. The influence of such cultural models is manifest in the social identities of individuals, in the goals that motivate them, and in the objectives and activities around which social groups and resources are mobilized. The task of cultural, historical and psychosocial inquiry is to understand the processes of motivation and mobilization that affect decisions and commitments concerning life chances in a particular society. In the Third World, this means moving beyond the focus on obstacles to Western-style educational mobilization and its economic utilization to examine the alternative directions in which individuals and organizations are investing their energies and resources.

One value of culturally informed analysis resides in its capacity to make sense of the 'contradictions' apparent in Third World societies. There is, for example, the contrast between India's measurable status as a poor, underdeveloped country as shown on Table 7.1 (low GNP per capita and literacy, high infant mortality) and the fact that India is a major industrial producer, currently self-sufficient in food production, a source of scientists and engineers, and a nation with democratic elections – characteristics usually found in highly developed countries. Another contradiction is presented by India's educational system, which is notorious for its overexpansion at the expense of quality, yet from which creative artists, scientists and mathematicians, and technical specialists – many of them at the highest levels of competence – regularly emerge. At a different level, there is the apparently contradictory role of Hinduism, which seems to bind India together as a nation,

181

while dividing its people by religious affiliation, caste and gender. All of these tendencies have to do with the Indian style of integrating diversity – at every level from the individual personality to the nation, and in domains ranging from therapeutic practices to political drama – without imposing uniformity. This style, and the processes involved, have been explored by a wide variety of scholars – Sanskritists, anthropologists, historians, political scientists, psychoanalysts.[2]

A lesson to be learned from these investigations is that agrarian models of the life span (e.g., as presented in Hindu texts) continue to provide meaning even for Indians sophisticated in Western ways. Criticizing and reinterpreting the tradition they share with the rural majority, they do not necessarily reject it. On the contrary, urban Hindus tend to organize their family lives in accordance with Hindu models (Vatuk, 1981). Men, for example, limit their sexual activity to prevent the loss of power embodied in semen, and women stop bearing children once their resident daughters-in-law begin doing so – with important consequences for India's birth rate. Older men retire from occupational activity to pursue spiritual careers as pilgrims to Hindu shrines. Thus reproduction, work and retirement are experienced through a conceptual framework derived from Hindu traditions.

The incorporation of multiple symbol systems and social identities in an Indian society heavily influenced by Western models of education, occupation and bureaucracy for 150 years, involves complex adjustments and compromises at local as well as national levels. Identification with local groups based on language, religion, region and caste remains strong and limits the building of a national consensus for human development along the lines of Japan or China. Yet Indians mobilize themselves in other ways, at other levels and for other purposes that involve the realization of human potentials. Their situation is not validly seen as stuck between where they used to be in 1800 and where we are now; it represents an alternative pathway between its own agrarian traditions and its distinctive place in the modern world.

Mexico presents a different set of apparent contradictions that invite cultural inquiry. In contrast with India, Mexico is a 'middle-level' developing country, with much higher income and literacy and much lower death rates. Unlike India, two-thirds of the Mexican population lives in the cities, but like India, the countryside is heavily populated with poor, little-educated people for whom agrarian social identities are salient. Mexico has a centralized and authoritarian political system, but much of public life is unregulated to the point of anarchy. Lifestyles of European and North American origin are widespread, yet nationalist feeling is strong and folk religion and folk medicine are thriving. The understanding of Mexican contradictions begins with an appreciation of the historical continuities underlying apparent discontinuities. Political power, as Paz (1972) pointed out, has not changed its location from the Aztec empire to the present government. Successive colonial and independent governments have situated their regimes in the same places, capitalizing on the earlier compliance of the population to commands emanating from the center of Mexico City, where the Aztec emperor reigned. Mexico's cultural style, developed in centuries of colonial and post-colonial isolation, is one in which European institutions and images provide the public settings for symbolic action in which indigenous meanings are preserved. Compromise institutions like the pilgrimage to Guadeloupe, which is outwardly and officially Roman Catholic but continuous with pre-Columbian beliefs and practices, exemplify this style. It permits the joint participation of people with differing social identities. Despite the outward unity in politics and religion, however, active loyalties are bound to ties of kinship, patronage and economically defined interest groups, with little left over for the nation.

Nigeria also defies easy categorization. Its annual GNP per capita of more than $1,000 puts it far above most countries of sub-saharan Africa in apparent economic development, yet its very high birth and death rates show that its population has hardly begun the demographic transition. (These figures are in any event rough estimates, since Nigeria has not had a national census since 1973, and it was not 'deemed adequate for making an accurate population estimate', US Bureau of the Census, 1983, p. 132.) Despite its large-scale oil production and other industrial development, Nigeria's population is 80 per cent rural, and its cities have few adequately functioning modern services. The low rates of literacy and school enrollment shown on Table 7.1 are belied by the fact that Nigeria's southern states are the most educationally developed part of sub-saharan Africa in terms of universal schooling, attendance at secondary schools and universities and the number of people who have studied abroad. Yet even in the south, the educational and cultural sophistication of the people contrasts with the lack of public services and safety found in other contemporary states at equivalent levels of educational development. Its political contradictions are particularly symptomatic of Nigeria's situation. A civil war was fought successfully to preserve national unity, with amnesty granted to the secessionist leaders, yet ethnic divisions continue to block effective national integration. Nigeria recently became the first African country to return from military to civilian rule, yet its elections were followed by another military coup.

The cultural factor is fundamental to an understanding of Nigeria's uneven state of development. With approximately 250 groups defined by language, culture and territory, and at least five or six significant ethnic blocs, Nigeria as a nation seems an arbitrary colonial creation. The English language is needed to communicate across the many language boundaries, but the world defined by English – i.e., the federal government and the modern city – does not command the primary loyalty of Nigerians. Loyalties and social identities remain resolutely local, tied to the ethnic territories from which people came, even when they are living elsewhere. Symbols associated with these ethnic loyalties motivate individuals and mobilize groups to function as interest groups seeking political and economic advantages. The population is 80 per cent rural, and even those who are permanent urban residents return to their rural homes to participate in festivals, group decisions, and economic activities. Perhaps most significantly, wealthy businessmen and professionals who live in the city seek traditional chieftaincy titles, build retirement homes and contribute to public works in the villages or small towns from which they came. This permanent connection of the modern elite to their rural kin and home communities prevents the rural-urban division found in Mexico and much of India. It indicates, however, that local identification remains much stronger than the loyalty needed by the government to build federal integration and pursue goals of human development at the national level.

This brief review shows that these three Third World countries all face problems of integrating culturally diverse populations within a federal structure of government. Their methods of integration differ, but all involve delicate but necessary compromises with interest groups that command more loyalty than the federal government itself. Such compromises reduce the government's ability to act effectively on behalf of the population as a whole, particularly when the action would benefit groups or regions that have been historically less developed than others. In effect, the leaders of these three states have less power and legitimacy than the leaders of Meiji Japan or revolutionary China, even when – as in the case of Mexico – they appear to have more. Lacking a powerful constituency for the common good, the government becomes another interest group, which furthers cynicism about its leaders.

Third World people, in these three countries as elsewhere, are not waiting for their governments or international agencies to do something about their life chances. They are actively striving for goals meaningful to them as members of families, kin networks, ethnic and other local groups, and as participants in patron-client relationships. Identifying with such an organization and its indigenous (largely agrarian) symbols, they view their interests from its perspective. This is what motivates individuals and mobilizes them for social purposes. Formal education, employment and participation in economic markets may be involved, but within a context set by group membership and permanent relationships. Thus the personal benefits gained are not reducible to their economic value but entail the security, respect and continuity obtainable through the group that represents potential support and validates individual accomplishments.

The strength of local ties and identities, then, may be an obstacle to national educational mobilization, not because people are uninterested in some of its values, but because they have already invested their energy and other resources in collective efforts at improving the lives of their children within a sub-national group. In this context, it may be impossible to identify with programs on behalf of children outside that circle. The government may mount programs for human development, as indeed the governments of these three countries have done in recent years, but they cannot always count on the kind of support from the people, or even the bureaucracy at its lower levels, that would guarantee successful implementation. When motivation is organized toward local ends, national programs are likely to suffer.

The other side of the coin, however, is that the majority of people are gaining benefits from their identification with sub-national groups which could not be replaced if they gave up such identification to seek their fortunes in the new academic-occupational hierarchy as participants in the labor market and the national state. They know that the resources are too scarce to guarantee them employment or other advantages, and their strategy is to maximize the range of possible benefits by seeking education and employment without giving up the permanent attachments that give their lives meaning. Just as they accept antibiotics without rejecting folk healing, Third World peoples adapt by keeping the advantages they already have while taking whatever new ones they can get.

The difficulty for policy-makers is to understand that there are advantages in the indigenous organizations and attachments of Third World peoples, even as they work against national integration. In their local reference groups, people find not only communities of interest but a moral order that fosters virtue and enforces moral norms. This is simply missing at the national level. Most Third World states are, as national societies, neither virtue-centered nor rights-centered, in Wong's (1984) terminology, and their successful initiatives toward national human development will probably have to await the construction of a moral community, based on models of virtue or rights, at that level.

III: Past and Future Worlds: Prospects for Educational Development

---

The myths and realities of Western experience set limits to the social scientific imagination, and modernity becomes what we imagine ourselves to be.

Lloyd I. Rudolph and Susanne Hoeber
Rudolph, 1967, p. 7.

Every human being knows his own world better than any outsider (including the expert who makes policy).

Peter Berger, 1976, p. xii.

8

IMPROVING HUMAN CONDITIONS: POLICY DILEMMAS IN CULTURAL CONTEXT

How can a cultural perspective assist the policy-maker who seeks to improve human conditions? First, by facilitating the recognition that any 'improvement' is not only relative to the time, place and condition of a particular people but also accompanied by other changes that may detract from the benefits they will experience from planned intervention. In other words, the policy-maker guided by a cultural perspective is more likely to engage in a wide-ranging analysis of probable costs and benefits to intervention in the appropriate local contexts, rather than assuming that what constitutes improvement in one context will be so everywhere – or that its human costs can be overlooked. This chapter explores the implications of such an analysis for the most common kinds of programs involved in human resource development, namely those concerned with education, health, child labor, and the position of women.

A cultural perspective can also help the policy-maker imagine culturally sensitive methods of realizing human potential. Knowing local definitions of human potential and the subjective conditions for their realization, the policy-maker is better able to design programs adjusted to pre-existing motives that will facilitate implementation. The next chapter explores this advantage of cultural analysis, using evidence from previous chapters to illustrate the cultural contexts of implementation.

Cultural analysis complicates the planning of policy interventions, exposing dilemmas that may otherwise lay hidden but which are perilous to ignore. The doctrine of universal human rights, for example, is an established rationale for the extension to other countries of life chances developed in the West, but it is potentially contradictory to the equally established principle of self-determination for all peoples through independent nationhood. If the customs of a country deprive its people (or a category of people) of their rights, some will claim that outside intervention is needed to protect individual rights, while others will argue that national self-determination protects a country from such intervention. Do individual rights transcend the right of a nation to determine its own public morality? Can and should human rights be enforced across national boundaries? These are dilemmas that are not easily re-solved, and we do not pretend to do so. We do believe that confronting such ethical dilemmas is necessary and that cultural analysis clarifies their local meanings in a way that assists the formation of intelligent policy.

CONFRONTING DILEMMAS

History is more powerful than policy – thwarting, magnifying and diverting initiatives for change without respect for the intentions of those who planned them. Albert O. Hirschman (1971) has shown how economic development projects considered failures according to the narrow criteria of their planners nevertheless had beneficial 'side effects' on the economies of the countries they were intended to benefit. The lessons learned from these projects support his 'bias for hope', based on a broader view of human improvement in which 'side effects' can become central. Unfortunately, however, the reverse also occurs, i.e. 'successful' projects (according to narrow criteria specified in advance) have undesirable 'side effects', harm-ing their intended beneficiaries and casting doubt on the wisdom of the policies that lie behind them. Policies will and should be judged in terms of their net effects, their social and psychological costs as well as their economic gains, their long-term impact as well as their immediate feasibility.

When it comes to human development, policy analysis of the broader sort is hindered by several factors. One is the lack of scientific understanding that would permit forecasting accurately a full range of beneficial and harmful effects. We have more know-ledge than we use effectively, but its certainty and generality are easily overestimated.

Other obstacles to a balanced evaluation of policies designed to reform human development concern the biases involved in analyzing them. Many published analyses of policy proposals are written by their proponents, who are naturally reluctant to emphasize probable drawbacks. Furthermore, most of us in the West are biased in favor of the extension of 'life, liberty and the pursuit of happiness' (as the Declaration of Independence called it) or freedom of choice and human rights (as enshrined in more recent, international declarations) to all peoples. Children of the eighteenth-century Enlightenment, we believe in its civilizing mission to share the benefits of literacy, rationality, and technology, as we construe them, with all humanity. We are thus inclined to support initiatives that promise to do so, without anticipating ill effects.

As policies are put into practice, however, questions arise about their unintended as well as intended effects, and a deeper understanding is achieved through the debate between critics and advocates of programs. This has occurred concerning educational expansion: Once accepted as representing an unqualified good for all societies, it is now subject to serious criticism and debate (Simmons, 1980). Much of the controversy is focused on economic outcomes, but the broader social impact of educational expansion has also been analyzed in critical terms (Dore, 1976; Dahrendorf, 1979). These analyses raise a general issue concerning the transfer of policies promoting human development from Western to non-Western contexts: Will the outcomes be as beneficial in the latter as they are held to be in the former, and will there be costs unanticipated by the Western experience?

In this chapter we ask this question of international policies, actual and proposed, that flow naturally from Enlightenment doctrines of human rights. Issues of the costs in non-Western contexts are raised about programs designed to expand schools, save lives, abolish child labor and liberate women. We begin with school expansion because the debate mentioned above has already assembled arguments and evidence on this topic.

EXPANDING SCHOOLS

Over the last two centuries, education has emerged as the leading institutional vehicle of hope for the world's peoples: Hope for a more civilized and democratic society (as conceptualized by political theorists from the Enlightenment to the present), hope for more skilled and productive workers (in both capitalist and socialist states), hope for personal advancement (in non-Western as well as Western countries). Few political appeals have been as popular as the building of schools and universities – new foci for the aspirations of nations, regions and ethnic groups. But hopes are not necessarily fulfilled, and in the case of education, more hopes have been aroused than can be fulfilled. Thus the effects of educational expansion have not been uniformly positive and have generated serious criticisms.

At the core of these criticisms is the fact that the schools that have been spread throughout the world are not simply a new means of transmitting literacy, numeracy and other skills and virtues, but represent a new model of social organization: the academic-occupational hierarchy described in Chapter 4. In this model, schools endow individuals with the qualifications that determine their respective places in a social order increasingly dominated by bureaucratic institutions. Schools do not just teach children, they evaluate them in ways that affect the lives they will lead, the roles they will play, the advantages to which they will have access. The academic-occupational hierarchy carries with it a model of the life span that inspires new social identities and motivates individuals toward new forms of competition, work and family life. As peoples of the industrialized world have come to spend more and more time in school and in bureaucratic occupations, the limitations and losses involved in living according to this model have become increasingly evident. And while Third World peoples have been creative in devising life-styles and social identities that combine old (agrarian) and new (academic-occupational) models, they too have experienced costs as the result of policies of educational mobilization.

Such costs are unplanned and often disavowed; mobilization is publicly intended to benefit the individuals to whom schooling is extended as well as to the national society of which they are members. But the national drive to expand education imposes new standards for evaluation of self and others; creates new situations of competition, uncertainty and conflict; and gives a new shape to the life course of men and women. The educationally differentiated hierarchy of occupations, graded in earnings and social respect, tends to replace the local age-sex hierarchies of agrarian societies and impose a single uniform standard of socio-economic evaluation based on the superiority of professionals and managers over clerks and the superiority of clerks over manual workers. In European history, the rise of this occupational hierarchy was considered democratizing, as a merit system based on individual skill that replaced a feudal system based on hereditary status. In the Third World, however, it may work rather differently, as when a Nigerian horticulturist 'discovers' he is a mere peasant or when a skilled Mexican craftsman finds himself classified as an illiterate manual worker. The realization that one is at the bottom of a ladder that one did not know existed can be a rude shock, though it is mitigated in Third World societies by the continued existence of agrarian communities with alternative values and social supports.

The psychosocial costs of educational mobilization can be seen as due to three processes: 1) relative deprivation, 2) competitive pressures, and 3) the narrowing of life course values.

1 *Relative deprivation*

Any social hierarchy establishes ideal models at the top that are unattainable for the majority. Thus, wherever there had been a monarchy, a caste system, a feudal order or a landed or mercantile elite, the majority of people were accustomed to the idea that they and their children could never realize for themselves the ideal lives to which they gave respect and support. The academic-occupational prestige hierarchy was different, because it introduced grounds for hope: if your child did well enough in school he would enter the higher ranks and would gain access to an ideal life. The facts were (and are), however, that the chances of anyone from the bottom rising to the top through academic achievement are necessarily slight because the hierarchy is a pyramid with fewer places at the top, and the chances decrease over time as the supply of people educated to any particular level increases over successive birth cohorts in a society mobilizing for education. The hope has been that economic growth would expand the pyramid and make more places at or near the top, but educational expansion (in the West and Japan) and population growth (in the Third World) have generally outpaced employment opportunities. The result has been, as Dore (1976) documented, an avalanche of failed aspirations throughout the Third World which since he wrote has penetrated the industrial countries as well. Many are schooled but few are chosen for the positions to which they (based on the experience of previous cohorts) aspired. The resulting frustrations have added to the general level of discontent in many countries.

When the Western occupational prestige hierarchy comes to dominate the processes of social comparison in a community, the stage is set for deprivation at the level of personal experience: Nothing seems to matter except what position a person's father holds in the hierarchy and what his own future placement will be. This situation generates the familiar Western experience with social class, wherein linkages not bounded by class have withered away, and individuals are exposed to the sense that their social position represents not merely success or failure but merit awarded for public virtue. For the majority, whose positions are ranked low, this can mean – as many sociologists have pointed out – a sense of inferiority that is certainly undeserved and that can be psychologically damaging.

One effect of educational mobilization, then, is the creation of marginal categories. The structure is such that relatively few can attain the goals they have come to cherish, and all others are in some sense marginal to the success stories that represent the ideal educational and occupational career. Some are marginal because they started out at the bottom and remained there; some because they gained less altitude on the occupational ladder than they and their sponsors expected. Others are marginal because they never entered the competition, like housewives, or have lived beyond their years in it, like the retired. The sense of relative deprivation is keenest when everyone who goes to school is led to believe he or she has a chance to get to the top, only to find that competitive examinations eliminate the majority. This is the charge most frequently made against mass schooling (e.g., Illich, 1971), that it awards certificates of failure to the great majority of people. The intensity with which 'failure' is felt, however, depends on the alternative social identities available to the individual through ligatures, i.e. through his social links to reference groups in which position is not simply a mirror of personal achievement. Critics of capitalism may regard such alternatives in an industrial society as mere palliatives to 'cool the mark' of being a loser, but this judgment does not gainsay the psychological salience of non-occupational identities. From a different perspective, one could say that life chances are better in those industrial societies where more social linkages and alternative social identities are available than in those societies with an equally steep and competitive educational pyramid but fewer ligatures.

2 *Competitive pressures*

Another frequent criticism of education in contemporary industrial societies concerns the pressures they put on children (and their families) to intensify efforts and preparation for the competitions that will determine their future occupational careers. The Japanese 'examination hell' (Vogel, 1963) is probably the most striking example, but the phenomena of youth rebellion, adolescent identity crisis and juvenile delinquency have been widely interpreted as responses to the pressures of academic-occupational competition at its most intense point in the life span, namely during adolescence.

Perhaps the most consistent consequence of the competitive pressure, however, is the increased investment of families in the careers of their children. This can start at the onset of child-bearing, as when a Japanese mother drops out of the work force to become a full-time mother or an American couple selects a suburb in which to live for its educational advantages. Through the preschool and school years, parents invest money, time and labor in the quest for educational advantages that will assure their child a place as near the top as possible. When the child's academic performance is threatened by learning disabilities, conduct disorders or temporary failure in school, parents hire specialists and special schools to get him back on the track. This is where parents at higher income levels have a decisive advantage in countries without extensive welfare provisions, for the poor cannot afford to increase their investment sufficiently to compensate for every de-railment of each child's career, and the careers suffer accordingly. After the completion of schooling, higher-income parents in the United States continue helping their children financially, making it possible for them to move through the early phases of their careers expeditiously, and guaranteeing that the early educational advantages of the grand-children are not sacrificed to their parents' career strivings. All of this must be counted as a competition-induced family investment in the occupational careers of children. A similar case could be made concerning the contributions of non-working wives to the career development of their husbands, that is, that it reflects a family adaptation to competitive pressures in the academic-occupational sphere.

3 *The narrowing of life course values*

This category of costs to educational mobilization has not been discussed as such in the research literature but is probably the most fundamental and pervasive. The life course in industrial societies tends to be so organized by the occupational career that it can be seen – and often is seen by members of such societies – as consisting of three major phases: a) preparation for the career, b) pursuit of the career, and c) retirement from the career. The extension of mass schooling into adolescence and beyond and the infiltration of competitive pressures into the preschool years are symptoms of how considerations of career development have come to dominate the structure of lives of those who have not yet entered the labor market. For those who have entered and are pursuing careers, the primary problem is that of integrating their demanding occupational roles with their roles as spouses and parents. For those who have retired, particularly men who have given so much to their careers, the problem is doing without the work demands and the satisfaction of being productive and appreciated for it. Yet the very societies in which men find themselves at such a loss in their years of retirement are those in which life expectancy is longer than ever.

The cost factor in this structure of the life course is the lack of ligatures. Children are encouraged to focus on their own interests rather than the needs of others, and 'bread-winners' to put their careers ahead of their families. By the retirement years, the non-occupational social linkages may be so weak and/or so unsatisfying that they cannot compensate for the loss of career involvement – the dominant source of meaning in the life course. What has been lost is clearest in old age, when the agrarian elder plays a central role in family and community life, and the elder in an industrial society searches for a meaningful role to play. But the difference in building and maintaining social attachments begins in childhood and is prominent at every stage in the life course. The members of contemporary industrial societies, particularly in the West, have more of everything except relationships, and in the end these give life a meaning it cannot otherwise have.

Formal education, as it developed in the Western countries by the middle of the nineteenth century, has many advantages that facilitated its global spread and will assure its future survival. It has not, as we have seen, been an unmixed blessing, in its places of origin or in those to which it diffused, especially in the impact of its particular organizational form on social relationships. While it has almost always been assumed that the benefits from expanding education would outweigh any conceivable costs – hence its massive expansion at all levels in this century – an historical examination of the psycho-social costs in their socio-economic and cultural contexts would at least cast doubt on this assumption. It is this doubt that the policy-maker should bring to consideration of future proposals for expansion.

SAVING LIVES

In modern Christendom, saving lives has superseded saving souls as the most important sacred duty in the public domain. The use of medical technology to postpone mortality and improve health – wherever and whenever possible – is taken to be an unchallengeable moral principle in contemporary industrial societies. In terms of rights, the right to life is the paramount right, prerequisite to the others. The case for policies of public health, however, rests on rational as well as moral grounds. Healthy populations are more economically productive and militarily capable, less needy of government welfare services. Public health thus promotes national goals as well as being an end in itself.

There may be no case to be made against the extension of public health or the saving of lives whenever possible. But if policies are judged in terms of all their effects, not just those that were intended, it is conceivable that policies intended to promote public health might be judged unwise because of unintended effects that were harmful or noxious.

This is not merely a hypothetical possibility. Between 1945 and 1970, death rates dropped substantially throughout the world. The declines in infant and child mortality and maternal mortality were particularly sharp in Third World countries, where formerly they had been high. This was caused by two general factors, namely, rising incomes and public health measures. The first gave more families than ever access to improved housing and clothing, more nutritious food and modern health services. The second included preventive measures such as improved sanitation, clean water and immunization for childhood diseases, as well as more effective medical treatment involving antibiotics and other new drugs. In many countries, health services were extended to the rural areas, providing the poor with their first access to modern medicine. There is debate concerning how much each of these factors contributed to a longer life expectancy, and particularly to the improved survival of children. But there is no doubt that public health policies played a major, and in some cases critical, role.

There is also no doubt about the consequences of declining mortality in the Third World, namely, the rapid growth of populations in Asia, Africa, Latin America, the Caribbean and the Pacific between 1950 and 1980 – a growth which, even though mitigated by falling birth rates since 1965, will continue into the next century and has already resulted in widespread environmental degradation and deprivation. Retrospectively, the reduction in death rates without a concomitant effort to curtail the birth rate seems self-defeating, since it has helped destroy the resource base of rural inhabitants and created scarcities of employment, housing and other material amenities in the cities. Why was there no plan to accommodate this demographic threat without sacrificing the newfound prosperity?

No single answer can account for this world-wide phenomenon, but the general outlines are clear. Improving the health of the people was regarded by Western colonial policy-makers as a last benefit they could bestow, and by Western economic advisers as a prerequisite for future development. Furthermore, it proved popular with the people themselves and their leaders, since increased child survival rates are consistent with the fertility goals of agrarian cultures. Deliberate curtailment of child-bearing, however, being contrary to those goals, would have required a national effort of persuasion and was thus postponed. Insofar as policy-makers were unaware of the demographic consequences, they can be criticized for the single-mindedness of their devotion to saving lives without considering the possible effects on population – a mistake that no future policy-maker would want to repeat. Insofar as they were aware of the possible consequences, they tended to believe that economic growth would outpace population growth in the short run and that in the long run a drop in birth rates would automatically follow improved child survival and higher monetary income, without anti-natalist policy intervention. What they did not anticipate was how much population growth would occur before that 'automatic' drop, and how much sturdier are agrarian fertility preferences than Third World economies.

This sad and now-familiar story is fraught with lessons for public health policy, which requires a scientific perspective broader than preventive and curative medicine can provide. It is not certain, however, that the lessons have been learned. International agencies during the 1980s have become newly concerned with child survival in Third World countries, and have launched programs for more rapid reduction in infant mortality – often without effective linkage to policies of family planning or overt recognition that such unlinked efforts in the past were partly responsible for the present difficulties. Motivated by an ideology of human rights in which saving lives is a moral imperative, these efforts once again lack the broader perspective to anticipate unintended risks.

ABOLISHING CHILD LABOR

The abolition of child labor is a proud chapter in European and American history, and according to the UN Declaration of Human Rights and documents issued by the International Labor Office, this achievement should be shared with the rest of the world. The move to prohibit child labor in the West began with the large-scale use of children in textile factories and mines, working long hours under unhealthy conditions without parental supervision. Such practices conformed to no public moral standards, but were symptomatic of the breakdown of such standards during the early period of industrialization. Laws prohibiting child labor and making school attendance compulsory represented the ultimately successful attempt by reformers to constitute a new public order in which children would be protected from exploitation and relieved of the obligation to perform productive work. As we saw in Chapter 3, these reforms were accompanied by a strong ideological current in which children were increasingly idealized and childhood came to be viewed as a period of play and learning insulated from the world of work. More recently, children have been explicitly defined as having rights,

199

legally enforceable at least in principle, which parents and teachers must respect.

Since 1979, declared by the United Nations as the International Year of the Child, there has been increasing concern in international circles about child labor in Third World countries. The International Labor Office issued two books surveying and analyzing the problem: *Children at Work*, edited by Elias Mendelievich (1979) and *Child Work, Poverty and Underdevelopment*, edited by Gerry Rodgers and Guy Standing (1981). Other publications have been issued, e.g. *Child Labour: A Threat to Health and Development* (revised edition), edited by P.M. Shah (1985) of the World Health Organization. During 1984 and 1985 discussions have been conducted in several UN organizations toward the development of a concerted plan of action.

The focus of international concern is that child labor is very widespread in the Third World, that it is detrimental to the health and education of children and that it violates rights that are protected for children in the industrial countries. Cases of extreme exploitation, such as child prostitution and children performing heavy work on construction projects, receive particular attention as indicating the severity of the problem and the inability of national governments to do anything about it.

The UN agencies begin with the assumption that the ultimate objective of policy in this area is to achieve a total prohibition of child labor throughout the world such as exists in the industrial countries. But the traditions and realities of the Third World, as we have summarized them in Chapters 2 and 7, suggest that any such policy initiatives will prove problematic in several fundamental respects.

First, a number of Third World countries already have laws prohibiting child labor but do not enforce them. The laws are not enforced because child labor is socially acceptable, i.e. it is not seen as violating public standards of morality. There are several reasons for this, the most important being the agrarian tradition in which children work in domestic production units for their parents or master (in a master-apprentice relationship). As we have argued in Chapter 2, agrarian models of the life span assume that children will work for their parents and other elders as they make their way up the local age-sex hierarchy. Child labor in this sense, like respect and obedience, is a sign of moral virtue, a forerunner of long-term filial loyalty and a part of the intergenerational reciprocity of kinship and community. Since the majority of people in Third World countries continue to be guided by these agrarian models, they are not able to see child labor as criminal activity even where it may be illegal. Another reason child labor is socially acceptable concerns its class distribution. In countries like those of Latin America, it is the children of the relatively poor who work, while the children of the wealthy do not. In order for child labor to become socially unacceptable, the wealthy – who are influential in the urban sector of society – would have to disapprove of its prevalence among the poor and actively seek to eliminate it. But the wealthy do not identify sufficiently with the poor to do so; they are not disturbed by the plight of poor children and therefore provide no impetus for change. A final reason it remains socially acceptable concerns the moral status of law and the police in many Third World societies, namely, that they are not legitimate in the sense of providing moral validation for the populace. Thus a legal prohibition on child labor is not experienced as an act of public conscience with which people identify but only another rule imposed from above to be circumvented one way or another.

Second, child labor exists in a wide variety of forms in Third World countries: with and without parental supervision, in place of or combined with school-going, involving heavy or light work, etc. A blanket prohibition such as exists in the industrial countries would make no distinctions among these kinds on moral grounds, although from almost any point of view they should be distinguished.

Third, child labor is simply economically necessary for many families in the Third World, because their labor-intensive subsistence base does not permit them to do without it. Changing the legality of children's work without changing the economic conditions of family life for the rural and urban majority would have no effect on this basic factor favoring the maintenance of child labor.

In sum, the economic, political, social and cultural conditions of Third World countries currently favor the use of child labor, and there is no compelling evidence that these conditions will change. The impetus for change comes largely from outside, i.e. from international agencies and European countries who are outraged by the abuse and exploitation of children and the waste of their potentials. But if the history of social reform in the West and of socialist revolution in Eastern Europe and China is any indication, outrage must come from within the society to effect change. A serious international movement to abolish child labor is more likely to precipitate a confrontation between the virtue-centered morality of agrarian traditions and the rights-centered morality of the industrial countries than it is to have a widespread effect on the lives of children.

LIBERATING WOMEN

From the perspective of human rights, agrarian customs concerning the treatment of women constitute oppression. The place of women in the local age-sex hierarchy is inferior to that of men; in many agrarian communities, women spend their lives under the authority of their fathers and husbands and are virtually confined to the domestic setting. In others, women work much harder than men, in addition to being totally responsible for child care and household tasks. Furthermore, women are publicly represented as inherently inferior, unworthy of the best rewards that life has to offer, and deserving of exclusion from positions of privilege. The case for their liberation from these conditions is simple and straightforward: they deserve rights equal to those of men, and anything less is a violation of their fundamental rights as humans.

Is that all there is to the matter, as an assumption for improving the condition of women? We think not. Just as the apparently simple and straightforward case against child labor became complex upon cultural analysis, so the case for women's liberation becomes complex when examined in the light of agrarian traditions. To free women from their agrarian servitude involves changing their relationships and their social identities, their motives and their sources of pride. While a liberationist perspective sees their current position in the Third World only in terms of constraint and the denial of autonomy and choice, agrarian people, men and women, may experience it quite differently. For one thing, in most non-Western cultures, autonomy and choice are not as central to the ideal self as conceptualized for either sex, as they are in Western societies. Thus the fact that women are not autonomous does not distinguish them as sharply from men as a Westerner might think. For another, as we have argued in Chapter 2, agrarian peoples tend to conceptualize the potentials of life in terms of relationships, and women have at least as much access to the benefits of permanent relationships as men do. Furthermore, in the agrarian situation, the domestic setting defines a productive unit as well as one of consumption, and the importance of women in domestic affairs puts them closer to the center of vital activities than is the case in many urban-industrial situations.

In other words, agrarian women and men share constraints, relationships and domestic participation in ways that are not immediately apparent to an outside observer. The latter is more likely to notice and be impressed by the highly visible public symbols such as deference customs and men's houses which dramatically portray women as subordinate and inferior to men, but which may gain much of their force from their contrast with the underlying realities of relationship and domestic power. This does not deny the reality of women's work and confinement; it suggests that there is more to their lives than can be grasped without learning the terms in which they experience themselves as women.

In terms of Dahrendorf's distinction between options and ligatures, Third World women would certainly be seen as being poor in options and rich in ligatures. We have argued that ligatures provide some of the most important benefits in life, namely, support, structure and motivation and a sense of respect and continuity. Thus it is not only possible but altogether likely that women in some Third World settings experience their lives as highly satisfying even though Western observers would not. On the other hand, Dahrendorf emphasizes that life chances are constituted by the balance between options and ligatures and that a surfeit of one does not necessarily compensate for a deficit in the other. Yet he is speaking in a Western context, in which options are usually assumed to have a greater importance than ligatures – an assumption that does not hold in other contexts.

Thus a case can be made for or against the liberation of Third World women from their agrarian stations in life. The case for liberation is based on the claim that their rights are being violated by conditions that make them unequal to men. The case against it is based on the claim that these conditions provide deeply satisfying benefits which might be lost if they were 'liberated', i.e. if policies were set in motion to remove their constraints and enhance their freedom of choice. Both claims strike us as having some merit in the abstract, but we believe that this dilemma is one that can only be resolved in the context of a particular culture and a particular policy proposal.

One frequent proposal is to liberate Third World women through employment, but it is not a foregone conclusion that this would constitute an improvement in their lives. We need to know how women in a particular community experience their lives, how they feel about the relationships and duties that appear to constrain them, and how they view possible changes. We need to assess the possible impact of employment on their families and on the relationships they are likely to need in the future. In short, before embarking on a policy of creating jobs for women to help them, the policy-maker should investigate the cultural and psychosocial contexts of their current lives.

CONCLUSIONS

In this chapter we have reviewed actual and proposed improvements in the conditions of human development derived from concepts of rights, especially as they apply to Third World countries, where agrarian traditions embody virtue-centered concepts of the person, relationships and the life span. We found that what constitutes an obvious improvement from one cultural perspective may not be one from the other viewpoint and may have negative consequences that are unimagined or underestimated by its proponents. The policy-maker must face these dilemmas rather than minimize their importance, and use culture-specific historical and psycho-social information to clarify their particular forms and identify possible solutions.

9

REALIZING POTENTIALS: A COMPARATIVE PERSPECTIVE

In this book we have argued that human populations vary so widely in the goals of life and the preferred means of attaining them that no universal conception of social progress or personal satisfaction can accurately guide educational policy in the contemporary world. Seeking to integrate and illustrate evidence concerning the diversity of human conditions rather than constructing a model of the Human Condition, we have offered a preliminary framework for future research on education and human development. In contrast with most economic approaches, our framework calls for a pluralistic social science of educational development, informed by historical, cultural, socio-economic, political and psycho-social data, and bringing together knowledge of particular countries and regions with comparative perspectives. Despite this breadth, the framework has a focus provided by a series of concepts: life chances, cultural models of the life span, agrarian and urban-industrial societies, changes in the meanings of parenthood and schooling, educational mobilization.

Life chances are the options and ligatures (choices and social linkages) available to individuals in a particular society. The improvement of life chances in a given society has often been defined as the expansion of options – freedom to choose a mate, a job, a place to live, consumer goods – without recognition of the social ties that make life – and choices – meaningful. Once social ties are seen as sources of personal benefit to individuals, then the question of what would constitute improvement in their lives cannot be answered a priori, i.e. before understanding what their community defines as beneficial – their cultural models of the life span, public representations of the life worth living according to local standards. Agrarian societies, dependent on domestic food and craft production and organized largely as local hierarchies stratified by age and gender, generate models in which fertility, filial loyalty and social reciprocity are central ideals for the life span. Urban-industrial societies, in which work is organized in bureaucratic hierarchies, and families are stratified by their places in the hierarchy, generate models of personal achievement, social advancement and individual rights. The meanings of child-bearing, work, schooling, and local relationships vary accordingly, and establish radically different contexts for the meaning of life.

During the last 200 years, some agrarian societies have become urban-industrial societies, first in the West and then elsewhere, yet the world's population remains heavily agrarian. Agrarian and urban-industrial models of parenthood, schooling and the life span co-exist, within and between countries. No single pattern of change or co-existence prevails. Our examination of the evidence indicates that the pattern of change varied even among countries of the West; Japan and China present another set of contrasting examples not foreshadowed by the Western experience. Third World countries combine agrarian and urban models in a variety of unique ways that can be explained only in terms of their cultural traditions and current situations. A majority of countries have adopted educational mobilization as a national goal during the past century, but the world is now divided more extremely than ever along lines of educational quantity and quality. Our analysis suggests that Third World countries will not 'catch up' and questions the desirability of formulating policy goals in terms of extensions of human rights such as expanding schools, saving lives, abolishing child labor or liberating women – without regard to the social and psychological costs expectable from such policies in a particular cultural and socioeconomic context. In planning change for the improvement of people's lives, then, the understanding of cultural meanings and local cultural adaptations is as important to the policy-maker as economic feasibility analysis.

Others have arrived at similar conclusions. In a volume of anthropological case studies of economic development, Sandra Wallman (1977) states:

[Efforts] to improve conditions in underdeveloped/developing countries continue to assess that improvement quantitatively – more is good; growth is progress – and to rate each area in terms of its shortfall from some implicit 'developed' goal – *we* set the objective which *they* have failed to reach. These notions persist in the plain face of two paradoxes:

(1) However successful a particular region's development effort, the economic gap between it and its industrialized, technological superiors continually widens. 'Progress', far from being the explicit arrival point of the development process, tends to recede as one advances. Even the poor are beginning to realize that they cannot catch up with the rich. In many cases they are no longer trying.

(2) High GNP and/or rates of industrial growth are precisely *not* progress for the developed regions any longer – apparently bringing more ills than we yet know how to cure and certainly not 'satisfying' as such.

. . . We need . . . to discover what that group, society or part-society wants and/or expects to gain from particular changes, and to recognize what it is likely to lose, or to perceive as loss, in the process (Wallman, 1977, pp. 1–2).

In a study of population policies and their implementation in eight Third World countries, Donald P. Warwick (1982) states, 'A central thesis of this project was that culture impinges on every aspect of population policy, from the initial awareness of population as an issue to client perceptions of the services offered,' (p. 106). He concludes, 'Implementation . . . depends on the interplay between the program and the cultural setting,' (p.186).

The question of implementation brings us to the main subject of this chapter, namely, education and human development viewed as the realization of potential. In what follows, we examine this view from the perspective of our framework and formulate what we believe to be the psycho-social and political processes involved.

THE REALIZATION OF POTENTIAL

The purpose of education in our time has been most broadly conceptualized as the realization of potential – a term that is consistent with Enlightenment concepts of human perfectibility and inclusive of the diverse values pursued by individuals and groups. Thus education can be seen as permitting individuals to realize an array of possibilities ranging from the earning of income (in the microeconomics of human capital) to emotional growth (in the 'Human Potential Movement'). The inclusiveness of realizing potential as a concept in public discourse indicates the relativity of values within contemporary Western culture. At the international level, however, potentials are most often assumed to be equivalent and realization is dealt with quantitatively, e.g., with respect to minimal standards of schooling and literacy, without which it is assumed that a good life cannot be lived. This assumption, however, like other preferences regarding human potentials, is grounded in a particular cultural perspective.

Given the impossibility of finding a non-cultural location from which to examine matters like the meaning of life and the purpose of education, the realization of potential is a reasonable starting point. The concept of potential in its implications for the analysis of educational policy has been subjected to a rigorous philosophical analysis by Scheffler (1985) as another part of the Harvard Project on Human Potential. Here we construct a framework for integrating the historical and comparative information of the foregoing chapters and investigating further the processes involved in realizing potentials.

The realization of potential can be thought of as a category of variation among th world's peoples. Cultures recognize and value diverse potentials in human life and varying ways of realizing them. Agrarian cultures, while varying widely among themselves, recognize the reproductive and relational potentials of human beings as those most worth realizing. Fertility, filial loyalty and a multiplicity of local relationships are valued in themselves and as means to other ends, and they are celebrated in shared representations of virtue. Those who have few or no children, who cannot rely on their children, or who are isolated from community relationships, are counted as the most unfortunate – cases of wasted potential. In the educational discourse of Western industrial societies, on the other hand, the realization of potential tends to be identified with the development of skills in the individual. The academic-occupational prestige hierarchy endows academic performance – interpreted as a definitive sign of skill acquisition – with symbols of personal virtue and power that are conceived of as transcending local relationships. Those lacking skills are the unfortunate whose potential is wasted. Cultural models of the life span and of the benefits to be gained from living, vary in accordance with these differing concepts of potential.

This does not mean that human wants are infinitely variable. Everyone wants survival, health and material well-being. The pursuit of wealth, prestige and power knows no cultural boundaries. We have argued as well that security, respect and continuity are universally experienced as beneficial. But cultural models not only represent these benefits in a wide variety of symbolic forms but also rank them differently as goals worth pursuing and as associated with moral virtue.

The greatest point of contrast between agrarian models, as we have generalized them, and those of the urban-industrial West, lies in their social and moral assumptions. The public morality of agrarian peoples is centered on respect, duty, obligation and responsibility, in the context of the local age-sex hierarchies that constitute their permanent reference groups. The public morality of Western societies, especially since their urban-industrial transformation, is centered on individual rights enforceable throughout a nation. This morality of rights presumes that individuals will negotiate their social relationships (rather than inheriting them), that relationships will be contractual and that the State will enforce the contracts. In this context, it is the individual and the State that are permanent, not the network of local relationships, and the code of law is as salient in such contexts as the code of kinship and clientage is in agrarian societies. Given this contrast in the ideology of social life, it follows that personal goals and strategies for attaining them will also differ. It is the processes by which cultural models are translated into individual and collective action, particularly in patterns of education and human development, that is our focus in this chapter.

In reviewing the data presented in earlier chapters, we focused on two processes involved in the realization of potentials: motivation and mobilization. In each case, we find cultural variability, a psychological dimension and connections between microsocial and macrosocial levels.

MOTIVATION

Motivation is the central process in the realization of potential, because it refers to the personal commitment of attention, effort and other resources available to the individual, toward specific goals (and often in task-specific situations) over a period of time. Without this commitment, the goals defined as representing a person's realization of potential are unlikely to be attained. This is as true for intellectual goals as for any others, for a person's talents cannot be fully developed without the active participation of that person (Gardner, 1984). In other words, regardless of which potentials – reproductive, athletic, military, cosmetic, financial, contemplative, or cognitive, among many others – are selected for realization, their actual realization in the individual requires long-term motivated activity by the person himself and often by those around him as well.

From the viewpoint of socially organized programs in the realization of potential, motivation is the key process in implementation. Where fertility is valued and the realization of reproductive potential is an important goal, the motivated activities of adult men and women in reproductive unions, and of their immediate kin, are necessary for implementation of the goal. In a modern school system, the motivated activities of pupils, teachers and parents are necessary for implementation of educational goals. When the motives of participants are at variance with the goals, attainment suffers accordingly. In other words, processes like reproduction and education do not work automatically, nor as an uncomplicated reflection of institutional pressures, but involve the motivations of individual participants at the point most crucial to their effectiveness, that is, at the point of implementation.

Our assumptions concerning what motivates individuals extend 'economic incentive', in fact they are in opposition to the notion that the anticipation of material gain is the only motivator. Our concept differs also from formulations like those of McClelland (1981) that assume a universal set of motives (e.g. achievement, affiliation and power) in somewhat variable cultural clothing. Starting from a relativistic appreciation of the complex symbols that move women and men in diverse settings throughout the world, we cannot accept any interpretation of the motivating quality of those symbols that is not based on evidence concerning their cultural meanings.

Thus our concept of motivation is culture-specific. We assume that individuals in all societies acquire social identities based on cultural models of the life span available in the environments in which they grew up, and that these social identities include goals that motivate long-term commitments of attention and effort along certain pathways, according to a culturally organized plan or script. Although it is possible to interpret these culturally prescribed and locally symbolized pathways in terms of universal goals (economic gain, prestige, power, sexuality, aggression, etc.), the anthropological evidence suggests that their impact as motivators among different peoples is not predictable without knowledge of the local idioms that specify their meanings. Somehow or other, in ways that are continuing topics of anthropological inquiry, the peculiar symbolic forms and formats of popular culture exert a uniquely powerful force on the activities of peoples.

The evidence we have reviewed in previous chapters illustrates how culture-specific motivation operates to realize potential. The Japanese borrowed the Western model for realizing potential represented by the academic-occupational prestige hierarchy, but they implemented it in terms of ends and means familiar to most Japanese from indigenous models of learning and performance. Tacitly rejecting the Western concept of opposition between options and ligatures (i.e. individual freedom vs. social constraints), the Japanese sought to expand options along lines represented by Western education and industrialism without dissolving the social ties of rural life or the values of indigenous social hierarchies. The revision of imported bureaucratic institutions like school systems and industrial firms to accord with Japanese norms of interpersonal behavior permitted the models and identities that had motivated performance in villages and family production units to continue to do so in novel settings. The maintenance of long-term relationships, stable reference groups and permanent loyalties – in contrast to the contractual ideology of Western urban society – continues to operate as a collective goal and personal motive along with the achievement goals familiar to Westerners. In other words, the goals that motivate learning and work among Japanese pupils, teachers and workers are framed in relational contexts that look 'agrarian' – from a Western perspective in which 'rural' and 'urban' symbolize polarities of social relations – but which operate in an urban-industrial setting. This phenomenon, as described in Chapter 5, was not predictable from the Western experience of urbanization and industrialization.

The People's Republic of China, as reviewed in Chapter 6, provides another example of motivation in the realization of potential that could not have been predicted from Western precedents. In Maoist China the revolutionary government attempted to stand the academic-occupational prestige hierarchy on its head, elevating manual labor over scientific/technical/managerial work, in order to avoid the failure of European Marxist regimes to realize egalitarian goals. In this effort, the Chinese leaders had recourse to dramatic personifications of good and evil that were familiar to the Chinese people as ancient models of virtue and vice, inspiring social identities committed not only to virtuous activity but also to the struggle against vice. That many were effectively motivated this way in their economic and political activities cannot be doubted, though the costs of coercion, divisive conflict and loss of skilled manpower were ultimately too great for a large-scale society to bear. The radicalism of the Chinese experiment in re-defining the realization of potential in moral terms, without regard for the practical consequences, makes it look like an aberration of human history. If so, it is an aberration consistent with China's agrarian traditions of public discourse.

In the Third World countries, recent social change has been less subject to central control than in Japan and China, and motivations remain tied to local social identities. These societies are often classified by what they lack – economic development, literacy, strong governments – and they are often assumed to be undermotivated as well. But our review in Chapter 7 suggests that the differences between the Third World and the industrial countries is not in how much they are motivated but toward what. Their agrarian social identities motivate people to realize their reproductive and relational potentials in terms derived from indigenous agrarian traditions, while at the same time attempting to maximize advancement in modern educational and occupational careers. New social identities have arisen that include agrarian as well as imported goals. These combinations are different from their Japanese counterparts because the Japanese deliberately redesigned bureaucratic institutions as they imported them, whereas most Third World countries were so dominated by Western countries (or an internal European elite group, as in Latin America) at the time schools, factories and government offices were introduced that they could not re-design them to fit local norms and expectations. Thus the new social identities of Third World peoples tend to be 'dual identities' like their economies, more additive than integrative, in which individuals see their academic-occupational careers as leading to economic and prestige outcomes that can be converted, sooner or later, into the relational symbolism of agrarian communities. Third World peoples are as motivated as the Japanese, but the goals that motivate their performance in school and the workplace are more likely to be extrinsic to the imported models that remain prevalent in those bureaucratic institutions.

MOBILIZATION

Mobilization is not independent of motivation, but is a macrosocial process that can account for the ways in which motivations are distributed in a population. We have used the term 'educational mobilization' to refer to the concerted effort by a nation-state to move toward a goal of universal education and increasing the average educational level of the population. In a sense, every society can be seen as 'mobilized' to fullfill the goals defined as salient in its cultural models, insofar as individual activities and motivations are organized toward those goals. But we prefer to reserve the term 'mobilization' for the centrally coordinated process in which resources and activities are diverted from other purposes to a single goal and in which there is sufficient unity of collaboration between commitments at the microsocial and those at the macrosocial levels that the boundaries between 'popular' and 'official' efforts become unclear. While this usage is most common for the military mobilization of a country, we have argued that the same metaphor is appropriate for the educational development of most Western countries and Japan in the late nineteenth and twentieth centuries.

Mobilization is not characteristic of agrarian societies in the past or Third World countries today, in part because the social organizations and identities that motivate adults and inspire their loyalty are largely embedded in local and regional associations rather than national ones. In the history of Europe, the rise of the national state was not simply an administrative development; it was accompanied by the emergence of ideological politics and the capacity of the State to inspire loyalty that transcended localisms through the manipulation of meaningful symbols (Deutsch, 1953). Many contemporary Third World countries, however, lack this capacity because of the culturally diverse peoples residing within their borders. Neither their national governments nor their national policies can be characterized as 'popular' in the sense that applied to Western countries during the most intense period of educational mobilization. Thus collaboration between segments, sectors and levels of the society is highly problematic; the motives of policy-makers and the population are often at cross-purposes.

What is the solution? First, it is necessary to understand the historical specificity of the problem. Mobilization is not required for societies to attain goals of realizing potential at all times and places. Indeed, we have argued that agrarian societies permit the realization of potential in local terms and in the context of local communities. Mobilization is a means of unifying efforts to realize potential throughout a nation that is also a large-scale society. The inability of a society to unify such efforts nationally does not mean that the potentials of individuals will not be realized but only that goals and means for attaining them will continue to be diverse. If there is no national consensus concerning definitions of potential and the allocation of resources to realize them, then it may be better to optimize diverse local efforts than to attempt a national policy of mobilization.

Second, it is relevant to remember that educational mobilization as we have described it encompasses varied political means, not only central planning. The United States is probably the leading example of locally organized and controlled educational development in the West, and despite the inequalities resulting from this uncoordinated process, its history may have more lessons important to internally diverse Third World countries than has been recognized. Third, educational mobilization brings with it social and psychological costs, as indicated in Chapter 8, and these should be carefully balanced against the gains for Third World countries where it has not yet occurred. The imposition of a single standard of personal value and the diminished salience of local reference groups is particularly threatening to Third World populations that have experienced a net loss from educational mobilization, in spite of the gains accrued from it in other countries.

The history of educational mobilization in other non-Western countries is important for educational policy in the Third World. Our profiles of mobilization in Japan and China in Chapters 5 and 6 show two autonomous East Asian countries that formed nation-states with different priorities for the realization of potential and the place of education in national policy. Japan presents the picture of a carefully designed confluence between popular and official efforts to maximize academic achievement at every level. The collaboration between macrosocial and microsocial processes involving policy-makers, teachers and parents, was orchestrated from the top, but by officials who anticipated the conditions that would motivate performance in the classroom and at home. The segregation of overt competition in the system they developed (to impersonal examinations and the private efforts of parents) is a noteworthy culture-specific innovation that was attuned to Japanese standards of face-to-face behavior and helped the morale of teachers and pupils in the classroom. The Japanese history of educational mobilization can be seen as a politically coordinated process involving public investment and planning at the national level that took advantage of folk models and norms to motivate performance at the microsocial level. Whatever its limitations from a comparative perspective – e.g. the assumption of cultural consensus among all participants in the system – the further analysis of this process can only illuminate the problem of how educational policy-making can draw upon local culture for the improvement of schools.

Educational mobilization in China shared some of the most widespread goals – wiping out illiteracy, nation-building, developing the skills needed for industrialization and bureaucratic institutions – found elsewhere in the world, and some – like ideological indoctrination – found among Marxist and other authoritarian states. Its unique, and in the long run unsuccessful, attempt to reverse the prestige implications of education has already been noted. Its cultural distinctiveness, however, particularly in contrast with Japan, is most evident in the part education played in the polarization of public discourse along ideological lines. Japanese educational mobilization involved a multiplicity of compromises – between different models, different interests, different levels – arrived at through behind-the-scenes negotiation and quiet policy decisions. In China, however, discourse about the moral values and evils of education constitutes a public drama that polarizes opinion and involves extreme policy reversals. The traditional Chinese examination system for entrance to the Imperial bureaucracy was, after all, the original prototype of the academic-occupational prestige hierarchy, and it remains the context for Chinese discussions of educational policy. The Communist government, seeking to abolish privilege, was hostile to school-based qualifications for higher status, but also needed technicians and intellectuals, so it initially retained (and expanded) a hierarchical educational system. This made it vulnerable to the accusation of fostering educational privilege, which was unleashed during the Cultural Revolution, with cataclysmic consequences. In the late 1970s, formal education was resuscitated on pragmatic grounds, but not without ambivalence in some quarters. Education in China, then, has been an historical battleground for ideological conflict concerning equality and privilege, and the expansion of schooling was accompanied by overt debate and struggle to a degree that was unknown in Japan. Japanese reformers during the Meiji restoration were concerned with diminishing inequality too, but their efforts were not publicized. In China, the official policy of rejecting the values of the past made educational policy the center of a moral dialectic that has not yet played itself out.

The Japanese and Chinese cases show the different directions that educational mobilization can take, even within the framework of a strong national state, and with a population that is relatively homogeneous in culture. Their radically divergent styles of bringing about change show how important the cultural factor is in implementing an educational policy.

CONCLUSIONS

Our conclusions concern factors worthy of further research in the comparative analysis of educational development. On the microsocial side, there is the factor of sponsorship, i.e. the way in which parents, teachers and other mentors commit themselves to the realization of an individual's potential. It is clear, for example, that a distinctive feature of the Japanese case is the way in which mothers commit themselves to the educational performance of their children. The sheer quantity of attention to the child's school work and educational career – the 'time on task' by parents – can become a major variable in the implementation of an educational program. Thus expectable educational outcomes should be seen as a function not simply of public and private investment of economic resources but of the attention, management and assistance available to the child from sponsors during the preschool and school years. This would help specify the proximate conditions of educational motivation.

On the macrosocial side, we have been impressed with the importance of political and demographic factors rather than strictly economic ones in accounting for cross-national differences in educational development. The land area, population size and cultural heterogeneity of contemporary nation-states determine in large measure their capacity to expand their school systems. Small, homogeneous countries are better able to develop a consensus about education and to educate their populations than large, populous, heterogeneous ones. Strong, popularly supported governments are better able than weak ones to implement policies designed to improve people's lives. It takes a certain amount of governmental stability and legitimacy – lacking in many Third World countries – to mount any human development policies effectively. The effectiveness of a government's police and judiciary determines its ability to enforce laws protecting children or improving the lot of women. Too often these problems in the realization of potential are discussed and analyzed in economic terms, implying that they will yield to technical economic solutions, whereas, as Hirschman (1971) has emphasized, their political dimensions are critical.

Finally, there is the factor of collaboration between processes operating at the macrosocial level and those operating at the microsocial level. Our discussions of motivation and mobilization indicate how crucial such collaboration is for the implementation of any policy to improve the lot of an entire population. In the context of the contemporary nation-state, neither official policy nor grassroots voluntarism alone can be relied upon to realize desired potentials; they must work together, convergently and synergistically. This is where culture is the critical term, for if policy-makers and ordinary people share cultural models of life, education and social performance, the possibilities for their collaboration are enhanced, whereas cultural divisions between them will inhibit the implementation of policies. The problem of finding an ideological basis for such collaboration is one of many problems we have raised for comparative research on educational development.

NOTES

CHAPTER 2 VIRTUES AND VICES:
AGRARIAN MODELS OF THE LIFE SPAN

1 This chapter presents a theoretical model based on our interpretation of the ethnographic record. No attempt is made to cite its many sources in the literature of social anthropology and social theory. Some of the more direct influences have been the works of Robert Bellah, Peter Berger, Morton Fried, Clifford Geertz, Robert Redfield, Edward Shils and Max Weber. Our argument, in this and succeeding chapters, proceeds by alternating between the formulation of ideal types (such as 'agrarian culture', 'agrarian schooling' and 'educational mobilization') and our empirical critique of global generalizations. Thus the ideal types are heuristic devices to capture widespread historical tendencies without underestimating the theoretical importance of cultural variation.

CHAPTER 4 REVOLUTION IN SCHOOLING: FROM
MASTER AND DISCIPLE TO CAREER DEVELOPMENT

1 The evidence on agrarian schooling used in this chapter was drawn from unpublished review papers written for the Project on Human Potential by Susan Pollak (1981, 1982, 1983), B. K. Ramanujan (1983) and Leonie Gordon (1982), and from a workshop on Islamic education held at the Project offices on September 2, 1982. Attending the workshop were Ali Banouazzizi, Azziz Esmail, Roy Mottahedeh, Lamin Sanneh, and Daniel Wagner. The authors are solely responsible for the synthesis and illustrations presented in this chapter.

2 This continuity is now being harnessed to the goals of modernization by UNICEF and other development agencies who hope to work within the Qu'ranic schools to introduce 'modern' skill training. Kamal El-Sayed

Darwish, 'Developing Koranic Schools to Meet the Educational Needs of the Young Child' UNESCO, PreSchool Education Paper 23, 1981.

3   The theory of the 'three debts' has helped to foster the aims of Indian education. This theory states that when an individual is born, he incurs three debts: to the gods (paid by learning to perform sacrifices); to teachers and scholars of ages past (paid by learning their teachings and continuing the tradition) and to the ancestors (paid by raising children and teaching them the traditional knowledge.)

CHAPTER 5   EDUCATIONAL MOBILIZATION: THE CASE OF JAPAN

1   This broad generalization indicates our belief – based on all the historical and psychometric evidence we are aware of – that cross-national differences in the comparable test performance of school aged children and adolescents reflect environmental factors rather than innate abilities. The social processes referred to schematically as political will, economic investment and parental commitment can only operate, of course, through a school system in which learning is effectively organized to meet performance standards. The role of the school system is explained later in the chapter.

2   All but the last of these are island countries, with limited land areas, sharp national boundaries, and relatively homogeneous populations – geographical and cultural features that favor the implementation of mass education programs. This is a fact to bear in mind in considering the conditions that facilitate or inhibit educational mobilization.

3   Iwao in White and Pollak, 1986.

4   In the Husen and Comber and Keeves studies, Japanese children are shown to excel in math and science above all countries studied, and Japan shows least inequality in such achievements across the population.

5   The functional illiteracy rate is less than 1 per cent, whereas it is 20 per cent in the US.

6   In fact, however, the current generation of top managers are self-made', at least in terms of academic credentials. Of the top 2400 businesses, 2000 have presidents without college degrees. Later age cohorts are progressively more educational-credential-selected.

CHAPTER 6   SCHOOLING IN CHINA: MOBILIZING FOR VIRTUE

1   There are part-time courses available for all workers in academic subjects and in morality, and it is expected that all will pass the junior middle school equivalency exams. Workers are tested periodically and

offered promotions when they pass. They are not fired if they do not pass but are less apt to be promoted.
2 One effect of the one-child family which is particularly problematic and which was cited was several cadres concerned with the welfare of the aged is that each partner in a marriage will be responsible for supporting his or her parents: each marriage will have to bear the burden of four aged persons.
3 This description is a composite, taken in life history and family interviews with twelve Chinese women in the PRC and Cambridge, Mass., conducted between 1974 and 1982.

CHAPTER 7   LIFE CHANCES IN THE THIRD WORLD: THE LIMITS OF EDUCATIONAL MOBILIZATION

1 International development agencies provide loans for educational expansion, but the recurrent costs involved in operating their school systems outpace the growth of their economies.
2 See Veena Das, 1986; Prakash Desai, 1986; Ronald Inden, 1977; Sudhir Kakar, 1978; McKim Marriott, 1977; S. and L. Rudolph, 1967; Sylvia Vatuk, 1981 and A.K. Ramanujan, 1980.

BIBLIOGRAPHY

Abegglen, James. *The Japanese Factory*, Glencoe, Illinois: The Free Press, 1958.

Anderson, C.A. *The Social Context of Educational Planning*, UNESCO, International Institute for Educational Planning, August 1967.

Anderson, Ronald S. *Japan, Three Epochs of Modern Education*, US Department of H.E.W., Bulletin 1959, No. 11.

Anderson, Ronald S. *Education in Japan*. US Government Printing Office, Washington, DC, 1974, pp. 15–38.

Andors, Phyllis. 'Politics of Chinese Development: The Case of Women, 1960–1966,' Signs: *Journal of Women in Culture and Society*, 1976, vol. 2, no. 1, pp. 89–119.

Aries, Philippe. *Centuries of Childhood*, trans. Robert Baldick, New York: Knopf, 1962.

Arnold, F., Bulatao, R., Burikpakdi, C., Chung, B., Fawcett, J., Iritani, T., Lee, S. and Wu, T. *The Value of Children*: vol. I, Introduction and Comparative Analysis, Honolulu: East-West Population Institute, 1975.

Arnove, Robert F. 'Educational Policy in China and India: The Problems of Overcoming the Work/Study Dichotomy,' *Phi Delta Kappan*, vol. 65, no. 7, March 1984, pp. 473–8.

Beardsley, Richard K., Hall, John W. and Ward, Robert E. *Village Japan*, Chicago: University of Chicago Press, 1959.

Becker, Gary. *Human Capital*, 2nd edn, Chicago: University of Chicago Press, 1975.

Becker, Gary. *The Economic Approach to Human Behavior*, Chicago: University of Chicago Press, 1976.

Becker, Gary. *A Treatise on the Family*, Cambridge, Mass.: Harvard University Press, 1981.

Beijing Normal University Press. *One Hundred Examples of Successful Persons Who Rose above Misfortune*, 1981.

Berger, Peter. *Pyramids of Sacrifice*, New York: Anchor, 1976.

Bloom, B. *Developing Talent in Young People*, New York: Ballantine, 1985.

Bibliography

Boas, F. *The Mind of Primitive Man*. New York: Macmillan, 1938.

Breiner, Sander J. 'Early Child Development in China,' *Child Psychiatry and Human Development*, vol. 11 (2), Winter 1980, pp. 87–95.

Caine, Augustus Feweh. 'A Study and Comparison of the West African 'Bush' School and the Southern Sotho Circumcision School,' unpublished MA Thesis, Department of Anthropology, Northwestern University, 1959.

Caldwell, J. *Theory of Fertility Decline*, New York: Academic Press, 1982.

Caldwell, J. 'Direct economic costs and benefits of children,' in R. Bulatao and R. Lee (eds), *Determinants of Fertility in Developing Countries*, New York: Academic Press, 1983.

Carnoy, Martin. *Education as Cultural Imperialism*. New York: McKay, 1974.

Caudill, William and Plath, David. 'Who Sleeps by Whom? Parent-Child Involvement in Japan,' *Psychiatry* vol. 29, 1966, pp. 344–66.

Caudill, William and Weinstein, Helen. 'Maternal Care and Infant Behavior in Japan and America,' *Psychiatry* 32, no. 1, 1969, pp. 12–43.

Chatterjee, K.K. *English Education in India*, Delhi: Macmillan, 1976.

Chaudhuri, Nirad, *The Autobiography of an Unknown Indian*, Berkeley: University of California Press, 1951.

Cochrane, S. *Education and Fertility: What Do We Really Know?* Baltimore: Johns Hopkins University Press, 1979.

Colletta, Nat J. *Worker-Peasant Education in the People's Republic of China*, World Bank Staff Working Papers No. 527. The World Bank, Washington, DC, 1982.

Comber, L.C. and Keeves, John P. *Science Education in Nineteen Countries*. New York: John Wiley, 1973.

Conroy, M., Hess, R., Azuma, H. and Kashiwagi, K. 'Maternal Strategies for Regulating Children's Behavior', *Journal of Cross-Cultural Psychology*, vol. III no. 2, June 1980, pp. 153–328.

Craig, John E. 'The expansion of education', in *Review of Research in Education*, vol. 9, 1981, pp. 151–213.

Critchfield, Robert, *Villages*, New York: Anchor Press, 1981.

Croll, Elisabeth J. 'Social Production and Female Status: Women in China,' *Race and Class*, vol. XVIII, Summer 1976, no. 1, pp. 39–52.

Croll, Elisabeth J. *Chinese Women Since Mao*. Armonk NY: M.E. Sharpe Books 1983.

Cummings, William. K. 'The Effects of Japanese Schools,' *Education in a Changing Society*, A. Ktoskowska and G. Martinotti, eds, Sage Publications, 1977.

Cummings, William K. 'The Conservatives Reform Higher Education' in Edward R. Beauchamp, ed. *Learning to be Japanese,* Hamden, Conn.: Linnet Books, 1978, pp. 316–28.

Cummings, William K. 'The Egalitarian Transformation of Post-War Japanese Education' in *Comparative Education Review:* February, 1982, vol. 26, no. 1, pp. 16–36.

Cummings, William K. *Education and Equality in Japan*, Princeton University Press, Princeton, New Jersey 1980.

Dahrendorf, R. *Life Chances*, Chicago: University of Chicago Press, 1978.

223

Bibliography

Darwish, Kamal El-Sayed. *Developing Koranic Schools to Meet the Educational Needs of the Young Child*, Paris: UNICEF, 1981.

Das, Veena. 'The Work of Mourning: Death in a Punjabi Family', in *The Cultural Transition: Human Experience and Social Transformation in the Third World and Japan*. ed. by Merry White and Susan Pollak, London: Routledge and Kegan Paul, 1985.

Davis-Friedmann, Deborah. 'Current Chinese Approaches to Issues in Human Development: A preliminary foray,' unpublished MS prepared for Project on Human Potential, December 1980.

Desai, Prakash and Collins, Alfred. 'Selfhood in Context: Some Indian Solutions', in *The Cultural Transition: Human Experience and Social Transformation in the Third World and Japan*, ed. by Merry White and Susan Pollak. London: Routledge & Kegan Paul, 1985.

Deutsch, K. *Nationalism and Social Communication*, Cambridge, Mass.: MIT Press, 1953.

Di Bona, Joseph. *One Teacher, One School: The Adam Reports on Indigenous Education in 19th Century India*, Delhi: Biblio Impex 1982.

Doi, Takeo. *The Anatomy of Dependence*, Tokyo: Kodansha International Ltd., 1973.

Dore, Ronald. *City Life in Japan*, University of California, Berkeley, 1958.

Dore, Ronald. 'Talent and the Social Order in Tokugawa Japan,' *Past and Present* No. 21, April 1962.

Dore, Ronald. *Education in Tokugawa Japan*. Berkeley, University of California Press, 1965a.

Dore, Ronald. 'The Legacy of Tokugawa Education', in Jansen, Marius, ed., *Changing Japanese Attitudes Toward Modernization*. Princeton, NJ: Princeton University Press, 1965b.

Dore, Ronald. *The Diploma Disease*, Berkeley: University of California Press, 1976.

Dore, Ronald. *Shinohata: a Portrait of a Japanese Village,* London: Allen Lane, 1978.

Embree, John F. *Suye Mura,* Chicago: University of Chicago Press, 1939.

Fairbank J.K. ' "Red" or "Expert"?', *New York Review of Books*, 2 December 1982, p. 13.

Fei, Xiaotong. 'Chinese Modernization and Sociological Research,' Draft Manuscript, 1981.

Fei, Xiaotong. Discussion with Project on Human Potential Staff, Cambridge, Mass., January 1981.

Fine, Elizabeth. 'The Rise of Universal Education in the 19th Century,' Project on Human Potential, May 1983.

Foreign Press Center, *About Japan Series: Volume 8, Education in Japan,* Foreign Press Center, Tokyo, Japan, May 1978.

Fried, Morton. *The Evolution of Political Society*, New York: Random House, 1967.

Frolic, B. Michael. *Mao's People: Sixteen Portraits of Life in Revolutionary China*, Harvard University Press, Cambridge, Mass., 1980.

Fukuzawa, Yukichi. *Autobiography*, New York: Columbia University Press 1966.

Bibliography

Gardner, H. *Frames of Mind: The Theory of Multiple Intelligences*, New York: Basic Books, 1983.

Goldman, R.J. 'Early Childhood Education in the People's Republic of China,' *The Educational Forum*, vol. XLI, no. 4, May 1977, pp. 455–63.

Gordon, Leonie. 'Education in China: Traditional and Modern,' Project on Human Potential, November 1982.

Gould, S. *Ever Since Darwin*. New York: Norton, 1977.

Graff, Harvey J. *The Literacy Myth: Literacy and Social Structure in the Nineteenth-Century City*, New York: Academic Press, 1979.

Grove, Cornelius Lee. 'U.S. Schooling through Chinese Eyes,' *Phi Delta Kappan*, vol. 65, no. 7, March 1984, pp. 481–3.

The Guangming Daily: 17 May 1981, p. 3: 'Twenty Youths from Beijing and Tienjing at a Discussion Meeting Talking about their Experience in Attempting Self-study.'

Guangzhou Middle School 7, Interviews with principal and teachers, 3 May 1982.

Habte, Aklilu, Psacharopoulus, George, and Hayneman, Stephen P. *Education and Development: Views from the World Bank*, World Bank, 1983.

Hall, John W. 'The Confucian Teacher in Tokugawa Japan' in Nivison and Wright, eds. *Confucianism and Action*. Stanford: Stanford University Press, 1959.

Hallak, Jacques. *Education, Training and the Traditional Sector*, Paris: UNESCO, 1981.

Hamaguchi, Eyshun. *Nihonjin ni totte kyariaa to wa* (What 'career' means to the Japanese), Tokyo: Nihon Keizai Shimbunsha, 1979.

Hamaguchi, Eyshun. 'The "Man" Model and the Human Nexus of the Japanese,' Osaka University Human Studies Department, Publication 8, 1982.

Hane, Mikiso. *Peasants, Rebels and Outcasts: The Underside of Modern Japan*. New York: Pantheon, 1982.

Hanley, Susan B. 'Fertility, Mortality and Life Expectancy in Pre-modern Japan', *Population Studies* 28, 1 March 1974, pp. 127–42.

Havens, Thomas, *The Valley of Darkness: The Japanese People and World War II*, New York: Norton, 1978.

He, Bingzi. Interview with Author. Beijing, China, 12 May 1982.

Heneveld, Ward. *International Dimensions of Early Childhood Education*, UNICEF, Paris, August 1982.

Hess, Robert., Kashiwagi, Keiko., Azuma, Hiroshi *et al.* 'Maternal Expectations for Mastery of Developmental Tasks – Japan and the U.S.' in *International Journal of Psychology* 15 (1980) pp. 259–71.

Heyneman, Stephen P. 'Improving the Quality of Education in Developing Countries,' *France and Development*, 1983, pp. 19–21, World Bank, May 1982.

Heyneman, Stephen P. 'Education During a Period of Austerity: Uganda 1971–1981,' *Comparative Education Review* vol. 27, no. 3, Oct. 1983.

Heyneman, Stephen P. and Loxley, William A. 'The Effect of Primary-school Quality on Academic Achievement across Twenty-nine High- and Low-income Countries,' *American Journal of Sociology*, 88, 1983, pp. 1162–94.

225

Bibliography

Hinton, Harold C. (ed.) *The Peoples Republic of China: A Handbook.* Boulder, Co: Westview Press, 1979.

Hirschman, A. *The Strategy of Economic Development.* New Haven, CT: Yale University Press, 1959.

Hirschman, A. *A Bias for Hope*, Princeton, NJ: Princeton University Press, 1971.

Hirschman, A., *et al.* (contributors). *Toward a New Strategy for Development: A Rothko Chapel Colloquium,* New York: Pergamon Press, 1979.

Hoffman, L. and Manis, J. 'The Value of Children in the United States: A New Approach to the Study of Fertility,' *Journal of Marriage and the Family*, 1979, 41, pp. 583–96.

Hsu, Francis L.K. 'Psychosocial Homeostasis and Jen: Conceptual Tools for Advancing Psychological Anthropology', in *American Anthropologist*, 73, 1971, pp. 23–44.

Husain and Ashraf. *Crisis in Muslim Education,* London: Hodder & Stoughton, 1979.

Husen, Torsten. *International Study of Achievement in Math: A Comparison of 12 Countries*, New York: John Wiley & Sons, vol. 2, 1967.

Hussein, Taha, *An Egyptian Childhood*, London: Heinemann, 1981.

Illich, Ivan. *Deschooling Society.* New York: Harper and Row, 1972.

Inden, Ronald and Nicholas, Ralph W. *Kinship in Bengali Culture*, Chicago: University of Chicago Press, 1977.

Inkeles, A. *Becoming Modern.* Cambridge: Harvard University Press, 1974.

Iritani, Toshio. *The Value of Children: A Cross-National Study* (Japan), Honolulu: University of Hawaii Press 1979.

Ishida, Takeshi. *Japanese Society*, New York: Random House, pp. 44–9, 1971.

Iwao, Sumiko. Personal Communication, Tokyo, May 1982.

Iwao, Sumiko. 'Skills and Life Strategies of Japanese Business Women', in Merry White and Susan Pollak (eds). *The Cultural Transition: Human Experience and Social Transformation in the Third World and Japan,* Boston: Routledge & Kegan Paul, Boston, 1985.

Iwasa, Nobumichi. 'The Differential Practices of Babysitting in America and Japan,' unpublished paper, Harvard Graduate School of Education, 1983.

Izutsu, Toshihiko. 'The Structure of Selfhood in Zen Buddhism,' Sonderdruck aus Eranos-Jahrbuch XXXVIIII, 1969, Zurich 1971.

Jansen, Marius B. (ed.) *Changing Japanese Attitudes Toward Modernization*, Princeton, N.J.: Princeton University Press, 1965.

Jansen, Marius B. and Stone, L. 'Education and Modernization in Japan and England,' in *Comparative Studies in Society and History*, vol. IX, no. 2, Jan. 1967.

Japan Bureau of Statistics, Office of the Prime Minister. *Statistical Handbook of Japan,* Tokyo: Bureau of Statistics, 1977.

Japan Teacher's Union, 'What Japan's Education Should Be' in Edward R. Beauchamp, ed. *Learning to be Japanese.* Hamden, CT: Linnet Books, 1978, pp. 349–71.

Kakar, Sudhir. *The Inner World*, Delhi: Oxford University Press, 1978.

Bibliography

Kakar, Sudhir. 'Indigenous Psychotherapy and the Self in India,' paper presented at the annual meeting, Association for Asian Studies, Washington DC, 21 March 1980.

Kato, Hidetoshi. *Education and Youth Employment in Japan*, Berkeley, Ca.: Carnegie Council on Policy Studies in Higher Education, 1978.

Kato, Koji. 'The "Open School" Movement in Japan: Present Status, Problems and Comparative Considerations.' National Institute for Educational Research, April 1981.

Kawai, Hayao. 'Egalitarianism in Japanese Education,' in *Japan Echo*, vol. II, no. 4 (October 1975), pp. 27–35.

Kessen, William (ed.). *Childhood in China*, New Haven: Yale University Press, 1975.

Keyes, Charles F. 'The Proposed World of the School: Thai Villagers' Entry into a Bureaucratic State System', SSRC/ACLS Joint Conference on South East Asia, Penang, Malaysia, July 1983.

Kiefer, Christie. 'The Psychological Interdependence of Family, School and Bureaucracy in Japan,' *American Anthropologist*, vol. 72, no. 1, February 1970, pp. 66–75.

Kirst, Michael. 'Japanese Education: Its Implications for Economic Co-operation in the 1980's' in *Phi Beta Kappa*, June 1981, pp. 707–8.

Kobayashi, Tetsuya. 'Tokugawa Education as a Foundation of Modern Education in Japan' *Comparative Education Review* vol. 9, no. 3, October 1965, pp. 288–302.

Kobayashi, Tetsuya. *Society, Schools & Progress in Japan*, New York: Pergamon, 1976.

Kobayashi, Victor N. *John Dewey in Japanese Educational Thought*, Ann Arbor: University of Michigan, 1964.

Kojima, Gunzo. *The Philosophical Foundations for Democratic Education in Japan*. International Christian University: September, 1959.

Kondo, Dorinne. 'Industrial East Asia: The Role of Culture,' Cambridge, Mass.: Presentation American Academy of Arts and Sciences, 22 September 1984.

Kraus, Richard. 'Social Affairs' in Harold C. Hinton (ed.) *The People's Republic of China, A Handbook*, Boulder, Co: Westview Press, 1979.

Kumagai, Hisa. 'A Dissection of Intimacy: A Study of Bipolar Posturing in Japanese Social Interaction–*Amaeru* and *Amayakasu*, Indulgence and Deference,' *Culture, Medicine and Psychiatry*, 5 (1981), pp. 249–72.

Lanham, Betty B. 'The Mother-Child Relationship in Japan' in *Monumenta Nipponica* vol. XXI, nos. 3–4. Tokyo: 1966, pp. 322–33.

Lanham, Betty B. 'Early Socialization: Stability and Change' in 'The Study of Japan in the Behavioural Sciences' ed. Norbeck and Parman, *Rice University Studies*, vol. 56, no. 4, Fall 1970.

Leacock, Eleanor Burke. 'Education in Africa: Myths of "Modernization" ', *The Anthropological Study of Education*, Craig J. Calhoun & Francis A.J. Ianni, eds, Paris, 1976.

Lebra, Takie Sugiyama. *Japanese Patterns of Behavior,* Honolulu: University of Hawaii Press, 1976.

Lebra, T. and Lebra, W. (eds) *Japanese Culture and Behavior*, Honolulu:

University of Hawaii Press, 1974.

Lebra W., ed. *Transcultural Studies in Mental Health*, Honolulu: University of Hawaii Press, 1973.

Lecourtois, André. *Ecoles Coraniques et Enseignement Fondamental.* Paris: UNESCO, August 1981.

Lei, Zhenxiao and Wang, Tongxun. *Rencaiology*, Beijing, December 1979.

Levine, Kenneth. 'Functional Literacy: Fond Illusions and False Economies,' *Harvard Educational Review*, vol. 52, no. 3, August 1982.

LeVine, Robert A. 'Western Schools in Non-Western Societies: Psychosocial Impact and Cultural Response,' *Teachers College Record*, vol. 79, no. 4, May 1978

Levy, Marion J. *Modernization and the Structure of Societies.* Princeton: Princeton University Press, 1966.

Liang, Heng and Shapiro, Judith, *Son of the Revolution.* New York: Vintage Books, 1983.

Lifton, R.J. 'Youth and History: Individual Change in Post-war Japan,' *Daedalus*, Winter 1962, vol. 91, no. 1, pp. 172–97.

Lutz, Catherine and LeVine, Robert A. 'Cultural Concepts of Intelligence in Infancy' in Michael Lenis, ed., *The Origins of Intelligence in Infancy*, 2nd edition, New York: Plenum Press, 1983.

MacFarlane, A. *The Origins of English Individualism*, Cambridge: Cambridge University Press, 1977.

Makita, Kiyoshi. 'The Rarity of Reading Disability in Japanese Children,' *American Journal of Orthopsychiatry*, 1967, pp. 599–614.

Mao, Danran. Interviews with Author, Harvard University Graduate School of Education, Cambridge, Mass., 1 December 1981.

Marriott, McKim. 'The Open Hindu Person and Interpersonal Fluidity,' paper presented at the Association for Asian Studies, Washington D.C., 21 March 1980.

Marriott, McKim and Inden, Ronald B. 'Toward an Ethnosociology of South Asian Caste Systems,' in Kenneth A. David, ed., *The New Wind: Changing Identities in South Asia.* The Hague: Mouton, 1977.

Matthews, R. and Akrawi, M. *Education in Arab Countries of the Near East*, Washington, DC, 1949.

Mauger, P. *et al. Education in China*, London: Anglo-Chinese Educational Institute, 1974.

McClelland, D. 'Child rearing versus ideology and social structure as factors in personality development', in R.H. Munroe, R.L. Munroe and B. Whiting (eds), Handbook of Cross-Cultural Human Development, New York, Garland STPM Press, 1981.

McKeown, T. *The Modern Rise of Population*, New York: Academic Press, 1976.

Mendelievich, E. (ed.) *Children at Work*, Geneva: International Labor Office, 1979.

Ministry of Education, Tokyo. 'Japan's Growth and Education: Educational Development in relation to Socioeconomic Growth,' in *Comparative Perspectives on Education*, Robert J. Havighurst (ed.), Boston: Little Brown, 1968.

Bibliography

Miyazaki, Ichisada. *China's Examination Hell: The Civil Service Examinations of Imperial China*, New Haven, Conn.: Yale University Press, 1976.

Miyoshi, Masao. *As We Saw Them*, Berkeley: University of California Press, 1978.

Morsback, Helmut. 'Aspects of Non-Verbal Communication in Japan,' *Journal of Nervous and Mental Disease*, vol. 157, no. 4, October 1973, pp. 262–77.

Mosk, Carl. 'The Decline of Marital Fertility in Japan,' *Population Studies* 33, 1 March 1979, pp. 19–38.

Mosk, Carl. *Patriarchy and Fertility: Japan and Sweden, 1880*–1960, New York: Academic Press, 1983.

Munro, Donald. *The Concept of Man in Early China*, Stanford: Stanford University Press, 1969.

Munro, Donald. 'Man, State and School,' in *China's Developmental Experience*, Michel Oksenberg (ed.), New York: Columbia University Press, 1973.

Munro, Donald. *The Concept of Man in Contemporary China*, Ann Arbor: University of Michigan Press, 1979.

Murase, Takao. 'Naikan Therapy' in *Japanese Culture and Behavior: Selected Readings*, T.S. Lebra and W.P. Lebra (eds), Honolulu: The University Press of Hawaii, 1974.

Nakane, Chie. *Japanese Society*, Berkeley: University of California Press, 1972.

National Institute for Educational Research, *Basic Facts and Figures about the Educational System in Japan*. Tokyo: Ministry of Education, 1982.

Nishi, Toshio. *Unconditional Democracy: Education and Politics in Occupied Japan 1945–1952*. Stanford: Hoover Institute Press, 1982.

Notestein, F.W. 'Population – The Long View' in *Food for the World*, ed. by Theodore W. Schultz, Chicago: University of Chicago Press, 1945.

Numata, Jiro. 'Acceptance and Rejection of Elements of European Culture in Japan.' *Journal of World History*, vol. 3, no. 1, 1956, pp. 231–53.

Ohara, Shin. ' "Time" as Japanese Civil Religion,' *Look Japan*, pp. 1–5, October, 1979.

Parish, William L. and Whyte, Martin King, *Village and Family in Contemporary China*, Chicago: University of Chicago Press, 1978.

Parsons, Talcott. *The Evolution of Societies*, Englewood Cliffs, NJ: Prentice Hall, 1977.

Passin, Herbert. *Japanese Education: A Bibliography*, New York: Teacher's College Press, 1970.

Passin, Herbert. *Society and Education in Japan*, New York: Teachers' College Press, 1967.

Paz, O. *The Other Mexico: A Critique of the Pyramid*, New York: Grove Press, 1972.

The People's Daily 'It's an Urgent Necessity to Solve the Problem of Training Persons of Ability,' 26 May 1981, p. 5.

The People's Daily 'Starting Education from Childhood to Lay a Good Foundation of Training,' 28 May 1981, p. 1.

The People's Daily 'Keeping a Wide Field of Observation to Discover More

Bibliography

Talents,' 29 May 1981, p. 4.

The People's Daily 'Training Talents is a Strategic Task,' 30 May 1981, p. 4.

Pepper, Suzanne. 'Education and Revolution: The 'Chinese Model; Revised,' *Asian Survey*, University of California, XVIII, no. 9, September 1978, pp. 847–90.

Pharr, Susan. 'The Japanese Woman: Evolving Views of Life and Role' in Lewis Austin, *Japan: The Paradox of Progress*, New Haven, Conn.: Yale University Press, 1976.

Plath, David. 'Japan, the After Years' in Cowgill and Holmes (eds), *Aging around the World*, 1969, Appleton: Century, Crofts.

Plath, David. 'Cares of Career and Careers of Caretaking,' *Journal of Nervous and Mental Disease*, Nov. 1973, vol. 157, 5, pp. 346–57.

Plath, David. 'The Last Confucian Sandwich: Becoming Middle Aged.' *Journal of Asian and African Studies* X, 1–2, January and April 1975, pp. 51–63.

Plath, David. 'How Portable is Japanese Psychotherapy?' *Japan Interpreter*, vol. II, no. 2, Autumn 1976, pp. 237–50.

Plath, David. 'Bourbon in the Tea: Dilemmas of an Aging Senzenha' in *The Japan Interpreter*, vol. XI, no. 3, Winter 1977, pp. 362–3.

Plumb, J. 'The New World of Children in Eighteenth Century England,' in V. Fox and M. Quitt (eds), *Loving, Parenting and Dying*, New York: Psychohistory Press, 1980.

Pollak, Susan. 'Traditional Jewish Learning: Philosophy and Practice,' Project on Human Potential, October 1981.

Pollak, Susan. 'Traditional Islamic Education,' Project on Human Potential, March 1982.

Pollak, Susan. 'Of Monks and Men: Sacred and Secular Education in the Middle Ages,' Project on Human Potential, December 1982.

Pollak, Susan. 'Ancient Buddhist Education,' Project on Human Potential, April 1983.

Pollak, Susan. 'Education in Ancient Greece,' Project on Human Potential, July 1983.

Prime Minister's Office of Japan, *Japanese Children and Their Mothers: International Comparison*, Youth Development Headquarters, Prime Minister's Office, Tokyo, 1981.

Psacharopoulos, G. 'Educational Research at the World Bank'. *The World Bank Research News*, vol. 4, 1983, no. 1, pp. 3–17.

Ramanujan, A.K. Draft paper on Gurukula, Project on Human Potential, 1983.

Ramanujan, A.K. 'Is there an Indian Way of Thinking?' paper prepared for Workshop on the Person in South Asia, 16 September 1980.

Rawski, Evelyn. *Education and Popular Literacy in Ch'ing China*. Ann Arbor: University of Michigan Press, 1979.

Rencai Study Preparatory Group, *Rencai, Rencai!*, Beijing: 1980.

Reynolds, David. *Mortia Psychotherapy*, Berkeley: University of California Press, 1976.

Rodgers, G. and Standing, G. (eds) *Child Work, Poverty and Underdevelopment*, Geneva: International Labor Office, 1981.

Bibliography

Rohlen, Thomas. *For Harmony and Strength*, Berkeley: University of California Press, 1974.

Rohlen, Thomas. 'Is Japanese Education Becoming Less Egalitarian?' *Journal of Japanese Studies*, Winter 1976–77, vol. 3, no. 1, pp. 37–70.

Rohlen, Thomas. *Japan's High Schools*. Berkeley: University of California Press, 1983.

Rostow, Walt W. *The Stages of Economic Growth*. Cambridge, England: Cambridge University Press, 1960.

Rudolph, Lloyd and Rudolph, Suzanne H. *The Modernity of Tradition, Political Development in India*, Chicago: University of Chicago Press, 1967.

Rudolph, Lloyd and Rudolph, Suzanne H. *Education and Politics in India*, Cambridge: Mass. Harvard University Press, 1972.

Sanneh, Lamin. *The Jakhanke*, London: International African Institute, 1979.

Sanneh, Lamin. 'Autobiography', unpublished manuscript, 1982.

Scheffler, I. *Of Human Potential*. London: Routledge & Kegan Paul, 1985.

Schultz, T. *Investing in People: The Economics of Population Quality*, Berkeley: University of California Press, 1981.

Shah, P.M. (ed.) *Child Labour: A Threat to Health and Development*, (revised edition), Geneva: World Health Organization, 1985.

Shanghai Conservatory of Music. Interviews with administration and teachers, 7 May 1982.

Shiang, Julia. 'Reciprocity: Toward a Chinese Concept of Self,' unpublished manuscript, Project on Human Potential, Cambridge, Mass. December, 1980.

Shibata, Tokue. Private Communication, Tokyo, May 1982.

Shirk, Susan L. *Competitive Comrades: Career Incentives and Student Strategies in China*. Berkeley: University of California Press, 1982a.

Shirk, Susan L. 'The Decline of Virtuocracy in China,' in James Watson (ed.), *Class and Stratification in Post-Revolution China*, Cambridge Univesity Press, 1982b.

Shively, Donald. 'Nishimura Shigeki: A Confucian View of Modernization' in Jansen, Marius (ed.). *Changing Japanese Attitudes toward Modernization*, Princeton, NJ: Princeton University Press, 1965.

Sidel, Ruth. 'Early Childhood Education in China: The Impact of Political Change,' in *Comparative Education Review*, February 1982, pp. 78–87, vol. 26, no. 1.

Sikkema, Mildred, 'Observations of Japanese Early Child Training' in D. Haring (ed.), *Personal Character and Cultural Milieu*, Syracuse, NY.: Syracuse University Press, 1948.

Simmons, John. *Education, Poverty and Development*. Washington: World Bank, 1974.

Simmons, John (ed.). *Education Dilemma*, New York: Pergamon Press, 1980.

Singleton, J. *Nichu: A Japanese School*, New York: Holt, Rinehart & Winston, 1967.

Sivard, R. *Women: A World Survey*, Washington, Word Priorities, 1985.

Bibliography

Spratt, Jennifer and Wagner, Daniel, 'The Making of a Fqih' in *The Cultural Transition*, ed. by Merry White and Susan Pollak, London: Routledge & Kegan Paul, 1985.

Stevenson, Harold W. quoted in *New York Times*, June 17 1983, articles 'US Pupils Lag from Grade 1, Study Finds,' by Edward Fiske, pp. 1 and 30.

Stevenson, Harold W., Lee and Stigler, 'The Reemergence of Child Development in the People's Republic of China,' unpublished paper, 1981.

Steward, J. 'Multilinear Evolution' in A. Kroeber (ed.), *Anthropology Today*. Chicago: University of Chicago Press, 1953.

Stocking, G. *Race, Culture and Evolution: Essays in the History of Anthropology*. Chicago: University of Chicago Press, 1968.

Stone, L. *The Family, Sex and Marriage in England, 1500—1800*. New York: Harper & Row, 1977.

Sweeney, Arlyn G. 'An Investigation into the Factors Contributing to the High Literacy Rate in Japan,' Ed.D. dissertation, University of Southern California, 1978.

Taniuchi, Lois. 'The Psychological Transition from Home to School and the Development of Japanese Children's Attitudes toward Learning.' Unpublished Qualifying Paper, Harvard Graduate School of Education, 1982.

Taniuchi, Lois and White, Merry I. 'Teaching and Learning in Japan: Premodern and Modern Educational Environments,' Project on Human Potential, October 1982.

Thurow, Lester. *Dangerous Currents: the State of Economics*, New York: Random House, 1983.

Tobin, Joseph Jay. 'Dependence, Independence and Amae: American Reactions to Living in Japan,' presented to the Association for Asian Studies 31st Annual Meeting, Los Angeles, 31 March 1979.

Treiman, Donald J. *Occupational Prestige in Comparative Perspective*, New York: Academic Press, 1977.

Trotsky, Leon. *The History of the Russian Revolution*, New York: Random House, 1936.

Tsunoda, Tadanobu. *Nihonjin no No* (The Japanese Brain), Tokyo: Dai Shushoku kan Shoten, 1978.

UNESCO. *Statistical Yearbook*, New York: The United Nations, 1982.

United Nations, Department of International Economic and Social Affairs. *Patterns of Urban and Rural Population Growth*, New York: United Nations, 1980.

Unger, Jonathan. *Education Under Mao; Class and competition in Canton Schools, 1960-1980*. New York: Columbia University Press, 1982.

US Bureau of the Census. *World Population*, Washington, DC: Bureau of the Census, 1983.

US Department of Education. *Digest of Educational Statistics*, National Center for Educational Statistics, 1982.

van de Walle, E. and Knodel, J. 'Europe's Fertility Transition: New Evidence and Lessons for Today's Developing World,' *Population Bulletin*, 1980, 34, no. 6.

Vatuk, Sylvia. 'Authority, Power and Autonomy in the Life Cycle of the

North Indian Woman,' paper presented at annual meeting, Association for Asian Studies, Toronto, Canada, 13–15 March 1981.

Vogel, Ezra F. *Japan's New Middle Class*, Berkeley: University of California, 1963.

Vogel, Ezra F. 'Kinship structure, migration to the city, and modernization,' in *Aspects of Social Change in Modern Japan*, ed. Ronald Dore, Princeton, NJ: Princeton University Press, 1967.

Vogel, Ezra F. *Japan as Number One*, Cambridge: Harvard University Press, 1978.

Vogel, Suzanne. 'The Professional Housewife,' *Japan Interpreter*, vol. XII, no. 1, Winter 1978, pp. 17–43.

Wagner, Daniel A. and Lotfi, Abdelhamid. 'Learning to Read by "Rote" in the Qu'ranic Schools of Yemen and Senegal,' unpublished, December 1980.

Wallman, S. (ed.) *Perspectives on Development 6*, Cambridge, England: Cambridge University Press, 1977.

Wang, Tongxun and Lei, Zhenxiao. 'We want You to Become a Talented Person,' Rencai Group, Beijing, 1981.

Warwick, D. *Bitter Pills: Population Policies and their Implementation in Eight Developing Countries*, Cambridge, England: Cambridge University Press, 1982.

Wei, Zhangling, 'Chinese Family Problems: Research and Trends,' *Journal of Marriage and the Family*, November 1983, pp. 943–8. vol. 45, no. 4.

White, Gordon. 'Higher Education and Social Redistribution in a Socialist Society: The Chinese Case,' in *World Development*, vol. 9, pp. 149–66, New York: Pergamon Press, 1981.

Whyte, Martin King, 'Destratification and Restratification in China,' in *Social Inequality: Comparative and Developmental Approaches* ed. G. Berreman. New York: Academic Press, 1981.

Wolf, Margery. *Women and the Family in Rural Taiwan*, Stanford, Conn.: Stanford University Press, 1984.

Wolf, Margery. 'Child Training and the Chinese Family,' in *Studies in Chinese Society*, edited by Arthur P. Wolf, Stanford, Conn.: Stanford University Press, 1978.

Wong, David. *Moral Relativity*, Berkeley: University of California Press, 1984.

World Bank, *Education: Sector Policy Paper*, 3rd edn, April 1980, World Bank, Washington, DC.

World Bank, *World Development Report*, Washington DC: World Bank, August 1980.

World Bank, *World Development Report*, Washington DC: World Bank, 1982.

Wrigley, E. 'The Growth of Population in Eighteenth Century England: A Conundrum Resolved' *Past and present*, 1983, no. 98, pp. 121–50.

Wu, David Y.H. and Wei-Lan W. Wu. 'Child Rearing in China: Issues of the One-Child Family,' paper presented at the 82nd Annual Meeting, American Anthropological Association, Chicago, 16–20 November 1983.

Bibliography

Xia, Dr Shuzhang. Interview, Guangzhou, 2 May 1982.

Professor Y. Interview, Research Institute of Education, Guangzhou China, May 1982.

Yamada, Yuichi. 'Employee Education,' in *Crosscurrents* no. 2, June 1980, UNESCO.

Yanazumi, Masami and Nakae, Kazue (eds). *Ko Sodate no Sho* volumes I, II and III, (*Compendium of Child Rearing*). Tokyo, Heibonsha, 1976.

Yang, Martin C. *A Chinese Village*, New York: Columbia University Press, 1945.

Yuan, Professor. Interview, Department of Psychology, Guangzhou Teachers' College, 4 May 1982.

Dr Z. Interview, Peking, China, 12 May 1982.

Zeng, Dr. Interview, East China Normal University, 9 May 1982.

Zhang, Suchu, Ms. Discussion at Project on Human Potential.

Zhang, Suwo. Interview, Executive, All-China Women's Education. Beijing, 12 May 1982.

Zhang, Tian An. Interview, Head of Research Department. Ministry of Education, Beijing, People's Republic of China. 13 May 1982.

Zhao, Dr Fusan. Discussion at Project on Human Potential.

Zhu, Dr. Interview. East China Normal University, 9 May 1982.

INDEX

Abegglen, James, 115
aborigines, 11
abortion, 155
access to education, 133, 134
achievement: academic, 86, 95, 98, 103, 109, 110, 113, 123, 127, 129, 139, 140, 141, 143, 157, 164, 206; personal, 192, 206
adolescence, 53, 60, 195–6
adult development, 3
affect, 123–5
Africa, 24, 33, 44, 46, 63, 74, 126, 128, 169, 171, 198; North Africa, 30, 73, 75; Sub-Saharan Africa, 28, 30, 74, 183; West Africa, 30, 73; *see also country name*
age segregation in schools, 77, 83
aging, 41–2; *see also* old age
agrarian schooling, 73–82, 86; in Japanese context, 95, 97; and societal complexity, 73–4
agrarian societies, 24–49; defined, 24–32; transition from, to urban-industrial societies, 51–72, 207
agrarian values, 25–50; in contemporary Third World, 169, 173–6, 185; and Chinese virtue, 128–31, 143; in modern Japan, 95, 97–104, 126, 174, 192–3, 201–2, 208, 212
agriculture, 24, 27, 30, 32, 56, 98, 100, 138, 139, 157, 168, 173, 174

Alger, Horatio, 99
ambition, 26, 82, 98, 116, 165; materialistic, 156; *see also* aspirations
anomie, 57
apprenticeship, 31, 56, 75, 76, 81, 82, 202
Argentina, 59
Aries, Philippe, 82
Arinori, Mori, 91
arithmetic, *see* mathematics *and* numeracy
arts, 40, 181
aspirations, 48; material, 58; national, 84, 192; general, 193–4
assertiveness, 66
attitude, *see* student attitude
auction model of development, 13–17
Australia, 11, 59, 63, 66
authority, 20, 30, 69, 70, 75, 76, 79–80, 123, 129, 151, 182, 202
autonomy, 26, 27, 39, 50, 57, 67, 70, 103, 121, 123, 127, 202–3; national, 89
Aztecs, 74, 183

backwardness, 12, 14, 169–70
Becker, Gary, 15
Berger, Peter, 187
biology, 38
birth control and limitation, 63, 64,